Drama and Curriculum

Landscapes: The Arts, Aesthetics, and Education

VOLUME 6

SERIES EDITOR

Liora Bresler, *University of Illinois at Urbana-Champaign, U.S.A.*

EDITORIAL BOARD

SCOPE

This series aims to provide conceptual and empirical research in arts education, (including music, visual arts, drama, dance, media, and poetry), in a variety of areas related to the post-modern paradigm shift. The changing cultural, historical, and political contexts of arts education are recognized to be central to learning, experience, and knowledge. The books in this series present theories and methodological approaches used in arts education research as well as related disciplines - including philosophy, sociology, anthropology and psychology of arts education.

For other titles published in this series, go to
www.springer.com/series/6199

John O'Toole · Madonna Stinson · Tiina Moore

Drama and Curriculum

A Giant at the Door

Springer

John O'Toole
24/9-19 Miller Street
Fitzroy North VIC 3068
Australia
j.otoole@unimelb.edu.au

Madonna Stinson
Nanyang Technological
University
National Institute of Education
1 Nanyang Walk
Singapore 637616
Singapore
madonna.stinson@nie.edu.sg

Tiina Moore
11 Thompson Crescent
Research VIC 3095
Australia
tiinamoore@dodo.com.au

ISBN: 978-1-4020-9369-2   e-ISBN: 978-1-4020-9370-8

DOI 10.1007/978-1-4020-9370-8

Library of Congress Control Number: 2008939879

Printed on acid-free paper

9 8 7 6 5 4 3 2 1

springer.com

To the worldwide community of drama educators,
who have been knocking at the door of curriculum for so long, with such
resourcefulness, imagination, artistry, scholarship, patience, and care.

Foreword

'Here's a knocking indeed!' says the Porter in Shakespeare's Scottish play (Act II, Scene 3) and immediately puts himself into role in order to deal with the demands of such an early call after a late night of drinking and carousal: 'If a man were porter of hell-gate . . .'. But what roles does the porter of curriculum-gate take on in order to deal with drama's persistent demands for entry? Ah, that depends upon the temperature of the times.

We, who have been knocking for what seems to be a very long time, know well that when evaluation and measurement criteria are demanded as evidence of drama's efficacy, an examiner stands as gatekeeper. When the educational landscape is in danger of overcrowding, we meet a territorial governor. And how often has the courtesan turned out to be only a tease because the arts are, for a brief moment, in the spotlight for their abilities to foster out-of-the-box thinkers? In this text, we meet these 'commissionaires' and many more. The gatekeeping roles and what they represent are so familiar that they have become clichés to us. We know them by their arguments, ripostes, dismissals, their brief encouragement and lack of follow-up. And we know that behind each one (however firmly they think they keep the keys) is a financial and political master whose power controls the curriculum building and everything in it.

The metaphor of drama as the giant Proteus standing outside the door of the curriculum, waiting, hoping, demanding to be acknowledged and given a room of its own serves this text well. It is a metaphor that readers will relish for its aptness and the opportunities it offers to look at this problem of access from multiple viewpoints. We have, of course, discovered ways to get to the other side of that door. We slide through the letter-box; we shuffle by as part of the crowd (and these days, there are a number of groups seeking a roof over their heads). Sometimes we just walk in boldly, disguised as something else – English and Language Arts have offered very comfortable and well-fitting cloaks. Occasionally, by assembling our arguments skilfully, the gatekeeper just stands aside and lets us in. But for many reasons, we rarely manage to stay for long or get past the hat stand!

Drama educators have tried on many guises and disguises in their efforts to become legitimate members of the curriculum collective and their efforts are beautifully and thoughtfully deconstructed for readers in this new look at the background and history of the long and difficult relationships between drama, theatre, and education. Both the history and the contexts for that history are woven so tightly together that, for most of us, we are familiar with only one or two of the strands that were used and can recognize only those patterns that speak to our own experiences. Standing firmly on the ground of their own practice, the authors have managed to encompass the position of drama and theatre education in such a way that international readers should have no difficulty in using this text as a matrix for examining their own situations. New and experienced researchers, practitioners, and teachers will find here a range of international references that will set them on a firm path to their own discoveries and stimulate new debates in the reconfiguration of theory into practice and vice versa.

The discussion of how drama has flexed and shaped itself to fit the latest curriculum fashion offers readers further evidence that whatever the demands, drama has found ways – honest, inventive, and appropriate – to demonstrate how that fashion can be served. When you work in a discipline that promotes 'the Big Lie', as Dorothy Heathcote often referred to it, manipulating the truth in the interests of gaining access has never been an option. But in our desire to get in the door, we can be distracted. In our anxiety to be heard, we learn others' languages and sometimes forget the power of our own. In our efforts to make things clear for other people, we forget that the art we practice is, of itself, deeply complex. The authors' discussion of these accommodations makes me realize again just how much drama offers as an enabler of learning both as subject and as a service. It also makes me wonder if we would have grown so strong without the constant need to prove and reprove the value of drama as a living pedagogy.

This text provides 'maps' for the kinds of terrain that must be travelled again and again. It reminds us of areas of difficulty and challenge, and the importance of being aware of subterranean political shifts and changes as they affect curriculum documents, particularly those that are constructed over extended periods of time. The book also serves as a guide and manual for the curriculum continuum from classroom drama through to applied theatre. To know how one school encourages the use of drama as a learning medium for almost all curriculum subjects provides a note of hope and reassurance to those of us who work in this demanding and richly rewarding field. It is a fulfilment of the wish that Madeleine Grumet expressed in 1995, 'Because drama is a way of knowing, an exploration and a performance of understanding, it needs to be at the very heart of classroom inquiry' (p. 10). This is one example only. Certainly there are others but not enough yet, I sense, to satisfy Dr. Grumet, the authors of this book nor, indeed, any of us who use the student-friendly, gloriously risky, whole person challenges of drama and theatre as classroom methodologies.

The questions raised, the passionate search, and the illuminating discoveries offer a plot full of tensions, surprises and the crazy logic that makes this story so entirely human and recognizable. As you read, you may want to keep in mind one of the Dalai Lama's teachings on how to live well. He writes, 'Remember that *not* getting what you want is sometimes a wonderful stroke of luck' (2008) – but then, drama has always been about paradox.

Victoria, British Columbia   Juliana Saxton

References

Grumet, M. (1998). Research conversations: Visible pedagogies/generous pedagogies. In J. Saxton & C. Miller (Eds.), *Drama and theatre in education: The research of practice/The practice of research* (pp. 7–11). Victoria, BC: IDEA Publications.

Stevenson, L., & Deasy, R. (2005). *Third space: When learning matters*. Washington, DC: Arts Education Partnership.

Acknowledgements

The authors have many people to thank, without whom this book would not have been written, or would have been much poorer.

First, we must thank Liora Bresler, whose idea the book was, and who provided encouragement, sage advice and endless patience. Next and equally, we owe a great debt to Juliana Saxton, for supporting the book from the original proposal, and giving us the wisest and most eagle-eyed of editorial scrutiny on the draft manuscript. We would also like to thank Gavin Bolton and Laura McCammon for supporting the proposal, and for their helpful comments.

We are grateful to numerous Australasian drama education pioneers in all States for their help in writing the book, particularly Chapter 8. Although, owing to limitations on space and the capacity of an international readership to be absorbed by local history, not all have been cited, their perspectives and memories have combined to provide a simplified but we hope coherent and textured overview of the very diverse and complex growth of drama in Australasian education. The following people were formally or informally consulted in writing that chapter:

Michael Anderson (NSW)
John Carroll (NSW)
John Deverall (Victoria)
Kate Donelan (Victoria)
Sue Elmes (Queensland)
Anne Gately (NSW)
Janinka Greenwood (New Zealand)
Brad Haseman (Queensland)
John Holmes (South Australia)
John Hughes (NSW)
Ida McCann (Tasmania)
Frank McKone (Australian Capital Territory)
Angela O'Brien (Queensland & Victoria)
Peter O'Connor (New Zealand)
Robin Pascoe (Western Australia)
Beth Parsons (Tasmania)
Paul Roebuck (NSW)

Megan Schaffner (Tasmania)
Jenny Simons (NSW)
Heather Smigiel (Tasmania & South Australia)
Paul Stevenson (Victoria & Queensland)
The late Robin Thomas (Queensland)

We are also grateful to David Warner and the students, staff, and parents of Eltham College, Victoria, for their bold support for drama in their curriculum, and to Madonna's colleagues in the Queensland School Curriculum Council, especially Carolyn Harrod and Jim Tunstall.

Finally, we must acknowledge with thanks the patience and support of Springer, who have waited for a long time.

Contents

Introduction 1
by John O'Toole
Signs of the Times. 1
How to Read this Book. 3
The Book as Curriculum 5
Reference 7

Part I   Background and Context

1 **Strange Bedfellows: Drama and Education** 11
by John O'Toole
Play and Pre-School 11
Traditional Performative Education. 13
Greeks Beware of Drama Bearing Gifts 14
The Pattern Repeated: Medieval and Renaissance Theatre 18
Four Strands of Purpose 23
References 26

2 **Curriculum: The House that Jack Built** 29
by John O'Toole and Madonna Stinson
A Grammar Lesson 29
Transported to Australia 31
The Twentieth Century 33
From the 1950s: Curriculum Gets Serious 34
Resistance, and Stirrings of Change 37
Curriculum Sea-Change? 40
Or Curriculum Little Change? 42
References 43

Part II   Theories and Practices

3   Drama and Language 49
  by John O'Toole and Madonna Stinson
  The Ambivalent Role of English 49
  Progress with Progressive Education 54
  With the Progressives in Retreat 58
  Speech and Drama. 60
  Drama for Second- and Other-Language Learning 63
  References 67

4   Drama for Development and Expression 71
  by John O'Toole
  Child's Play Again 71
  Creative Dramatics and Creative Drama. 72
  Creativity Worldwide 78
  Revisiting Developmental Claims 81
  Movement and Motor Development 88
  Drama for Healing – Therapy and Psychodrama 89
  References 93

5   Drama as Pedagogy 97
  by John O'Toole
  Marvellous Miss Johnson 97
  Wind of Change: Hurricane Heathcote 101
  TIE/DIE in the Swinging Sixties 102
  Process Drama and the Curriculum 104
  Drama, Values and Social Change. 108
  Adult Drama for Learning 110
  Theatre for Development and Liberation 111
  References 113

6   Civil Wars 117
  by John O'Toole
  The Battle of the Paradigms 117
  References 125

7   The Three Pillars of Art 127
  by John O'Toole
  Drama and Music 127
  The First Pillar: Appreciating Drama 128

The Second Pillar: Performing Drama 131
The Third Pillar: Making Drama 134
Resolving the Conundrum: The Whole Curriculum 140
References 142

Part III Drama in Action in Contemporary Curriculum

8 Doorway Politics: Cracking an Education System 147
by John O'Toole and Madonna Stinson
Part One: Queensland – A Case Study 147
Drama in the Driveway 149
In Through the Porch 152
Part Two: Widening the Case Study 154
The Extra-Curricular Pass-Key (in from the Garden) 155
Speech and Drama as a Pass-Key 156
The English Pass-Key 156
Sharing a Pass-Key 157
Fifth Columnists and Insiders 158
Overseas Influences... 159
State and National Associations............................... 160
Tertiary Education Influences 162
Theatre's Patchy Influence 164
Renovating the House, or Just Redecorating? 165
References 167

9 Drama as Macro-Curriculum: Peeking Behind the Closed Doors
   of Drama Syllabus Development 169
by Madonna Stinson
The Queensland Context 169
Consultation 171
The Curriculum Design 172
Phase One: The Design Brief................................... 174
Phase Two: The Outcomes Development Phase...................... 175
Phase Three: Trialling the Curriculum in Schools 177
Politics and the Draughts of Change 178
Constraints 180
References 182

10 The HistoryCentre: A Micro-Curriculum 183
by Tiina Moore
Background 183
A Timely Convergence 184
An Interdisciplinary Curriculum 185

The History Centre 186
St. Rhyio by the Sea 186
Reflective Practice 189
Twilight Role 190
The Physical Environment 191
References 192

11 Pasts, Present and Futures: Which Door Next? 193
by John O'Toole and Madonna Stinson
Applied Theatre 193
Culture, Politics and Technology 197
Drama Research and Drama as Research 199
What Is 'Appropriate'? 203
References 207

Author Index 211

Subject Index 215

Introduction

John O'Toole

> 'There's no sort of use in knocking,' said the Footman, 'and that for two reasons. First, because I'm on the same side of the door as you are; secondly, because they're making such a noise inside, no one could possibly hear you.'
> 'Please then,' said Alice, 'How am I to get in?'
> 'Are you to get in at all?' said the Footman. 'That's the first question, you know.'
> ... 'But what am I to do?' said Alice.
> 'Anything you like,' said the Footman, and began whistling.
> (Alice in Wonderland)

Signs of the Times

In an interesting sign of the times, on the very morning that we began writing this book, in a university meeting elsewhere a senior drama lecturer sat down a little nervously with a small committee entrusted with planning the 'new generation' teacher education program for her faculty. She was filled with hope (to improve drama's tenuous position in the curriculum) and fear (that it might be further undermined), the two emotions as usual poised in delicate balance. The scale tilted toward hope as she noted that, very surprisingly, all five of the committee members came from the areas of arts, language and literacy or creative curriculum. In a unique, temporary and aberrant turnaround from what would be seen as 'normal' in the traditional organisation of such a curriculum development committee, there was nobody directly representative of the scientific or social scientific communities, which traditionally form the backbone, and often the entire body, of education faculty decision-makers.

She smiled warmly at another colleague with an arts background, and he returned her smile encouragingly – another tip of the scale towards hope, but it was premature. As the meeting progressed, the balance tilted back towards fear as to the dismay of both of them they found themselves locked in conflict. Our heroine recognised a familiar territorial battle. She represented Drama (and by implication Subject Disciplines), he represented Curriculum. Curriculum theory and practice

J. O'Toole et al., *Drama and Curriculum,* Landscapes: the Arts, Aesthetics, and Education 6, DOI 10.1007/978-1-4020-9370-8_1,
© Springer Science+Business Media B.V. 2009

were his particular expertise, and he had been responsible for what in the previous program was one of the largest course components. Philosophically the two were as one – he strongly believed in the 'aesthetic' and 'artistic' curriculum theories of Elliott Eisner, Maxine Greene and their followers, and his own school-teaching history was visual arts and a smattering of drama. Yet they were on opposite sides in a bitter skirmish over the territory of teaching, which is the territory of time not space, as they fought, ironically, for the same cause of aesthetic education.

She was demanding an increased contact time in the primary and early child-hood courses, beyond the current 18 hours for drama discipline-based studies, which seemed to her quite risible, for giving the students the artistic skills firstly to under-stand the dramatic implications of an aesthetic pedagogy and curriculum, then to implement it. Her colleague was equally convinced that any reduction of his 100 hours to purvey the principles and effective planning of that same aesthetic cur-riculum would be deeply to the students' detriment. She perceived that he had a limited grasp of the elements of art-form that was well-meaning but inadequate to understand the complexity of aesthetic curriculum, and completely unrealistic in terms of grappling not only with the commonalities of the arts but with the quite distinct demands of visual arts, music, literature, drama, dance and media. He saw her insistence that an aesthetic curriculum means just that, a curriculum founded on artistry, as special pleading, and a cheap and improbable grab for the centre of the curriculum, which has traditionally always lain elsewhere. With a conscientious concern for all the traditional key learning areas in the curriculum, he felt he had bigger fish to fry. He had history on his side in the territorial wars. All she could do was point to the constant complaints from students that they did not have enough time for the arts.

That's how it is in the schools too, only many times more so. And so it always is, it seems, right round the globe. The scene above could have been played out in almost any education faculty in the world. Drama and curriculum are some-how natural enemies. Certainly drama has been until recently excluded from the central curriculum of most schooling systems, and mainly exists on the margins: strongly in so-called 'co-curricular' or 'extra-curricular' activities (i.e., those that take place outside 'normal school-time'); fragmented within English or literature courses; occasionally as the poor third creative art in liberal studies courses; and otherwise embedded, if anywhere, only in the early childhood area.

Ironically, in the not-so-distant past, most of our teacher education students would have had much more drama than now they do. And that was before scholars like Elliot Eisner and Maxine Greene had formulated that same aesthetic curriculum that our heroine's colleague teaches so dutifully, and before drama gained whatever establishment it has in Australian schools (which are the main location of this book). This contemporary deficit is especially true in secondary teacher education, where unless they are drama specialists, preservice teachers are unlikely to get any access to drama at all. Back in the 1970s and even 1980s, all student-teachers in Aus-tralia took classes including some drama activities, which were sometimes called communication, sometimes drama or sometimes speech and drama. These were popular and generally quite uncontested territory. Pretty well everybody accepted them unreservedly as helping the students to develop the personal and interpersonal presentational skills necessary for a teacher/performer, to foster those skills in their own school classes, and to establish sufficient understanding of group dynamics to generate a lively, controlled dialogue in classes. Yet they have vanished almost completely, driven out by new invaders demanding temporal territory, time for inclusive education, for special needs education, for ethics and safety and health, research and reflective practice, professional practice studies, more time for teaching strategies, more time for. . . curriculum.

To look at the stand-off between those two like-minded colleagues, and begin the complex process of deconstructing it, alternative lenses are needed to show that the situation need not be so polarised. We must examine the nature of drama itself, and what, if any, is its relationship to learning, and therefore its claims to a share of the schooling territory. We must also examine the history of western schooling – and particularly the ideological, political and economic basis of the curriculum, which has existed since the establishment of compulsory schooling. And we must scrutinise the word 'curriculum' itself, where in this apparently solid word reassuring to parents and old school principals we shall discover a miasma of paradoxical, problematic, contradictory meanings, connotations and associations.

How to Read this Book

Our story of drama in curriculum draws on two metaphors. The people who make curriculum often unconsciously use one of them in the phrase 'curriculum-building'. We think that this metaphor is often unwittingly made true, and curriculum is conceptualised, established and built like a house, where certain kinds of knowledge take up permanent residence, while others are occasional visitors, and some are rarely or never invited. To capture the spirit of drama, we were attracted by the Greek myth of the Titan Proteus, the old man of the sea who tended Poseidon's seals. Proteus could change himself into any shape he pleased (hence 'protean'). This is the magic capacity of drama, in fact its central function: through fiction, we can rearrange reality temporarily to look like whatever we want it to, then change it at will into an altered or a different fiction to fit our purpose. Putting the two metaphors together seems to us quite apt to describe drama's protean (and titanic) efforts to be seen as a welcome visitor or even a resident in that house, and this is a central narrative throughout the book. Proteus had another magic characteristic, which is relevant to our story, too: if seized and held, he would foretell the future. As we follow Proteus in his assaults on the door of the house, we will try to seize hold of him within the pages of this book and we hope that by the end, we may have held him long enough for at least some possibilities for the future to be revealed.

The book is divided into three parts.

Part One (Chapters 1–2) sets the scene and gives the background and context to the relationship between drama and curriculum. Chapter 1 traces and maps through history the paradoxical, continuing but uneasy kinship of drama with education, starting with its position as a natural part of the family in some traditional societies. In Western society, Plato was the first to show it the door, and it's been in and out ever since, rarely fully ousted or regathered, as we see in Chapter 1. In order to focus specifically on its relationship with 'curriculum', in other words what happens in the establishments where learning happens officially, it is necessary to understand exactly what this relatively modern term means, and how it manifests itself in current and recent schooling systems worldwide; this is the purpose of Chapter 2.

Part Two (Chapters 3–7) is the conceptual and philosophical hub of the book, which tries to disentangle the many reasons why people do drama, and how these have intersected in schools through the twentieth century and into the twenty-first century. When drama and theatre do make an appearance in schools, it is for a bewilderingly knotty diversity of purposes, knotty because some of these threads of purpose blend into each other, while others appear contradictory or incompatible. We believe that the multiple threads can be untangled and plaited into four strands of related purposes, which can usefully be distinguished from each other. The first three represent major paradigms of purpose that are on the whole distinct, although we will show how they are frequently woven into and through each other. The first (first only in the order they appear, not in priority) we are calling the *linguistic/communicative* paradigm: developing language through drama; this is dealt with in Chapter 3. Equally important is the *expressive/developmental* paradigm: growing through drama, which is dealt with in Chapter 4. The third is the *social/pedagogical*: learning through drama, the subject of Chapter 5. In one way or another, these three dominated drama in schools – and all educational contexts – through the twentieth century, and each had its impassioned and articulate adherents, for drama teachers down the ages have been nothing if not both passionate and vocal. Probably inevitably, those territorial pressures caused rifts and feuds, when the paradigms seemed irreconcilable. The most serious of these is dealt with in Chapter 6. However, by the end of the century, another way entirely of looking at the purpose of drama in schools had become current, a concept derived from the broader field of arts education philosophy. This we have defined as the *aesthetic/cognitive*: the art form of drama, studying and practicing all dimensions of what humans do when they participate in drama and theatre. That may seem deceptively simple, even obvious, but there is of course more to it than that. Chapter 7 demonstrates that the theory and practice within this paradigm effectively unpicks the knot that caused the very uncivil war, resolves the apparent dichotomy and can subsume all the other paradigms. To change the metaphor again, drama besides being a shape-shifter is a many-headed monster, and invariably fulfils a number of purposes at the same time. In a drama activity whose primary purpose is seeking to develop some aspect of their language, the students will probably be simultaneously engaged in other aspects of language development, in developing personal and social skills, in a pedagogy, which brings in many areas of curriculum, and in developing dramatic skills and knowledge.

Part Three (Chapters 8–11) changes the focus and to some extent the tone of the book, demonstrating through a series of stories how drama in all its manifestations has shape-shifted into contemporary education. Chapter 8 takes the context the authors are most familiar with as a case study, first telling the story of how Queensland metamorphosed from one of the world's more traditional and mechanistic education systems into one of its most progressive, with drama embedded at all levels; the salient features of this are analysed and applied to a widened case study incorporating all Australian states, to show how those key features are necessary for drama to establish itself in formal education systems. Key features notwithstanding, there are still plenty of curriculum gatekeepers to be overcome, bribed or otherwise disarmed, in order to establish a consultative drama curriculum for a whole state schooling system, as Chapter 9's first-hand story illustrates. The alternative is to fly under the radar, and make of drama what the earlier chapters claim for it: namely, the centre of your own curriculum. This is what Chapter 10 describes, with the down-to-earth narrative of one teacher's use of drama to teach virtually everything to her students. Chapter 11 ponders the future, trying to bear in mind both drama's propensity to shape-shift and education's thoroughly ambivalent attitude towards it.

The Book as Curriculum

We are also aware that this book can be seen as a curriculum document in itself. If that is the case, then as authors we should try to put our money where our mouth is, and construct the book itself as the kind of dialogical curriculum which we endorse in its pages. The notion of 'educational book' starts off where the notion of 'curriculum' usually starts: it is on the face of it a presentation of knowledge, written by us who know (and are impelled to tell you) for you who do not (and presumably do or should want to find out). It is ostensibly authoritative as it is authored, and it is ostensibly monological – you can't enter the discussion, exchange your own knowledge, dispute our assertions or question our authority. However, some form of dialogue is still possible, and we have tried to construct the book accordingly. For a start, it is multiply authored, and the authors have both worked and talked a lot together, and we continue to develop our ideas on curriculum (not least through the process of writing the book). Second, we have consulted many other authorities and sources of information – we have discussed with those authorities such as books and curriculum documents and curriculum users, which we refer to and quote. Third, we have been and still are engaged ourselves in the process of making curriculum at many educational levels. And fourth, the book has grown and changed, organically. It started out, like many a traditional curriculum outline or lesson plan, as a quite trim, tightly organised and clearly defined document, a chapter in a big and very authoritative Handbook on arts education (O'Toole & O'Mara, in Bresler 2007).

Expanding that chapter to a book has been rather like actually teaching the lesson: the transformation has changed the neat dynamics, and the structure too. The book has grown lots of bits, at least two unexpected chapters and some quite new ideas; the nicely distinct paradigms started to fuzz at the edges and overlap more and more;

the shape has been re-arranged, a number of times; and this re-arrangement has resulted in a 'new' resolution of an established problematic that quite startled us. Even as we write this preface, we're still finalising the order of chapters to make the most sense to ourselves and our readers. There are so many interdependent components, but some have to be explained before others (for example, is it best to say first what curriculum is, how it works or where and why it happens?).

The book makes no claim to be comprehensive, and we freely admit to being positioned educationally, ideologically, culturally and geographically. We draw on personal experience as well as the literature in the field. We have been influenced by what Proteus has washed up on our shores from the twin oceans of curriculum and drama experience. We have tried to fashion something coherent from the driftwood and shells we found and hope that it will be useable by others.

We hope the book has a wide relevance, but it is not universal. We shall be looking at the phenomenon of drama curriculum mainly in its manifestations in Australia, to a lesser extent the United Kingdom, and lesser still the USA, Canada, Africa, South East Asia, and other systems. We have three reasons or excuses for this:

- First, obviously, the authors are all Australians, who have all worked in the UK as well, and we're writing about what we know best.
- Second, the book needs a focus of evidence and practice that we are in a position to provide, which we hope will be recognisable, will resonate with readers' own different contexts, and will be easily transferable to them. The overwhelming majority of educational literature published by this and other major publishers has strong and usually unacknowledged US-centricity or Anglo-centricity for which we are all used to making allowances, and we plead your similar indulgence.
- Third, perhaps our most important and we hope most convincing excuse is that Australia is one of the few countries which has established drama more or less throughout the curriculum, at all levels and all schooling systems in all states – and has had some sort of continuous establishment for over 20 years. Canada has too, and Taiwan, New Zealand, and some Scandinavian countries are among those that now have a well-supported official commitment to drama throughout the school years. In the USA and UK, the situation is far more patchy, though for different reasons that will be touched on in this book. Elsewhere, we believe that drama is mainly outside the door to the curriculum, still. We hope we might be wrong, and if you have evidence that we are, dear reader, then it's time for you to write the next book – on that drama curriculum.

Meanwhile, in another sign of the times, back at that 'new generation' faculty committee stand-off, less than a year later, neither of those warring academic colleagues were still on the committee. Nor did the committee exist. Their territorial battle had been subsumed in an entirely new curricular paradigm imposed by the scientists making a triumphant comeback. Both had seen some gains and losses to their beloved areas, dictated by factors that were entirely extraneous to either but dominant over both. Our heroine's primary drama time had shrunk even further, as she had feared, to an even less adequate 12 hours teaching. In some compensation, the time allocation for her secondary drama specialist teachers – which she already viewed as comparatively generous – had been doubled. As usual, she accepted the swings and the roundabouts, made up her quarrel with her colleague, and set about finding some new doors to penetrate deeper into this supposedly 'new generation' house of curriculum, where she realised she was still in the entrance hall.

To help our heroine to reflect on why this is drama's position and she what might do about it, we hope it will be worth reading this book. Time and time again, drama confronts curriculum doorkeepers who are, like the frog footman at Alice's palace door, masters of not listening, and of sophistical argument. Drama, the giant that shape-shifts, in spite of its Protean qualities, is still at the door.

Reference

O'Toole, J. & O'Mara, J. (2007). Proteus, the giant at the door: Drama and theatre in curriculum. In Liora Bresler (Ed.), *International handbook of research in arts education.* Amsterdam: Springer.

Part I
Background and Context

Chapter 1
Strange Bedfellows: Drama and Education

John O'Toole

Play and Pre-School

Historically, drama has had a long and equivocal relationship with education, formal and informal.

This relationship is probably at its richest, most universal and least noticed in dramatic play. From the moment when a child plays 'peekaboo' with its parent or another adult, three of the foundations of drama are being laid: the (1) *shared agreement* to (2) *pretend* that produces (3) *pleasure*. Jerome Bruner, following Piaget, defined the importance of peekaboo as identifying the point at which an infant can demonstrate that it understands the permanence of objects (1976: 271–285). In terms of drama – or proto-drama – the delight that the child gets from peekaboo and shares with the adult is one of the first manifestations of the pleasure of *social playing*: it shows that the child also paradoxically understands that the permanence of objects can be temporarily suspended (i.e., *pretend*) and that this action is *pleasurable* if the pretence is *shared*. Perhaps too there is an element even in peekaboo not only of *play* but also of *display* that relates to the beginning of understanding of the pleasure of performance and the notion of audience that emerges soon after with the unmistakeable expressions of pretend: 'Look at me – I'm flying'. Whether that is true or not, peekaboo is a flying start, and from then on the child builds on this foundation structures of dramatic play of increasing sophistication and artistry. Simple pretend quickly incorporates fantasy and narrative, and the child both generates and shares the means of controlling the pleasurable and increasingly sociable expression of these. By now, hundreds of other researchers have investigated the specific learning effects of dramatic play, from Smilansky's (1968) classic work with disadvantaged children in the 1960s to Betty-Jane Wagner's 30-year quest to chart especially the language effects (1998).

The early years of childhood are full of dramatic play. Educational psychologists and philosophers have much more enthusiastically acknowledged the crucial cognitive, sensory, emotional and kinaesthetic learning that takes place within play during these formative years than the guardians and commentators of the school curriculum. The Czech education philosopher Jan Comenius in the 1650s, working as headmaster of a school in Hungary, suggested that school should be a joyful

J. O'Toole et al., *Drama and Curriculum,* Landscapes: the Arts, Aesthetics,
and Education 6, DOI 10.1007/978-1-4020-9370-8_2,
© Springer Science+Business Media B.V. 2009

place where children learn through play, and in this as we also shall see later, he very specifically included dramatic play and plays. As Anna-Lena Østern notes:

> Comenius writes about how play, a free, creative and orderly activity, is natural for the human being, is authentically human, and is social:
> 'Play/acting reinforces a stronger life than any other. All children learn remains more strongly in their minds when they act themselves and especially when they say and perform for many other people, on the stage; and they learn better together with others than they do alone' (Østern 2007: 235).

In the eighteenth century, Friedrich Froebel declared that 'Play is the highest expression of human development in childhood for it alone is the free expression of what is in a child's soul' (in Lowenfeld 1991: 91). By the end of the nineteenth century, the Swiss philosopher Groos (1899/1976: 68) suggested that 'young animals do not just play – they have their childhood in order to play'. The twentieth century's two most renowned and influential educational psychologists, Jean Piaget and Lev Vygotsky, both acknowledged and wrote extensively about learning and dramatic play, the first exploring its role in the formation of understanding of symbols, rules and social structures, and the second asserting its importance in the development of language (e.g., Piaget 1962 & Vygotsky 1933/1976) and as one of the building blocks of his philosophy of the socially constructed nature of learning.

The notion of curriculum is often much more fluid in early years' contexts, anyway, and much more open to drama. In what was for systemic education a highly unusual initiative in 1975, the founding Director of the Queensland Pre-school Education Branch, the late Gerald Ashby, strenuously and successfully opposed the development (or imposition) of any kind of formal curriculum, written or otherwise. This department's decision was embraced by a young teacher joining this new department as:

> its leaders who were bold enough to suggest that we should facilitate young children's learning, based on their love of engaging with the real world, rather than that the regular indoctrination process of 'real' learning that occurred in other sectors at the time (McGowan 2007).

Not coincidentally, as a major part of his strategy for the new pre-schools, Ashby generously funded a local theatre, La Boîte, to provide a theatre-in-education company, ECDP (the Early Childhood Drama Project), to work with schools and children developing both interactive performances for schools and teaching resources for play (Education Queensland 2005: 8). The absence of curriculum and the ECDP both lasted for about 8 years, but vanished for quite different reasons: the Queensland Department of Education predictably could not handle what they saw as a vacuum (Ashby had long moved on) and with relief, prepared multiple curriculum documents. Even then, they were cautious about it – Ashby's influence remained strong:

> Preschool curriculum was seen as emergent, that is, as being developed by the teacher within an observational framework based on thorough understanding of typical patterns of human development, while recognising unique aspects of development for each individual, and with scope for significant input from children themselves and from their parents. Within

this approach, the teacher was expected to draw on relevant knowledge disciplines rather than be directed by them (ibid: 12).

Twenty-five years on, 'Early childhood education in Queensland state schools is characterized by quality curriculum, pedagogy, assessment and reporting' declares the same Department proudly (Education Queensland 2007). Almost simultaneously with that hardening of curriculum, La Boîte theatre decided that it did not need or want the ECDP or theatre in education in that form anyway, nor even the Department's money, and disbanded it. To its credit, the Department has continued to sponsor a theatre-in-education team for Early Childhood, KITE, to this day, in a number of evolving forms – one that is very explicitly harnessed to curricular ends.

Dramatic and proto-dramatic forms of play as learning also form the field of examination of scholars of adult human behaviour, such as Clifford Geertz (1976), with his exploration of extreme forms such as 'deep play', later expanded upon as 'dark play' by Schechner (1993: 36), who brings it back home to drama and theatre.

The word play, and dramatic play itself, quickly disappear, however, in the space of modern schooling that 'curriculum' inhabits. As we shall see, schools do have a place for play – the 'playground', which is physically and conceptually marked out as separate from the 'classroom'. Children come *into* the school *from* the *play*ground, to do school*work*, which is different from play ... indeed, by rarely challenged assumptions of over a century, its opposite or converse. Julie Dunn is one of the few writers who have followed the study of pre-school play into later years of schooling – and, significantly, she had to do it in a co-curricular context (2002).

Traditional Performative Education

It was not always so, and many traditional education systems have depended on dramatic play, formalised and performative storytelling, dance and theatre, and specialised genres such as praise poetry, as significant drivers of learning. You might say that the word 'curriculum' is too formal and pretentious a title for this organic societal process; however, the sharing, passing on and building upon the wisdom of the tribe seems to us a pretty good definition of the word. Recent African scholarship seeking to reclaim and understand traditional performance forms has identified how important the performing arts have been for developing young people's understanding, especially of mores and moral imperatives: Chris Odhiambo, facing orthodox modern pedagogy in Physics with exasperation, turns and affirms in Piagetian terms the contemporary relevance of

> the indigenous art forms ... encompassing all the learning domains ... essentially dramatic/theatrical in nature. Indeed, they can be viewed as a fusion of epistemology, work and play, in which assimilation and accommodation are kept in balance by the guidance of narrator/singer/dancer/artist and which translated into the contemporary pedagogical set-up becomes the classroom teacher (1999: 144).

Qoopane (1990) describes how this happens at community level through the sharing of traditional and current stories during regular evening gatherings. Kennedy

Chinyowa (1999, 2001) analyses the pedagogical importance of children's games and traditional narratives. In South Africa, Dalrymple (1996), in consciously tapping into these traditional forms to generate student-driven community learning, shows their applicability in one of the most pressing concerns of contemporary African curriculum: health education, and specifically preventing the spread of HIV-AIDS.

> They use their own voice, their own ways of saying things, to tell their parents. These young people know how to dance, they know their folk dances; in some of the more rural areas there's no sport, so this is what they do in the afternoons – the whole range of traditional dances. So when we said to them, 'Well, how would you put across the [HIV-AIDS] message?' they picked on these – and praise poetry as well, that's very popular – and they changed them, and they made them about HIV-AIDS. And so when the parents come to watch, they can read the form: the message is new, but the form is theirs. They are very excited about it and they give the young people their support (Dalrymple 1996).

The relationship of traditional performance forms and contemporary curriculum in the realm of community and adult education has morphed into the genre now known as *Theatre for Development*.

Greeks Beware of Drama Bearing Gifts

The origin of formal drama in western society is obscure, and was so even for Aristotle, who was writing his *Poetics* in about 330 BC, and who describes the varying claims of drama's antiquity from all over Greece. Aristotle's title, of course, is significant, since though he is writing mainly about highly sophisticated performances of tragic theatre, even he makes no clear distinction between poetry and drama. This should not be as surprising as it seems to contemporary Western ears, and would not be at all surprising to the African storyteller/performers mentioned above. Poetry has always been performed, long before it was ever written down, and the poetical storyteller and actor were one and the same (incarnate in the legendary Thespis), since any storyteller naturally drops into the first person, and takes on and enacts the characters of those s/he is describing and enacting. One of Aristotle's candidates for drama's direct ancestor is the dithyramb, or harvest festival celebration poetry. At some time, this became tied up with the rites of worship of the god Dionysus, telling stories from his life – and, therefore, in one broad sense, educational. This pattern linking drama with educating audiences about religion is one that was to recur over a millennium later in Western theatre.

The dithyramb also sets another pattern, which is the main theme of this book, that of the nervous ambivalence with which professional educators have viewed drama ever since. As Harwood (1984: 39) points out very pertinently to our purposes, 'the entrance of Dionysus into the theatre's evolution is decisive'. The dithyrambs, apparently, used to get out of hand (Dionysus was god, among other things, of revelry and wine), and by Aristotle's time were probably in decline anyway, as by then sophisticated and still rapidly changing forms of tragedy and comedy were both flourishing. So was the nervous ambivalence, and the lingering sense that slightly below the surface of drama lie those frenzied and anarchic rites, ready to emerge and imperil the fragile structure of civilisation ... and yet, maybe there is some good in it. Aristotle certainly thought so, and it is instructive to compare his attitude to drama and education with that of his own tutor, Plato.

Plato could be regarded as the first Western philosopher of curriculum, since in his vision of a perfect state, *The Republic* (c.360BC), he argues at great length about the qualities needed for its citizens and, therefore, to be instilled in its children. Being the founder of the first Academy, he had both theoretical and practical interests in curriculum. Plato, in spite of his enthusiasm for play in education, had a more reluctant admiration for grown-up drama, and finally decided almost entirely to banish the poets (i.e., dramatists) from his ideal Republic, as we shall see. It is worth spending a little time with Plato, because that text mirrors the ambivalence of his successors, down to those today who would banish drama from our schools, or keep it safely on the margins of the curriculum. Book 3 of *The Republic* shows exactly how down the ages, educators have all too often misunderstood the very nature of drama, both overestimating its dangers and underestimating its power, and completely missing its central paradox concerning the relationship between fact and fiction, reality and illusion. In hindsight, it is astonishing that Plato of all people missed it, since his major philosophical legacy consists of destabilising our perceptions of what reality and truth are, proposing an alternative, paradoxical and deeper, but unseen, spiritual reality. The length and tortuous logic of his argumentation on drama suggests that he really is uneasy about it, perhaps as regretful as he is determined to keep it out of the perfect state.

He attacks on two fronts, both central elements of drama: narrative and mimesis (imitation), and he attempts to deal with both the substance and form between which he assumes a simple and direct relationship. In terms of narrative, he takes the case of those storytellers who sing and perform the reprehensible deeds of some of the gods. He makes the assumption that to hear of something is the same thing as firstly to believe it, and secondly to want to do it. So he demands that

> We will not have them trying to persuade our youth that the gods are the authors of evil, and that heroes are no better than men

because

> They are likely to have a bad effect on those who hear them, for everybody will begin to excuse his own vices ... and therefore let us put an end to such tales, lest they engender laxity of morals in the young.

Moreover,

> Poets and storytellers are guilty of making the gravest mis-statements when they tell us that wicked men are often happy, and the good miserable; and that injustice is profitable when undetected ... these things we shall forbid them to utter and command them to sing and say the opposite.

He then turns his attention to imitation, at first in the indirect form of the first-person spoken narrative, pointing out that the actor/narrator cannot have real experience of the character he is assuming (actors were all male, in Plato's mind at least). Therefore, the more characters he tries to assume, the less authentic they will be ... which Plato then transfers into the real life of the narrator:

> No one man can imitate many things as well as he would imitate a single one. Then the same person will hardly be able to play a serious part in life, and at the same time to be an imitator and imitate other parts as well, for even when two species of imitation are nearly allied, the same persons cannot succeed in both, as for example the writers of tragedies and comedies.

By now he is getting quite a head of steam, and recycles the point he made earlier about narrative, especially for the potential leaders of the state – the 'guardians':

> If they imitate at all, they should imitate from youth upward only those characters that are suitable to their profession – the courageous, temperate, holy, free and the like; but they should not depict or be skilful at imitating any kind of illiberality or baseness, lest from imitation they should come to be what they imitate .... Neither should they imitate the actions or speech of men or women who are mad or bad; for madness, like vice, is to be known but not to be practised or imitated.

Now we're getting to the crux of his argument. Not only must the Guardians-to-be, for the same reason, not

> imitate a woman quarrelling with her husband ... or when she is in affliction, or sorrow ... and certainly not one who is in sickness, love or labour ...

... but Plato's just about to grasp the wrong end of another stick entirely.

> Neither must they represent slaves, male or female ... neither may they imitate smiths or other artificers, or oarsmen or the like .... How can they, when they are not allowed to apply their minds to the callings of any of these?

In other words, not only you are debasing yourself to try and act lowlife, but if you haven't lived it, you can't play it authentically. Instead,

> When he comes to a character which in unworthy of him, he will not make a study of that ... he feels such an art, unless in jest, to be beneath him, and his mind revolts at it.

Plato then graciously steps back to concede that there are in fact actors who are capable of taking a wide range of characters good and bad, and performing them convincingly; even that this 'pantomimic' style (imitating everything), though the opposite of what he is recommending, is:

> very charming, and ... is the most popular style with children and their attendants, and with the world in general.

However, (of course)

> Such a style is unsuitable for Our State, in which human nature is not twofold or manifold, for one man plays one part only.

And so, with a wonderfully elegant and respectful regret he waves it away:

> When one of these pantomimic gentlemen, who are so clever that they can imitate anything, comes to us, and makes a proposal to exhibit himself and his poetry, we will fall down and worship him as a sweet and holy and wonderful being, but we must also inform him that in Our State such as he are not permitted to exist; the law will not allow them – and so when

we have anointed him with myrrh, and set a garland of wool on his head, we shall send him away to another city.

The only poets permitted to remain will be the

rougher and severer sort, who will imitate the style of the virtuous only.

Like many educators after him, he confused fiction with untruth. In his imaginary perfect Republic, human nature might not be manifold, contradictory and ambiguous, but in any real world it assuredly is.

Aristotle (c.330 BC), however, was a more empirical observer than his master Plato, and perhaps a better psychologist. Certainly he was much more supportive of drama and saw in tragedy an explicitly educational purpose which Plato would have actually approved. First, he insisted that 'Imitation, then, is one instinct of our nature.' He declared that Poetry, therefore, is a more philosophical and a higher thing than history: for poetry tends to express the *universal*, and history the *particular*. Very shrewdly, he saw much more clearly than Plato the complex interaction of content and form. He analysed how theatre's didactic message purpose must be purveyed equally through its intellectual power, by getting people to think, and through its emotional impact, by generating in the audience vicarious pity and terror for the tragic protagonist, dangerous emotions that were purged through the catharsis of the play's resolution.

It should imitate actions which excite pity and fear, this being the distinctive mark of tragic imitation. It follows plainly, in the first place, that the change, of fortune presented must not be the spectacle of a virtuous man brought from prosperity to adversity: for this moves neither pity nor fear; it merely shocks us. Nor, again, that of a bad man passing from adversity to prosperity: for nothing can be more alien to the spirit of Tragedy; it possesses no single tragic quality; it neither satisfies the moral sense nor calls forth pity or fear (330BC: Chapter 13).

For this, the contemporary drama educator and prophet of liberatory theatre Augusto Boal has famously dubbed Aristotle as creator of 'Theatre of Oppression', where the purpose of theatre is to keep people enslaved to the notion that their fate and oppression are immutable.

Aristotle's coercive system of tragedy survives to this day, thanks to its great efficacy. It is, in effect, a powerful system of coercion (1979: 46).

In this, he is rather unkindly shooting the messenger. Aristotle didn't invent classical tragedy, or even write it – his *Poetics* is merely a very sophisticated empirical analysis of a phenomenon that he considered important. And the greatest of the classical tragedians, such as Sophocles and Euripides, transcend the strictures of either Aristotle or Boal, as great writers always do – the fates of Antigone, Philoctetes, Phaedra and Medea are too ambiguous, complex and deeply thought-provoking to be reduced either to a simplistic cathartic release or to an equally simplistic reinforcement of oppression. Aristotle makes the point himself, and in his detailed analysis is not afraid to contradict his master Plato:

Unity of plot does not, as some persons think, consist in the Unity of the hero. For infinitely various are the incidents in one man's life which cannot be reduced to unity . . .. Nor, again, should the downfall of the utter villain be exhibited. A plot of this kind would, doubtless, satisfy the moral sense, but it would inspire neither pity nor fear; for pity is aroused by unmerited misfortune, fear by the misfortune of a man like ourselves. Such an event, therefore, will be neither pitiful nor terrible. There remains, then, the character between these two extremes, that of a man who is not eminently good and just, yet whose misfortune is brought about not by vice or depravity, but by some error or frailty . . .. A perfect tragedy should, as we have seen, be arranged not on the simple but on the complex plan (Chapter 13).

The Pattern Repeated: Medieval and Renaissance Theatre

Over the next millennium and a half, the same pattern replayed itself. Plato's spirit infused the early Christians, in more derogatory language – and again Dionysus got the blame, along with his artistic and celebratory fellows in the pagan pantheon, particularly Venus and Apollo. Following Plato's measured if mistaken logic but without his courteous dismissal, Christian theologians like Tertullian and St Augustine of Hippo saw no educative potential in theatre. They leapt to the conclusion that since those old gods were not dead but re-invented as 'devils', then 'Dionysus the old god is lord of the theatre, therefore the theatre belongs to the devil . . . and the devil will enter the audience's mind'. That was Tertullian. Augustine just chortled at the collapse of theatre: 'the theatres are falling almost everywhere, those sinks of uncleanness . . . lewd and sacrilegious practices'.

The authors are grateful for the very recent information and insight in the above paragraph to Li Chyi-Chang (2008: 95–102), one of the burgeoning new Taiwanese community of drama education scholars. This shows, if nothing else, how Proteus gets around, and drama's ups and downs find resonances worldwide. Li draws the same conclusions as we have about the pervasiveness of Plato's belief that immoral behaviour will be copied by the spectator (98) and Aristotle's more beneficent influence (95).

It has been customary in recent years to change the nomenclature of the period following the fall of the Roman Empire from 'Dark Ages' to 'early Middle Ages'. However, in the contemporary theatre terminology of a theatre being 'dark' when no production is happening, they were Dark Ages indeed. The post-Roman church happily banned drama, and theatre disappeared as a public art-form. Of course, drama lurked on in the lives of the new rulers. Thespis now spoke other languages as the storytellers of the Norse and Celtic sagas, and mimesis was alive and well among the carnivals and folk-rites of the underclasses, such as the Nordic Yul-Plays (Eriksson 2002).

However, with typical ambivalence, not all in the church had totally dismissed drama in those theatrically dark ages, and it was its educational potential that encouraged the same church once more to bring it out as a distinct art-form (though not this time in quite such a frenzied cult as Dionysus), at the turn of the millennium. The writings of the Greek and Romans, including their plays, as well as Plato and Aristotle, were preserved by monastic communities around Europe, and the poetry was certainly read. The early medieval church re-discovered the performative possibilities of enacting stories from scripture for the edification of the audience or congregation – as a musical, no less, complete with stage directions, costumes, props, choruses and tenor solo:

> Let four brethren dress themselves; of whom let one, wearing an alb, enter as if to take part in the service; and let him without being observed approach the place of the sepulcher, where, holding a palm in his hand, let him sit quietly. While the third responsory is being sung, let the remaining three brethren follow, all of them wearing copes and carrying censors filled with incense. Then slowly, in the manner of seeking something, let them move toward the place of the sepulcher.
>
> These things are to be performed in imitation of the Angel seated in the tomb, and of the women coming with spices to anoint the body of Jesus. When therefore the seated angel shall see the three women, as if straying about and looking for something, approach him, let him begin to sing in a dulcet voice of medium pitch:
>
> Whom seek ye in the sepulcher, O followers of Christ?
>
> (Ethelwold Bishop of Winchester, c. 965, Regularis Concordia, in Gassner 1987: 37).

This *Quem quaeritis* (Whom seek ye) trope, as it is known, and similar enactments around Europe produced by monastic orders, like the Benedictines, are generally regarded as the starting point of modern British and European drama, and they clearly have an educational function. They must have been a roaring success, for within a couple of hundred years, they were turned from Latin into the local vernaculars, and fully dramatised into the form usually known as Miracle Plays. As they became more complex, they incorporated lay members as extras, and then they spilled right out of the churches and into secular production.

Companies of travelling players took them up, and schools followed, bringing drama back into formal education with a rush. The Miracle Play of Daniel was both written and performed in 1140 in a Beauvais 'scholars' festival' and the Cornish Cycle of plays 'derives mainly from Glasney College, Penrhyn' (Coggin, in Li 2008: 117). Then in larger cities, the citizens' trade guilds were roped in to help cover the increasing cost of staging. This is probably how the plays got their rather misleading alternative title of 'Mystery' plays, from the French word 'mystère' meaning craft (in middle English 'maistrie' or mastery of the craft). Although some historians construe the word as referring to the ineffable 'mystery' of Christianity, these plays' very purpose was in fact to illuminate, not mystify – to bring religion right down to earth. Some guilds took the responsibility for particularly apt stories, such as the Shipwrights' for Noah's Flood, or macabrely the guild of Pinners (nailmakers) for the Crucifixion. By the fifteenth century, both lay and clerical writers were involved, as the marvellously rich melange of vernacular and religious dialogue in plays like the Wakefield Second Shepherd's Play or the York Play of the Crucifixion indicates.

> 2nd Shepherd: Hail sovereign saviour, that all things has wrought
> Hail, I kneel and I cower. A bird I have brought
> Bairn that ye are.
> Hail little tiny mop –
> Of our creed thou art top.
> At thy mass I shall stop –
> Little day star.
> (Adapted from middle English by the author)

They developed into cycles of plays covering, for the edification of the whole population, the major events of the Christian scriptures from the Creation to the Resurrection and beyond. They were usually performed on Christian festivals such as Corpus Christi Day (or days, since the full cycles could take a couple of days to fully enact). Sometimes they were performed on a set stage in the market place; other producers embodied the ongoing narrative quality by having each staged separately with the audience moving from one to the other, or even reversing the process and celebrating the processional flavours of the day by having the stages erected on moving carts. However diverse, some of the most well-preserved cycles show the unifying hand of writers or producers, such as the anonymous Master of Wakefield, who was probably a cleric.

Although the movement lasted for hundreds of years, it was not without its critics from the start and it was not long before those who distrusted the power of fiction raised the old objections. A very education-minded nun, Herrad of Landsberg, with a penchant for visual art, was attacking the new drama as early as 1050 in her *Garden of Delights*. Three hundred years later, the Dean of Theology at the University of Paris (also a curriculum gatekeeper, incidentally), described it in 1445 as:

> A gin-trap of the devil which draws people to the belief of the Antichrist. I witnessed with my own eyes men and women weep at the sights before them and gave credence to many lies as well as truths by their means ....[1]

Aha, here we are again – more intemperately than Plato, but the same conflation of dramatic fiction with untruth, and the same fear of the power of drama to cause real-life manifestation of evil by imitating it. Like Plato, however, the Dean was not without grace, and knew how to bring it down by patronising it:

> It should not be played, for though it was plausible to years ago, and would now also of the ignorant sort be liked, yet now in this happy time of the Gospel I know the learned will mislike it.

Shades of Plato and the pantomimes.

By the Dean's time, not only had the dramas become much more lavish and expensive, but new and more explicitly educational forms were evolving, partly perhaps to counter the kinds of arguments put above. These didactic 'morality' plays depicted vices and virtues symbolically personified. The moral educational purpose was hardly subtle, as in the most famous English example of the genre, *Everyman*, where the eponymous hero with his good mate 'Fellowship' encounters various nasties like 'Death', 'Goods', and even 'Kindred' before 'Knowledge' and 'Good-deeds' save him and deliver him to a friendly angel. Not all have happy endings – some are more cautionary tales, like *The Morality of Wisdom*, whose main characters 'Soul' and 'Wisdom' carry on an elegant but hardly electrifying dialogue with 'Mind', 'Will' and 'Understanding' – until Lucifer comes along to liven up the

---

[1] These quotations from the Reverend Dean, and the later ones in similar vein by Archbishop Grindal, the author retrieved as a part of the research for a production involving Medieval theatre in 1979. I have been unable to verify the references.

discussion a bit, and beguile the latter three into sin . . . and the play ends with them celebrating their beguilement with a lively dance.

And that kind of two-bob each way, so typical of drama's paradoxical and playful nature, led eventually on the one hand to the rich ambiguity and complex moral debate of the great Elizabethan and Jacobean dramatists. Their way was actually prepared for them in advance by the universities and even the schools themselves, as the indispensable Li Chyi-Chang's detective work reveals (2008: 120–124). Back in the thirteenth century, Thomas Aquinas laid the groundwork for a rediscovery not only of Aristotle but also of dramatic play and its place in education. In the fourteenth century, Erasmus used drama in his educational ventures. In the fifteenth century, one Vittorino da Feltre set up a new school in Mantua originally wonderfully titled 'The Pleasure House' – then amended more cautiously to 'The Joyful House'. He brought into his curriculum not only play, play-reading and 'demonstrating' (of Plautus, Terence, Euripides and even Aristophanes) but also play-writing – in Greek and Latin, of course (128). Sir Thomas More, the English 'man for all seasons' who fell foul of King Henry VIII over Anne Boleyn, was more than a dabbler in drama, and drama education too. He wrote plays as a young man and was a close friend of Erasmus. He even 'founded a small university' and 'He himself was Head of the Drama Department' (147). His enthusiasm for drama was quite common at the time, it seems. It is well-known that one of the earliest surviving play-texts in 'modern' English, Nicholas Udall's *Ralph Roister Doister*, was presented to Queen Mary in 1553 by Udall's Westminster College students. This was a knockabout romantic comedy, not in the least 'improving'. What Plato would have said about this!

The disapproving spirit of Plato and Tertullian was still alive and gathering its forces against this outbreak of mirth and play in the school corridors. The killjoy descendants of Herrad of Lansberg and the Dean of Theology in Paris had crossed the floor during the Reformation, and though Luther himself encouraged play and even plays, the fast-growing Puritans set out to banish Proteus from their establishments once again – especially the dramatic education of the people represented by the Miracle Plays. Flushed with the self-righteousness of the Reformation, Archbishop Grindal of York firstly denounced drama as an outmoded Catholic practice – 'bending to lewd Papish profanities' – then invoked Plato's arguments to damn it:

> There is in this play called Corpus Christi Play many things used which tend to the derogation of the majesty and glory of God, the profanation of the sacraments and the maintenance of superstition and idolatry.

He was probably instrumental in having the Bishop of Chester incarcerated in the Tower of London for continuing to permit his local play festival (one of the most complete and sophisticated of all the cycles that have survived). Throughout Elizabeth's and James's reign, bodies responsible for the citizenry's welfare like the City of London dithered and banned it, then unbanned it, and then banned it again. They were torn between the growing ferocity of these fusillades against drama and the genuine and entirely cross-class enthusiasm for it from their monarchs themselves and their nobles down to the groundlings who thronged the open-air theatres. Came the revolution, and the triumph of Oliver Cromwell; all the theatres were closed in 1642 for nearly 20 years and not opened again till the restoration of the monarchy by the enthusiastic theatre-goer Charles II in 1660. Drama, in Britain anyway, went underground again.

However, it generally fared better on the European continent, with the morally improving fare of neo-Classical tragedy and with Italy's Commedia dell'Arte tradition and Molière in France keeping the flag of satire flying. Against the fulminations of the Calvinists, 'suitably pious plays performed in Latin became a regular feature of religious education on the continent', as Gavin Bolton informs us in his fine short history of drama education (2007: 46). It was again mostly the Catholics, especially the Jesuits, maintaining the torch. Significantly it was the Jesuits, as the religious order most concerned with the schooling of young people, who kept drama alive – though how ironic that the plays were now back in Latin, for the educated only. And even then, they were not safe from the killjoys. A dissenting French Catholic priest complained, echoing the Dean of Theology in Paris over a hundred years earlier, that they were 'contrary to the gospel and to our statutes', but went much further in his critique:

> that the plays are usually pitiful, that they waste a lot of time, that they distract the mind, that they wreak havoc with studies, over-excite the mind and go to the head (in Bolton 2007: 46).

As Bolton points out dryly, 'the antipathy it expresses towards school drama, and the reasons given for that hostility, have never entirely disappeared even to the present day'. Many drama teachers in contemporary schools will quite regularly deal with just these accusations, expressed perhaps in slightly less shrill form, by principals, parents, media, and colleagues teaching more sedate or sedentary subjects.

And yet, and yet …. Throughout the sixteenth and seventeenth centuries, the notion of 'teatro mundi' was entirely current, most famously encapsulated in English in 'All the world's a stage, and all the men and women merely players'. One visionary at least saw its implication for education, and actually put it into practice. Comenius not only suggested that school should be a joyful place where children learnt through play, but his specialty was educational theatre. In his pamphlet *Scholae Pansophicae* (1650), he demanded four theatre plays every year in school, and in *Scola ludus* (c.1650/1974), he attempted to encapsulate all the knowledge of his time within eight plays, which the children performed throughout the school. Among his other maxims are

- The one who wants to change what is happening on the stage of the world, firstly must educate man.
- The future sits at the school bench. What they play today becomes serious tomorrow.
- Our life is a play, the world a theatre, and school must be a prelude to life.
  (Comenius, adapted from Østern 2007).

However, while educational philosophers to this day continue to extol the visionaries like Comenius and Froebel, schooling systems have never followed their vision. In England at the same time as Comenius, when the restoration of King

Charles II brought theatre back with a wave of popularity, under a monarch even more enamoured of it than his forebears, it is hardly surprising that the ongoing ambivalence kept drama out of the schools virtually until the twentieth century, at least in any kind of dramatic form.

Aeschylus and Sophocles, even Terence and Plautus (suitably trimmed), did find their way into schools, safely pinned to the page as Greek and Latin texts. That way they could be useful as texts for translation, rather than as anything that might overexcite the mind and go to the head. Dead classic vernacular writers like Racine and Corneille, Shakespeare and Marlowe (well, some of their plays) could be safely regarded as morally improving texts. When compulsory schooling got under way in Britain and its colonies by the 1870s, there was little other sign of drama in the new curricula that were being designed. Sophocles and Plautus receded into the private schools. Those new curricula were emerging as a response to the ideals of the nineteenth century, and a shift from the education of an enlightened populace was being replaced by a utilitarian education for a literate but compliant workforce. This was cruelly immortalised by Dickens in *Hard Times*, but is still alive today, where in many countries a good class is a quiet class, and learning is socially approved (and socially improving) knowledge, usually about, as Dickens said: 'Facts! Give the boys nothing but facts!' to be transmitted by people called teachers, and accepted passively and uncritically by the learners. True, Arts still held a public position as Science's complement, especially in festivals, exhibitions and public events, but theatre especially was much more likely to be represented frozen in the carved friezes over the porticos of nineteenth-century college buildings than manifest inside the doors.

It is hard to keep drama out altogether, though its capacity to shape-shift like Proteus meant it kept reappearing in glimpses. It was usually found hanging around the doorways, as it still does, in pre-school dress-up corners and play spaces, in out-of-school plays, dance-drama displays and masques, in Christmas nativities, in 'let-your-hair-down' excursions and end-of-term rags. Teachers following the ideas of Froebel and Montessori discovered that their philosophies of the importance of self-expression, of play, and of activity learning often led in one way or another to or through the world of make-believe.

Four Strands of Purpose

At this point, moving into the twentieth century, it becomes unhelpful to try and follow the history as a single sweeping story, since during the twentieth century and the beginning of the twenty-first, drama makes not one entrance on to the curriculum stage, but many, through several different doors. The sections and chapters in this book pick up the story as drama and theatre make their re-emergence into the formal curricula of schooling throughout the twentieth century in a number of quite different shape-shifts, or manifestations, with very different purposes and outcomes ascribed to them. There are ironies abounding: because drama does take many forms, these have sometimes been lined up with philosophical, ideological or pedagogical purposes very much at odds with each other. Uncomfortably for those dominant paradigms, the forms of drama and its effects on learners have a habit of evolving into each other, and looking remarkably like something that is supposed to be quite different, or even something to be disapproved of. Sometimes, the way through the classroom door has been under the uneasy hegemony of an accepted discipline, such as English, languages, health, religious studies or physical education. Other arts already established in the curriculum, such as music, visual arts and in recent years media, have been ambivalent allies, often fearful of drama as a cuckoo that might take over their tenuous territory in the nest.

To try and chart these complex and often contradictory dynamics and influences, we have arranged the map according to what we see as drama's four major and relatively self-contained paradigms of purpose within a curriculum (though resonances and overlaps will be spotted all over the place). In addition, we try to address the notion of drama in the contemporary curriculum from both ends: how in yet another (more evolutionary) shape-shift, we will see drama can become in itself a micro-curriculum; and how, within the constraints of the rapidly changing contemporary curriculum scene, designing a statewide drama macro-curriculum entails dealing with a greater than ever range of competing possibilities, constraints, opportunities and threats.

In a few places – such as New Zealand, most of the States of Australia, a few States and Provinces of North America, Denmark, Taiwan – drama has achieved at least a notional full place among the standard subjects offered within a school curriculum, through all the years of schooling. These are still the exceptions. In many countries, it flourishes in the pre-schools and kindergartens, but then is left behind outside the classroom door. This is particularly true in economically developing or ambitious countries, such as most of those in South-East Asia, which have until very recently adopted or maintained the basically utilitarian aims and structures of the colonial educational systems, including the passive absorption of facts calculated to produce effective engineers, business managers, lawyers and scientists. These aims and structures fitted in quite comfortably, too, with the willing and unquestioning acceptance of the wisdom of elders that was demanded by some forms of traditional teaching, such as Chinese Confucianism.

In some systems, such as some authorities in the United Kingdom and other systems in North America and Europe, drama has a half-life embedded somewhere and semi-acknowledged, as part of English, or as something called 'expressive arts' or 'integrated arts'. This can be a highly creative fusing of art forms, as scholars such as Madeleine Grumet describe (2004), in a sense getting back towards the artistic continuity of those traditional societies where art, music, drama and dance are all part of the efflorescence of imaginative activity. Too often, it is just the result of a timetable compromise where the arts have been squeezed to the margin of the overcrowded curriculum. This is done by those who neither value them nor understand the entirely discrete sets of high-level cognitive, affective and technical understandings and skills necessary to engage in any one of the art forms, before it is possible to discover what they might all have in common as art forms. In that manifestation, 'expressive arts' usually means one of the following three things:

(a) a teacher using this time to teach whichever of the arts s/he happens to know about or be trained in – and that is least likely to be drama (Freebody 2005) – while trying gamely to insert token representation of the others;
(b) a battle for territory among the arts practitioners, which is usually won by the established and trained (and again that is rarely drama);
(c) a kind of low-skill arts muesli, where drama might be utilised in acting out bits of scenes dramatised from a story in front of a painted backdrop with a musical accompaniment.

Elsewhere, drama can be offered as a specialist study, even in special 'performing arts' schools, usually at the secondary level. In England again, drama suddenly re-emerges as a fully fledged, named secondary subject, where students are somehow expected to have been absorbing it through osmosis since they last met it in their early years of schooling.

In many countries, drama appears in the curriculum in another form entirely. In France, there is almost no such thing as a drama teacher, but instead, there are very well-developed partnerships ('partenariats') with performing artists, who see it as an important part of their professional responsibilities to engage with young people in their schooling through residencies, regular visits, special performances and so forth. Britain, USA, Canada and Australasia are among the countries with well-developed traditions of theatre-in-schools companies, with the actors and directors sometimes working directly to curricular briefs, as in the form known as 'theatre-in-education'. In economically developing countries, such as Thailand, groups such as the Maya Centre and Makhampom Theatre usually target children in socially and educationally disadvantaged regions.

Almost everywhere in the world, drama flourishes as extra-curricular activity: in school musicals and high-profile promotional events, in drama clubs, speech training, self-expression, emotional development and confidence building. It has its own life in the early childhood play corner. It excites and sometimes daunts English teachers. It is used for training procedural knowledge and strategic and managerial skills in vocational training, invariably under different names like 'role-training' and 'simulation'. Drama's stigma as something 'artistic', and therefore unpredictable, soft and unreliable, is vividly alive in the world of adult training and instruction. Those great military exercises where nations prepare for war by having simulated invasions, and where police squads prepare their probationers for hijacks and human relations by role-playing, are actually just drama at work. In the aftermath of crises, drama is one of the means often turned to help populations, and especially children, deal with the trauma of natural disaster or war. One form of dramatic activity has been developed into a rigidly controlled practice and annexed by the world of clinical psychiatry as 'psychodrama'. Under another title, 'Theatre for Development', drama attracts millions of dollars for communicating to village and rural populations. It lays claim to being a pedagogy as much as an art form, with implications across the school curriculum. It is being re-discovered in cyberspace through role-play structures and massively multiplayer interactive games like *Everquest* (Carroll 2004: 72) and more recently *World of Warcraft* and *Second Life*.

How do you wrap up all those somewhat conflicting manifestations in any coherent way in the overcrowded school timetable, how do you rationalise them, make a curriculum out of them or even badge them, and how on earth do you teach them, where most teachers have themselves had little or no exposure to drama in their own education?

References

Aristotle (c.330 BC) *The Poetics*. Variously translated and published.

Boal, A. (1979). *Theatre of the oppressed*. London: Pluto.

Bolton, G. (2007). A history of drama education – a search for substance. In L. Bresler (ed), *A Handbook of Research in Arts Education*. New York: Springer.

Carroll, J. (2004). Digital pre-text: process drama and everyday technology. In C. Hatton & M. Anderson (Eds.) *The state of our arts: NSW Perspectives in educational drama*. Sydney: Currency Press.

Chinyowa, K. (1999) Theatre for life: the educative function of traditional and modern children's games in Zimbabwe. *NJ – The Journal of Drama Australia, 23*(1) 71–83.

Chinyowa, K. (2001) The Pedagogical dimensions of an African Narrative Performance. *Drama Research*, 2 13–25.

Dalrymple, L. (1996) Transcribed from verbatim, in *Reflections in the River: The IDEA 95 Video*. Brisbane: IDEA Publications.

Dunn, J. (2002). *Imagined worlds in play*. Unpublished PhD thesis. Brisbane: Griffith University.

Education Queensland (2007) *Early Childhood Education Unit Homepage*. http://education.qld.gov.au/strategic/advice/earlychildhood/index.html. Accessed 25 February 2007

Education Queensland (2005) *The story of pre-school*. Brisbane: Department of Education and the Arts. http://education.qld.ov.au/etrf/docs/story_of_preschool.doc Accessed 7 April 2007. p. 8.

Eriksson, S. (2002). Christmas traditions and performance rituals: a look at Christmas celebrations in a Nordic context. *IDEA Journal/Applied Theatre Researcher, 4*. http://www. griffith.edu.au/centre/cpci/atr/content_journal_2003.html

Freebody, K. (2005). *Mentoring evaluation report: Arts Syllabus Implementation Committee*. Brisbane: Education Queensland: Mt Gravatt/Holland Park District.

Gassner, J. (Ed.) (1987) *Medieval and Tudor Drama*. New York: Applause Books.

Geertz, C. (1976). Deep play: notes on the Balinese cockfight. In J. Bruner, A. Jolly & K. Sylva. (Eds.) (1976) *Play : its role in development and evolution*. London: Penguin.

Groos, K. (1899). The Play of animals: play and instinct. In J. Bruner, A. Jolly & K. Sylva. (Eds.) (1976) *Play : its role in development and evolution*. London: Penguin.

Grumet, M. (2004). *No one learns alone*. In Nick Rabkin & Robin Redmond, *Putting the arts in the picture: reframing education in the 21st century*. Chicago: Columbia College.

Harwood, R. (1984) *All the world's a stage*. London: Methuen.

Li, C.-C. (2008). *Brecht's epic theatre in drama education*. Unpublished Ph.D. Thesis. Canberra: Australian National University.

Lowenfeld, M. (1920 republished 1991). *Play in Childhood*. New York: Mac Keith.

McGowan, G. (2007) *Pre-school days – teachers remember*. Queensland Department of Education, Training and the Arts. http://education.qld.gov.au/etrf/farewell/preschool_days.html Accessed 6 April 2007.

Odhiambo, C. (1999) New wine in old wineskins: exploiting indigenous folk art form in our contemporary pedagogical practices in Kenya. In E. Mwangi, T. Otieno & O. Mumma

(Eds.) *Emerging patterns for the third millennium: Drama/theatre at the Equator crossroads.* Nairobi: KDEA.

Østern, A.-L. (2007). The future of arts education – a European perspective. *Journal of Artistic and Creative Education, 1*(1).

Piaget, J. (1962). *Play, dreams and imitation in childhood.* London: Routledge & Kegan Paul.

Plato (c. 360BC) *The Republic. Book 3.* Variously published.

Qoopane, F. (1990) *Traditional African village performance.* Unpublished M.A. Thesis. Dar ed Salaam: University of Tanzania.

Schechner, R. (1993). *The Future of Ritual.* London: Routledge.

Smilansky, S. (1968) *The effects of sociodramatic play on disadvantaged preschool children.* New York: Wiley.

Vygotsky, L. S. (1976/1933). Play and its role in the mental development of the child. In J. S. Bruner, A. Jolly & K. Sylva. (Eds.), *Play – Its role in development and evolution* (pp. 537–554). Harmondsworth: Penguin Books. Transcribed from a lecture in Leningrad 1933.

Chapter 2
Curriculum: The House that Jack Built

John O'Toole and Madonna Stinson

A Grammar Lesson

Having looked through the telescope of history at whether, where and how drama is seen as educational curriculum, let's turn the scope round and look through the big end starting with curriculum, right back down the tube to drama, which mostly looks pretty small.

Canadian drama educator and scholar Richard Courtney's (1980) book *The Dramatic Curriculum* is the most thorough investigation of the relationship between the words so far. For us, it was Courtney who in a casual conversation with a colleague in 1979 first helpfully started to de-stabilise the word curriculum by suggesting that instead of having, or being given, a 'curriculum', teachers and students should 'currick'.[1] It was a lovely and vivid neologism that in an instant crystallized drama teachers' inchoate unease with the word, and helped to deconstruct the assumptions that most of us unthinkingly carried around.

The principle of curricking, if not the word, was quite a popular notion in the late 1970s, and now even the most gravitas-endowed curriculum scholars such as Ted Aoki use the same metaphor:

> Aoki's interdisciplinary erudition enables us to understand curriculum . . . as a verb (rather than a noun) . . . . 'The other curriculum world,' Aoki continues, 'is the situated world-as-lived that Miss O and her pupils experience'. (Pinar 2005: 1, 14)

In an attempt to be helpful in explaining this new grammar to teachers who conceived curriculum as very much a noun, Courtney held workshops explaining that the word is descended from the Latin verb 'currere', that is to run, and that 'you, your students, time and the material were all running along together and that was what made a curriculum' (Saxton 2008). Juliana Saxton, now herself the doyenne of Canadian drama educators, goes on to note that 'It is of course absolutely understandable now, but then . . . served only to make us feel deeply resentful and cheated. We needed to know what we should be teaching, not have some sort of Phys. Ed. lecture!'

---

[1] Anecdotally reported by Paul Stevenson, 1981.

J. O'Toole et al., *Drama and Curriculum,* Landscapes: the Arts, Aesthetics, and Education 6, DOI 10.1007/978-1-4020-9370-8_3,
© Springer Science+Business Media B.V. 2009

Plainly, for her as for most of us then and now 'Curriculum' *is* a noun, a very large, abstract and static one, its form un-mutated from its Latin origin. We still pluralise it in the Latin way, as 'curricula' . . . that is if we think of it as plural: its most common use is very singular and with the definite article – 'THE curriculum'. That the Latin itself is a form of the verb 'to run' is more of an irony than a help. Curriculum is still commonly seen to be something that has an immutable substance – the 'body' of knowledge that students are expected to acquire, or at least which teachers are supposed to offer them. The curriculum is solid and authoritative because it has been laid down by other people, who know and have the power. Neither Plato nor the medieval monks had any doubt about that, and that is certainly how millions of teachers and students round the world view their respective tasks today: teachers receive a curriculum that has been laid down; they teach that and students learn it. Their own prowess is judged by how well the students have learned that chunk of officially approved, literally 'given' wisdom. It is very hard to change, and even harder to see what running has to do with it. Certainly this was how curriculum was conceptualised up to, in and beyond the middle of the twentieth century, which is the departure point for most books and courses on formal curriculum and curriculum development – and, incidentally or not, for formal drama within that curriculum. But first, a little ancient history.

Taking up where the last chapter finished, it is worth briefly visiting the ancestral home of today's curriculum, the nineteenth century. That is when in some Western countries like Britain and its colonies such as Australia schooling systems and curricula both became national and formalised, crystallising in compulsory universal education around the 1870s in both the countries. There was of course enormous diversity even within those two composite nations, and readers may find that the following paragraphs and this chapter, which primarily relate to the rise of curriculum and the appearance of drama in Australia and to a lesser extent England and the USA, differ from their own national curriculum. However, we believe that readers are likely to find parallels across the developing countries of the industrial revolution, and those nations' attitudes to the arts in general and drama in particular – attitudes that have been carried whole or gradually evolving through the schooling systems of the twentieth century, and in some instances, the twenty-first century.

It occurs to us that the sense of curriculum as being something solid – as a 'thing' – is a product of the recent Western paradigm of compulsory (and largely free) education for all children between certain ages. The inevitable compulsion and the legal requirements for these new education systems to replicate and perpetuate the social and economic hierarchies built into Western societies dictate what is essential to learn. The corollary of that is the primacy of assessment – both *how* we assess and how we *report* on assessment. The hierarchies are sustained and reinforced by the rank ordering (and hence valuing) of individuals based on the narrow curriculum that schooling is able to offer. Political slogans like 'No Child Left Behind' thinly disguise this beneath an egalitarian veneer ('No child left behind' what? . . . and in any case, it is highly contentious as to whether and how much that US initiative worked). Another and equally egregious slogan current in Australia,

'Essential Learning Standards', reminds us that we still live by educational coding and valuing that are the results of political processes and exigencies: 'essential' to whom and for what?

Transported to Australia

Australia provides us with a convenient starting place, with the single, very concrete event of the arrival of the white settler population in 1788. Prior to this, the curriculum had been the gradual lifelong acquisition by the indigenous peoples through the tuition and initiation by their Elders of the necessary, time-honoured wisdom and skills of living and knowledge sustainment – the Dreaming. This was carried on very largely and integrally through the arts, through a seamless web of painting, dance, music, storying, and singing, which even included fairly formalised dramatic performance quite akin to Western forms (Marshall 1991). That indigenous curriculum was of course to be largely extinguished by attrition, by neglect, and sometimes by force, through the next two centuries. In its place, a new schooling system and curriculum had to be invented – or imported – for the new Settlers, still and for many years hence harking back to their own ancestral lands.

From the time of the arrival of the First Fleet in 1788, according to one estimate, there were 36 children at Botany Bay, evenly divided between the children of convicts and those of marines (Barcan 1980: 9). From the start, schools, set up in huts or even tents, were seen as necessary mainly to stop these children running wild, so curriculum was a secondary consideration. Schools were founded in Sydney in 1789, Parramatta in 1791 and Norfolk Island in 1792. However, voluntary immigration and settlement followed fast on the establishment of the convict settlements, besides the release and 'ticket-of-leave' arrangements that left many ex-convicts and their families unable or unwilling to return to Britain. These new populations not only generated more kids that had to be stopped from running wild, but parents with aspirations for them. From about 1803 'academies' for the middle class were opening, with explicit and sometimes competing curricula. John Mitchell and James MacConnell opened one in 1805, teaching:

> English grammatically, Writing, Book-keeping after the Italian mode, French grammatically, and mathematics (Barcan 1980: 15).

Girls' schools provided a housewifely curriculum, though those which were more ambitious offered the 'polite accomplishments' considered suitable for middle- and upper-class girls in contemporary England, which seems to be where any of the arts are first mentioned.

> In addition to reading etc. Mrs Williams pledges herself expeditiously to teach plain and fine needlework, marking, Tambour work etc. (Barcan 1980: 18)

For the bulk of the population, the curriculum comprised absolutely the basics of what the society at the time perceived settler youngsters would need. In Sydney Public Schools in 1820, the curriculum was essentially reading, writing, arithmetic and religious instruction. The boys might learn some gardening and the girls some needlework. The more privileged, in the emerging 'grammar schools', might expect some kind of compromise between practical commercial and European classical curriculum, again with no time for the arts (Barcan: 35/36). However, for the top end of the social ladder, the curriculum slowly liberalised and very advanced ideas began infiltrating. By 1872, the 'outstanding Catholic College in Australia', St Mary's College for Boys, Lyndhurst, in addition to languages and classics, a library and a museum, taught elocution (a cousin of drama, as we shall see) and held leisure-time drama classes.

This might be the first reference to drama within (or nearly within) the formal school curriculum in Australia. That's almost a century after theatre arrived, which was with the very first convicts. Right from their landing in the First Fleet to found the bizarre and dysfunctional colony, the convicts themselves made their own theatre, enthusiastically. Within 5 years, there were thriving theatres in Sydney and on Norfolk Island. This should not be surprising, as Robert Jordan's (2002) authoritative account indicates, since the British theatres of the times were eclectic in their class appeal, and moreover, a proportion of the convicts were pickpockets and prostitutes for whom the theatre was one of their favourite workplaces – and who professed a love of the drama for its own sake too! On the other hand, contrary to the impression created by Thomas Kenneally's novel *The Playmaker* or Timberlake Wertembaker's popular dramatic adaptation *Our Country's Good*, the military and the early settlers were largely uninterested in either theatre or what the convicts did with their spare time. It was instead these middle classes, the clergy and the forces of law and order, who repeated the usual pattern of fear and suspicion that theatre might be seditious or lead to riot, and suppressed these brave pioneer theatres. So it apparently took over 80 years before drama was deemed safe to bring into schools – and as a pursuit for the gentry, no longer for the poor or 'middle people'.

Back down the social ladder, 1872 was also a very significant year for those poor and middle people, with the passing of the Education Act in Victoria, which guaranteed education for all, and:

> laid the foundations of universal, state-controlled, secular elementary schooling. It was the first legislation of its kind in the Australian colonies, and has come to represent the growth of the secular-liberal society in Australia (Grundy 1972: 2).

The Act was preceded and accompanied by a storm of controversy, and as Denis Grundy points out 'has figured prominently in one hundred years of acrimony over the rights and duties of citizens and parents in the education of their young' (1972:2). Virtually none of this ballyhoo was concerned in the slightest with curriculum, except in one single subject: Religious Instruction. The whole battle was a politico-religious one, pitched and fought over religious and interdenominational control, management of schools, and of course whether, how much and whose religion should be taught. The result was a rout for all the religious advocates: 'In every state school secular instruction only shall be given and no teacher shall give any other than secular instruction' (Government of Victoria 1872: Section 12).

The other states followed, and to this day Australian state schools guard their secularism stringently, though religious schools were permitted to continue and flourish under their own systems. Apart from that statement above, the Act itself is entirely silent on what actually should comprise this Education, with the only definition wrapped up in a dozen or so words in an appendix: 'Reading, Writing, Arithmetic, Grammar, Geography, Drill, and where practicable, Gymnastics; and Sewing and Needlework in addition for Girls' (Government of Victoria 1872: Schedule 1). Not much succour for those looking for culture, the arts – or even science – in that basic curriculum, significant because it was, literally, 'the basics'. Ironically, basic though it was, subsequent simplification by populist politicians of 'the basics' to 'the three Rs' has even shorn those original basics of Drill and Gymnastics – the 'mens sana in corpore sano' (healthy mind in a healthy body) that the nineteenth century so admired – as well as the broadening subject of Geography and the practical skills for girls.

It was the template for the bulk of the population, a subsistence diet reduced to what were seen as the essentials for a literate, numerate and otherwise undemanding workforce. Not for the riff-raff the aesthetic cultivation of Lyndhurst, or of the Catholic Girls Convents, where the students' 'cultural curriculum' might include 'music, singing, drawing, painting and dancing, poetry, callisthenics ... and dramatic performance' (Barcan: 166). Quite quickly, however, even those basic State curricula did find themselves infiltrated by some arts. By 1883, the primary curriculum in most states included poetry (in Tasmania and Victoria, in the lower grades, rather charmingly labelled 'rhyme').

The Twentieth Century

Music and visual arts crept in over the next decades, spurred on by the giant presence and influence of educational theorists in the first half of the twentieth century like John Dewey, Herbert Read and Louis Arnaud Reid, each of whom wrote extensively and authoritatively on both education and art. Music and art were aided and found a natural place too in the progressive education movement espoused by such as Dewey, where children learn by doing, holistically; where knowledge does not come just from the outside in, but the child's experience forms part of that scaffold for learning.

Perhaps surprisingly, drama didn't get far on coat-tailing either the Arts-inclined scholars or progressive education (well, not till much later). No further than the Christmas Nativity and the firmly extra-curricular school play or concert party. At least, there was little public manifestation of drama in schooling systems, although a few crucial pioneers and their publications, mostly from the UK, were to lay the groundwork for later and rapid expansion. So, in Australian schools, it was left for many decades to the private and religious schools to continue to offer drama, sometimes in the curriculum, more often on the edge as an optional extra, and frequently in the form known as 'speech and drama'.

In the first half of the twentieth century, much curriculum across the Western world was devised for the specific requirements of subjects that already existed in the curriculum, often according to what end-users like employers or universities felt to be needed and/or what was examinable. This was invariably done by committees or sometimes individual 'experts'; so a Maths committee decided what maths would be taught and examined. Conversely, even then many progressive educators saw curriculum as something that was made up as you went along (Nelson: 120) – a notion that was to return in new and more sophisticated form from the 1960s to the 1980s as progressive education was revisited. One of the figures to challenge both these piecemeal approaches to curriculum in the 1920s was American Harold Rugg, who was, not coincidentally, a civil engineer turned social studies educator. 'If there were one word to describe Rugg's theories of curriculum making, it would be *design*' (Nelson 1998: 119). The engineer's eye for synthesising individual parts into a whole mechanical system underpinned his approach to the curriculum: 'Curriculum is really the entire program of a school's work. It is the essential means of education' (Rugg 1936: 18).

> The curriculum, then was to be scientifically 'narrowed down', but not fixed. The setting of educational goals was a matter of judgments . . .. Curriculum makers would select and develop specific goals based on the 'correct' social observations, and knowledge that Rugg felt curriculum makers must possess . . .. This plan would include objectives, experiences to achieve these objectives, subject matter for the experiences, intended outcomes. (Nelson 1998: 122)

In other words, curriculum was to be constructed by experts, who would see both the wood and the trees, and design programs for schools and teachers to implement for the benefit of their students. He crystallised this into '10 Principles of curriculum design', focused on social studies, since he strongly believed that 'to keep issues out of the school program is to keep life out of it' (this and the 10 Principles – Nelson 1998: 124).

Interestingly, the ninth of those principles is that 'meaning must be built through dramatic episodes'. This might be an extraordinarily prescient vision of the drama pedagogy that was not really to emerge for another 70 years, and was then to be applied most assiduously to Rugg's own passions of social studies and issues-based education. On the other hand, it might just have been metaphorical, which is certainly how curriculum designers have regarded it, as neither dramatic episodes nor any other forms of drama have figured much since Rugg in mainstream curriculum design.

From the 1950s: Curriculum Gets Serious

Before we look at how and when drama started seriously knocking at the curriculum door in Australia, Britain and elsewhere, it would be appropriate to pick up the broader curriculum story itself at around the same time, in the years after the Second World War, when radical change was in the air – change down to the roots, at least in theory, and then slowly in practice. Drama's emergence is part of that slow evolution.

In 1949, Ralph Tyler (1949) crystallised the structuralist approach to curriculum. His book *Basic Principles of Curriculum and Instruction* (1949) was prepared as a syllabus for his US university class. Still in print after more than 50 years, this text was selected by the 'Professors of Curriculum', as one of the two publications that has had the most influence over the field of curriculum and has been called the 'bible of curriculum making' (Jackson 1992). Tyler articulated what at the time seemed a very humanely learner-centred approach, which was 'linear-rational' as he called it. It was founded on 'objectives', which led to the preparation, effective organisation and implementation of 'learning experiences' that would be evaluated in terms of how successfully those objectives, and those alone, had been achieved (Tyler 1949). These words and this sequence still ruled curriculum writing in Australia up until the early 1990s. In themselves, the objectives were comprehensive and divided into five wide-ranging types: objectives based on learners needs; on contemporary life; on subject specialists; on philosophy and values; and on theory of learning (3–43). There were four sets of Learning Experiences: to develop skill in thinking; to acquire information; to develop social attitudes; and to develop interests (68–82). The last we might consider rather curious now – suggesting that what a student is interested in becomes a learning objective, rather than a point of engagement and motivation, i.e., the end of the curriculum, rather than its beginning.

That word 'objectives' opens a can of worms of grammatical and semantic questions, as can be seen looking back with the hindsight of a drama teacher both conscious and proud of the sophisticated understanding of the subjective and objective implications that we have now thoroughly mapped.

There is one rather gallant, if laboured and unsophisticated, attempt by a leading curriculum theorist to marry Rugg's ninth principle with Tyler's practical classroom curriculum. Hilda Taba was a graduate student of Tyler, and her classic *Curriculum Theory, Development and Practice* (published in 1962, but the ideas come through from much earlier) also shows the influence of Rugg's theories. In this book, there is not a lot about any of the arts, although Taba does struggle gamely with the notion of creativity, and where to put it in a structuralist curriculum:

> Whenever the development of creativity is mentioned, thought immediately turns to the creative arts... One could also reverse the argument and maintain that the development of creativity is as important in mathematics as in creative arts, but it will be a creativity of a different sort (Taba: 183).

Later on, she does venture just once into Rugg's tempting territory of 'dramatic episodes'. In an exemplar of the study of 'Primitive peoples' (sic):

> The concluding activities consisted of dramatizing the contrasting aspects of recreation, education, and law in the primitive and modern cultures . . .:
> Let the boys list the skills boys in primitive societies need for hunting... let the children practice some of these physical skills on the playground... small groups of children might enjoy creating some dances...
> [and in conclusion:]

Have the children dramatize situations that show a sharp contrast between primitive and modern activities, such as

Recreation:

A modern family going to a show
A primitive family telling of a hunt with songs etc.

Education:

Modern children learning to read at school
Primitive children listening to a storyteller . . .

Law:

A father recovering his stolen car in court
A chief telling his tribe who gets the slain animal. . . (368–373).

Just prior to this, she again comes close by suggesting another history task as

After having studied conditions and feelings during the Civil War, a synthesis might be made by writing a letter such as a Southern belle might write to her boyfriend at the front (368).

which is a nice early example of what drama educators now term 'writing-in-role' (cf. inter alia Ackroyd 2000). For the next decades, the curriculum devisers, the examination systems, the education faculties and the teachers themselves within the dominant schooling systems more or less unquestioningly used Tyler's language and internalised his structures. Even the reintroduction of progressive notions like the importance of learning through process, and incorporating subjective and emotional learning into the curriculum, did not shake the hegemony. In post-1970 Queensland, which had just established what was and still is a remarkable and quite revolutionary school assessment system, we all had to write new syllabuses and work programs in terms of four sets of objectives, starting with 'content objectives' and 'skills objectives' – nothing difficult about that, as Tyler would have confirmed. It got harder when we had to prescribe 'process objectives' (which being an oxymoron, caused a lot of puzzlement, but which we dutifully concocted somehow). Finally we had to prescribe 'affective objectives'; most teachers, being in any case much more used to excluding emotions from the classroom and curriculum than encouraging and trying to measure them, put these straight in the too-hard basket and the curriculum authority was forced into the anomalous position for an examining board of demanding that they be prescribed and identified, but not assessed.

Objectives-based curriculum dominated schooling systems until the 1980s at least, sometimes even into the new century, although the philosophy, scholarship and rhetoric of curriculum have all undergone a sea-change, with challenges coming both from inside the academy and from the other side of the educational fence. Arts and drama educators are new and not very loud spokespersons inside the systems. They have, however, been among the most voluble and energetic in challenging the appropriateness of doing all one's planning in terms of pre-ordained objectives limited enough to be attainable, then tailoring learning experiences and assessment just to test whether those objectives have been reached. Let alone other objectives, or some other learning entirely, as visual arts educator Elliott Eisner (1967: 85–91) pointed out. Just like visual arts, drama doesn't work like that. From the earliest contestations, drama educators have been right in there, tiny currents in the sea-change.

Resistance, and Stirrings of Change

And the contestations started early. In 1924, American satirist and social commentator H. L. Mencken wrote about schooling:

> to fill the young of the species with knowledge and awaken their intelligence? . . . Nothing could be further from the truth. The aim . . . is simply to reduce as many individuals as possible to the same safe level, to breed and train a standardized citizenry, to put down dissent and originality. That is its aim in the United States. . . and that is its aim everywhere else. (1924, in Gatto 2003)

In 1939, the wonderfully named J. Abner Peddiwell (actually Harold Benjamin) wrote a slim and wicked satire on orthodox schooling called *The Saber-tooth Curriculum including other lectures in the history of paleolithic education* (Benjamin 1939). This pointed out the kind of immutable Parkinson's Law which operates, where education systems become geared up to teach the knowledge and skills required to deal with any social need or threat (such as sabre-toothed tigers) just about the time that the society has dealt with the need or threat (i.e., the beast has become extinct), but then continue to teach those skills for generations until the next threat has been identified and dealt with!

In England, radical thinker and educator A.S. Neill founded the famous alternative school Summerhill in 1921, chronicling it in a number of books (e.g., *Summerhill: a Radical Approach to Child Rearing* 1960). In Australia, alternative community schools sprang up: Preshil in Melbourne was founded as early as 1930, though they are mostly from the 1960s onwards. These cater principally for two social groups outside the mainstream. Some of them, like Summerhill, were and are for the children of the well-enough-heeled and educated to be free-thinking, such as Brisbane Independent School, founded in 1967, whose mission is 'to nurture, develop and trust our pupils' innate love of learning and positive values', and Currambena School in New South Wales. Others like Strelly Aboriginal Community School in Western Australia cater for the opposite end of the social class scale, especially those caught in economic and cultural vicious circles. Nearly all these alternative schools share two key characteristics: (a) they are far more democratic in structure than standard schools, endeavouring to maximise the involvement of the community, the parents and the children themselves in the decision-making and management; and (b) they invariably privilege and promote the arts far more than the standard schools. In a way, their underlying assumptions are the flipside of those underpinning the orthodox curriculum – if the arts are marginal or superfluous to the standard curriculum, then they should probably be central to the alternatives – that's a part of what makes them alternative.

The social liberation and desire for change that was 'blowing in the wind' of the 1960s saw the beginning of a flood of influential books, some of which had roots much earlier in this alternative counter-culture to Tyler's and the official curricula. Its ideals became adopted by disgruntled teachers and education writers, especially teachers of the socially disadvantaged, with titles that made their ideology quite clear. In the USA, John Holt spent 11 years teaching and observing how children behaved in schools, analysed it and came to the conclusion in *How Children Fail* (1964) that children instinctively want and know how to learn, and that the main obstacle to this is schooling; so he proposed his own system of radical home schooling. Neil Postman and Charles Weingartner wrote *Teaching as a Subversive Activity* (1969), focusing on giving children what we could now call agency over language, which became for a decade a bible for progressive teachers, especially English teachers, longing to break out of the straitjacket of curriculum.

Looking at the two sides of the class tracks, Basil Bernstein observed the built-in linguistic advantages of middle-class children in conventional schools. The literate and literature-influenced linguistic codes of the middle-class teachers and the books they used, which he called 'elaborated codes', severely disadvantaged the children of poorer and working-class children, who used 'restricted codes' (e.g., Bernstein 1973). Since, he maintained, people speak and act in response to the expectations of those whom they are speaking to, schools curricula should be changed so that these working-class children could be given access to those elaborated codes. That promptly stirred up a hornet's nest, which is still buzzing. Some critics suggested that blaming the children and their parents for what was the failing of schools and their teachers was a cop-out. A much larger fusillade of social critics pointed out that working-class and socially disadvantaged children do have elaborated codes of their own, but just different ones – for example, mainly oral, inflective and allusive ones, less dependent on wide vocabulary and postliterate verbal syntax. These critics pointed out that it was about time schools and teachers gave due respect to and became familiar with the equally sophisticated codes of speakers from across the tracks, instead of perpetuating the dominant white middle-class accents and dialects, etc., etc. The debate continues in a thousand academic books and websites.

From a quite different direction – outside both of what at the time we liked to call the 'First World' of economically highly developed countries and their hegemonic education systems – came Brazilian Paulo Freire, with his 'liberation pedagogy' expressed in the still influential *Pedagogy of the Oppressed* (published in English in 1970). This argued for a quite new approach to universal literacy. Freire demanded that the growing voice of the poor and oppressed in economically disadvantaged countries, which we liked to call the 'Third World', be given better means of expression. By implication, this pedagogy points out that orthodox Western education systems and curricula not only always support the status quo, but reinforce existing power systems and hierarchies of selective privilege.

Freire was not alone. There was something of a spate of books at the time, including *Deschooling Society* by Ivan Illich (1970), a distinguished educator with one foot in each of the 'First' and 'Third' worlds – a philosopher and theologian from Austria who became a radical educator and spokesperson for Latin America. He attacked the patronising neo-colonialism of rich countries, churches and charitable agencies, which disempowered and exploited with their patronage. He passionately argued that schooling needed to be de-institutionalised in order that society could begin to be de-institutionalised.

> Schooling served, at least in Puerto Rico, to compound the native poverty of half of the children with a new interiorized sense of guilt for not having made it. I therefore came to the conclusion that schools inevitably are a system to produce dropouts, and to produce more dropouts than successes . . .. In the minds of the people who financed and engineered them, schools were established to increase equality. I discovered that they really acted as a lottery system in which those who didn't make it didn't just lose what they had paid in but were also stigmatized as inferior for the rest of their lives. (1988/1997)

Almost simultaneously with this bombshell came Everett Reimer's (1970) even more pungently titled *School is Dead: Alternatives in Education*. Reimer and Illich had met in 1956 and around the time their books were published they worked together in the Centre for Intercultural Documentation. Reimer's scathing summing up of the worth of the efforts of Tyler and the millions of schools and schoolteachers working in similar systematic and systemic curricula was, among many pithy aphorisms:

> Schools learned long ago that the way to keep children from thinking is to keep them busy. (52)

Around this time, too, the phrase 'the hidden curriculum' gained currency. It was crystallised as a book title by Benson Snyder (1971) (though it has been variously attributed), and discussed as a concept by many of the above, including Freire, Postman and Illich. Snyder asserts:

> Covert, inferred tasks, and the means to their mastery, are linked together in a hidden curriculum. They are rooted in the professors' assumptions and values, the students' expectations, and the social context in which both teacher and taught find themselves. (1971: 4)

Another set of critiques from outside the education systems actually came from the world of theatre, a profession full of practitioners as balefully sceptical about education as education is about theatre. One of the most savage and widely quoted was by Bertolt Brecht, a quotation that was enthusiastically reprinted as an introductory framing quotation to a highly respectable textbook for English teachers:

> The young person in school is monstrously confronted by the BARBARIAN in unforgettable form. The latter possesses almost limitless power. Equipped with pedagogical skills and many years of experience, he trains the pupil to become a prototype of himself. The pupil learns everything required for getting ahead in the world – the very same things that are necessary for getting ahead in school: deceit, pretending to have knowledge one does not have, the ability to get even without being punished for it, speedy acquisition of clichés, flattery, subservience, a readiness to betray ones fellow to the higher-ups, and so on, and so on . . .. The pupil has got to recognise the teacher's weaknesses and know how to exploit them, for if he doesn't he'll never be able to defend himself against having a whole rat's nest of completely worthless intellectual rubbish crammed into him.
> (Brecht, Dialogues in exile, as frontispiece to *Team Teaching and the Teaching of English* by Anthony Adams - again, significantly, in 1970).

Less surprisingly, this very quotation was used in exactly the same way a few years later in a swashbuckling piece of advocacy for a new dramatic pedagogy, Albert Hunt's *Hopes for Great Happenings* (1976).

Curriculum Sea-Change?

However, by the 1970s, even within the universities and centres of curriculum development, there was a sea-change happening in curriculum theory, based on the realisation that what curriculum designers set out to have taught is not necessarily the same thing as what teachers teach or learners learn. A constructivist paradigm of educational philosophy has largely replaced the structuralist one. Curriculum in this paradigm sets out to privilege learning and learners' needs and experiences over teaching imposed content, and the negotiation and transformation of knowledge over its transmission. Perhaps after all, curriculum is, or can be, a verb – as we have suggested.

The first wave of the sea-change consisted of descriptive theorists, who attempted to come to understand how curriculum development actually takes place in school settings. For them, the importance lay in the relationships between the steps and procedures that are followed in the curriculum development process. Adding to Tyler's trio of society, school and subject matter, Schwab (1973: 502–505) offered five 'bodies of experience' for consideration in curriculum development: learners, subject matter, milieus, teachers, and the curriculum-making experience of the developers. His commitment was to the 'practical' matters of creating and enacting curriculum. The additions of 'milieus' and 'curriculum-making' experience acknowledge that curriculum is developed and diverse contexts and that curriculum developers and implementers bring with them a diversity of experience and expertise. Bruner (1963, 1977) proposed a 'spiral curriculum' where concepts and content are revisited with more complexity and depth at each succeeding level. His curriculum planning required the identification of the fundamental ideas and concepts of a discipline. These were to be introduced as concrete examples in the early stages of learning and create the foundations for more abstract learning at later stages.

Some of these descriptive theorists started to offer their own alternative models to the linear progression dominant in the Tyler/Taba models, and still a feature, really, of Bruner's. Macdonald, Wolfson, and Zaret (1973) proposed learning that is organised in a continuous cycle of exploring, integrating and transcending. They also identified self-evaluation as an important aspect of this concept. As early as 1971, Decker Walker proposed a 'deliberative' model of curriculum development suggesting that prior to the actual curriculum design, it is necessary to establish the platform upon which the curriculum will be developed and this involves a shared understanding of beliefs and theories about learning, and consideration of aims and procedures. That is followed by a process of deliberation whereby the curriculum developers consider precedents, costs and consequences; decide on the content needed; generate alternatives; and choose the most defensible.

The next wave was the explicitly critical-exploratory theorists, who, rather than describing and improving previous curricula, focused on their radical deficiencies and set out to provide something completely different. Already in 1967, Eisner had challenged objectives themselves in *Educational Objectives: Help or Hindrance?* and proposed an 'artistic model' of curriculum development, later expanded in *The Educational Imagination* (1979) and subsequent writings (e.g., 1994). Through the seven considerations he offered for curriculum development, Eisner introduced concepts entirely alien to Tyler, quite compatible with many of the resistance's contestations and, appropriately to his curriculum's 'artistic' title, much more akin to how drama might work. In discussing 'goals', he encouraged the consideration of affective and even 'unexpected' objectives that may arise during the learning process. In 'content', Eisner (1994: 138) pointed out that the very process of selecting content that will be included in the curriculum produces a 'null' curriculum, i.e., the knowledge that is not selected, and from which the students are, therefore, excluded. He suggested the transformation of goals and content into learning opportunities: 'the kinds of events that have educational consequences'. In organizing those learning opportunities, he rejected the linear 'staircase' model with its monodirectional, time-based orientation, and proposed a 'spiderweb' model in which the 'curriculum designer provides the teacher with a set of heuristic projects, materials, and activities whose use will lead to diverse outcomes among the group of students' (ibid.: 142). He encouraged integration of content areas rather than disciplinarity with the aim of connecting with the messiness of real life. Eisner also noted that the history of education has privileged written and verbal responses and so he encouraged a greater diversity of representational modes as part of the experience of learning and in the opportunities allowed for students to respond. He suggested that students should be able to show what they have learned through action (doing an experiment), alternative verbal and visual forms (poetry, film) or in modes that are non-verbal (images, music, dance [and what about drama ... harrumph, not mentioned, but maybe implicit]). Furthermore, evaluation should pervade the learning process rather than occur at the end-point, and is determined by the content and the learning opportunities that have been experienced.

Following the 1973 '*Reconceptualising Curriculum*' Conference, in Rochester, NY, instigated by William Pinar, the wave of critical explorers became a tsunami of 'reconceptualism'. Strongly influenced by social critical theory, by poststructuralist thought, and philosophers like Foucault, the reconceptualists such as William Doll Jr. (e.g. 1993), Nel Noddings and Michael Apple – and a host of others easily accessed via the works of Pinar or any of the above – were and still are concerned with domination, exploitation, resistance and what constitutes legitimate knowledge in contemporary society. They don't describe or even explore curriculum: they interrogate it:

> Whose knowledge is it? Who selected it? Why is it organised and taught in this way? To this particular group? (Apple 2004: 6)

They have seized and changed the focus of the argument, with writings like Noddings's (1992) *The Challenge to Care in Schools: an Alternative Approach to Education* and *A Morally Defensible Mission for Schools in the 21st Century* – Noddings (2006) does particularly eloquent titles. They consider what might be necessary knowledge in the future and the impact of globalisation and capitalism on the work of teachers, and they are explicitly political, rejecting any notion of schools and teaching being 'neutral' or 'politics-free' as self-deluding mythology, as in Michael Apple's equally pungently titled *Educating the 'Right' Way: Markets, Standards, God, and Inequality* (2006). Reconceptualists reject the modernist view of a stable-state universe and the belief that a better world can be accomplished through order and control. They criticise efficiency-oriented curricula for using schools as instruments of social control and highlight issues of gender (e.g., Grumet 1988), race (e.g., Castenell & Pinar 1993), social disadvantage and how power operates. They propose that curriculum must be autobiographical, drawing on the personal pasts, presents and futures of both teachers and students (e.g., Grumet 1987). They demand that curriculum be dialogic with teachers acting as public intellectuals (e.g., Giroux 2006).

Or Curriculum Little Change?

With such a basically consensual torrent of demands, proposals, rejections and critiques from curriculum makers over the last 40 years, has there been a sea-change in school curriculum? What, indeed, is a sea-change and where does the word come from? For those who can't remember, it's from Shakespeare's *The Tempest* Act 2 scene 1, from a song which the spirit Ariel is singing to young Ferdinand to put him under a spell:

> *Full fathom five thy father lies ...*
> *[he] doth suffer a sea-change*
> *into something rich and strange*

Actually, Ariel is lying. Ferdinand's father Alonso, King of Naples, is alive and well at the time, if seriously deluded. And there's much in common between Alonso and school curriculum. Alonso is an autocrat, ruthless, capable of malignant repression and exclusion, at times sentimental, easily swayed by arguments of political expediency, needing devoted maintenance and protection, and at the time we meet him, completely oblivious to the reality of his surroundings. If there's a comforting moral in the analogy, by the end of the play he has come to some sense of himself and his surroundings, and some glimmer of responsibility to his subjects, though you'd hardly say he's in control.

Over the last 40 years, this transformed concept of curriculum has slowly been percolating into the schooling systems in some countries including Australia. How slowly? We found the quotation from H.L. Mencken that started the *Resistance* section of this chapter in an article by a former three-time winner of the New York City Teacher of the Year, John Taylor Gatto: *Against School: How Public Education Cripples Our Kids, And Why* (2003). Gatto resigned the very next year after he won his third award – announcing in the Wall Street Journal that he no longer 'wished to hurt kids to make a living' – in order to write books and articles with titles like the above, and *Dumbing Us Down: the Hidden Curriculum of Compulsory Schooling* (1992). Much too slowly, it would seem, after 25 years of supposed sea-change.

The reasons for the slowness are not hard to discern. First, although the ideals, principles and rhetoric of the 'new' curriculum theories have been overwhelmingly adopted by the administrators and the teachers, the structures of schooling, and the constructions of knowledge into 'disciplines', 'subject areas', timetables and assessment schemes that underpin them are still designed for the one-way transmission of content and skills 'belonging' to those subject areas.

Second, the mainstream contemporary curriculum designers are hard-pressed to find a pedagogy that adequately translates their theories into practice. There *is* one at least, and it's called drama, as we shall explore throughout the rest of this book. It clings unregarded but limpet-like out there beyond the mainstream, still right on the 'sea marge, sterile and rocky hard' as Shakespeare put it in the same play, that liminal space where all important change agents can always be found. A few of the more visionary curriculum theorists like Ted Aoki recognise that space:

> This kind of opportunity for probing does not come easily to a person flowing within the mainstream. It comes more readily to one who lives at the margin – to one who lives in a tension situation. It is, I believe, a condition that makes possible deeper understanding of human acts that can transform both self and world, not in an instrumental way, but a human way (Aoki 1996: 333).

And a very few, like Madeleine Grumet (2004: 61), can not only discern the dramatic limpet more than dimly, but also pick it off the rocks:

> The children followed her instructions, but their suggestions were repetitive and empty, for they had no particular stake in each other's narratives. We asked the children, instead, to perform each other's stories. After enacting one little boy's description of a trip to the zoo . . .. this time they had wonderful language for the world of his story, for they had inhabited it with their bodies, memories and imaginations as they played the parts.

For most curriculum theorists and specialists, however, it is hard for them to see, from out there in the mainstream, exactly how the creatures of the shoreline can turn the 'dead body of the structural curriculum 'into something rich and strange'. That's why, mostly, the curriculum theorists are unaware of the pedagogy, the practice or the research literature of drama. And that, in the end, is what this book is about.

References

Ackroyd, J. (2000) *Literacy alive!: drama projects for literacy learning.* London: Hodder & Stoughton.

Adams, A. (1970) *Team teaching and the teaching of English.* Oxford: Pergamon Press.

Aoki, E. (1996). A lingering note. . . In: W. Pinar & R. Irwin (Eds). (2005). *Curriculum in a new key: The collected works of Ted. T. Aoki.* Mahwah, NJ: Erlbaum.

Aoki, E. (2005) Reflections of a Japanese Canadian teacher experiencing ethnicity. In: W. Pinar, & R. Irwin, *Curriculum in a new key: The collected works of Ted. T. Aoki.* Mahwah, NJ: Erlbaum.

Apple, M. (2004). *Ideology and Curriculum* (3rd ed). New York and London: Routledge Falmer.

Apple, M. (2006). *Educating the "right" way : markets, standards, God, and inequality.* New York: Routledge.

Barcan, A. (1980) *A history of Australian education.* Oxford: OUP

Benjamin, H. (1939). Saber-tooth curriculum, including other lectures in the history of paleolithic education, by J. Abner Peddiwell, PH.D. New York: McGraw-Hill.

Bernstein, B. (1973). *Class, codes and control.* St. Albans: Paladin.

Bruner, J. (1963). Structures in Learning. In: G. Hass (Ed.), Curriculum Planning: a new approach (5th ed.) pp. 243–267. Boston: Allyn and Bacon.

Bruner, J. (1977). *The Process of Education*. Cambridge, MA: Harvard University Press.
Castenell, L. & Pinar, W. (Eds.) (1993) *Understanding curriculum as racial text : representations of identity and difference in education*. Albany: State University of New York Press.
Courtney, R. (1980). *The dramatic curriculum*. New York: Drama Books.
Doll, W. (1993). *A postmodern perspective on curriculum*. New York: Teachers' College Press.
Government of Victoria (1872): *The Education Act*. Melbourne: Victorian Government.
Grundy, D. (1972) *Secular, compulsory and free – the education Act of 1872*. Melbourne: MUP.
Eisner, E. (1967). Educational objectives: help or hindrance? In D.J. Flinders & S.J. Thornton (Eds.) (2004). *The curriculum studies reader*. (2nd ed). New York: Routledge.
Eisner, E. (1979) *The educational imagination*. Upper Saddle River, NJ: Merrill/Prentice Hall.
Eisner. E. (1994) *The educational imagination*. (3rd ed.) New York: Macmillan.
Freire, P. (1970). *Pedagogy of the oppressed*. New York: Herder & Herder.
Gatto, J. (1992). *Dumbing Us Down: The Hidden Curriculum of Compulsory Education*. Gabriola Island, BC: New Society.
Gatto, J. (2003). Against school: How public education cripples our kids, and why. *Harpers Magazine*. September.
Giroux, H. (2006). Teachers, public life and curriculum reform. In F.W. Parkay, E.J. Anctil & G. Hass. (Eds.) *Curriculum planning: a contemporary approach*. 8th Edition. Boston: Pearson.
Grumet, M. (1987) The politics of personal knowledge. *Curriculum Inquiry, 17*(3) 319–329.
Grumet, M. (1988) *Bitter milk: women and teaching*. Amherst: University of Massachusetts Press.
Grumet, M. (2004). No one learns alone. In Nick Rabkin & Robin Redmond: *Putting the Arts in the picture – re-framing education in the 21*st *century*. Chicago: Columbia College.
Holt, J. (1964). *How children fail*. London: Pitman.
Hunt, A. (1976) *Hopes for great happenings*. London: Eyre Methuen.
Illich, I. (1970) *Deschooling society*. New York: Harper and Row.
Illich, I. (1997/1988) *Interview with Ivan Illich*. In David Cayley (1988) *IDEAS* Canadian Broadcasting Corporation Radio. Reprinted in *Skole, the Journal of Alternative Education*. Spring 1997.
Jackson, P. (1992). Conceptions of curriculum and curriculum specialists. In P. Jackson (Ed.) *Handbook of research on curriculum*. New York: Macmillan.
Jordan, R. (2002) *The convict theatres of early Australia 1788–1840*. Sydney: Currency P. 6.
MacDonald, J. B., Wolfson, B. J., & Zaret, E. (1973). Re-schooling society: a conceptual model. Washington DC: Association for Supervision and Curriculum Development.
Marshall, A. (1991). Comparative studies in performance training in traditional Aboriginal ceremony and contemporary Australian theatre. *QADIE SAYS*. Vol 16, No 2. Queensland Association for Drama in Education. 13–19.
Neill, A.S. (1960). *Summerhill; a radical approach to child rearing*. New York: Hart.
Nelson, M. (1998). *Rugg on Rugg. Journal of Curriculum Inquiry, 8*(2) 119–132.
Noddings, N. (1992) *The challenge to care in schools : an alternative approach to education*. New York: Teachers College Press.
Noddings, N. (2006). A morally defensible mission for schools in the 21st century. In F. W. Parkay, E. J. Anctil & G. Hass (Eds.), Curriculum Planning: A contemporary approach (8th ed.) pp. 17–22. Boston: Pearson Education.
Pinar, W. & Irwin, R. (2005) *Curriculum in a new key: The collected works of Ted. T. Aoki*. Mahwah, NJ: Erlbaum.
Postman, N. & Weingartner, C. (1969). *Teaching as a subversive activity*. New York: Delacorte Press.
Reimer, E. (1970) *School is dead: alternatives in education*. New York: Doubleday.
Rugg, H. (1936) *American life and the school curriculum*. Boston: Ginn.
Saxton, J. (2008). Informal notes commenting on this text. Unpublished.
Schwab, J. J. 1973. The practical three: Translation into curriculum. *The School Review, 81*(4): 501–522.

Snyder, B. (1971). *The hidden curriculum*. New York: Knopf.

Taba, H. (1962) *Curriculum development theory and practice*. New York: Harcourt Brace.

Tyler, R. (1949) *Basic principles of curriculum and instruction*. Chicago: University of Chicago Press.

Walker, D. F. (1971). A Naturalistic Model for Curriculum Development. *The School Review, 80*(1), 51–65.

Part II
Theories and Practices

Chapter 3
Drama and Language

John O'Toole and Madonna Stinson

The Ambivalent Role of English

This chapter describes what is perhaps the simplest of drama's four paradigms of purpose in learning contexts, the *linguistic/communicative*: its role in the development of language. In a new book on drama for English teachers published this year, one of the authors wrote:

> A contemporary classroom, and above all an English classroom, is a public performance space, where dialogue happens. And drama is the art of performance, of making dialogical performance text.
>
> Language itself – verbal, and also vocal and gestural language – is not only the primary instrument of human communication but also the prime medium of drama. Out of performed dialogue, new understanding emerges that is cognitive and embodied, personal and social, emotional and sensory and kinaesthetic, understanding that we can call 'learning'. This has always been theatre's job. It is also the job of the English teacher.
>
> The classroom is a public stage, where a narrative of learning is to be enacted, and so dramatic tension and focus are crucial. Children and students are all acting in this public performance space, and all should be equally engaged in the dialogue. The teacher herself is the key performer – but not the star – and so she must have some of the skills and range of an actor to command and shift focus, engage the students in the dialogue, inspire them with the story of what is to be learned, and above all model and embody their language learning. (O'Toole 2008: 14)

Obvious enough to most drama teachers, to many English teachers the above concept is an entirely foreign and quite threatening notion. If you investigate English (or first language) teachers anywhere, you will find exactly the same ambivalence about drama, and its uses in the classroom, as we have been identifying elsewhere. It may well be that these are actually accentuated in contemporary times, as the focus of English has shifted very strongly to written literacy and critical literacy, and so there is stronger emphasis than ever on the written word.

However, English teachers have always been more respectful, and protective, of spoken English than those of their colleagues who cherish the notion that the 'quiet classroom is a good classroom'. Their respect is usually enshrined in syllabuses, such as:

> Students learn to speak, listen to, read, view, write and shape texts to make meaning with purpose, effect and confidence in a wide range of contexts. They learn how language use

varies according to context, purpose, audience, and content, and they develop their abilities to use this knowledge. Students develop their ability to use language to talk about language and to reflect on and critique its use. (Draft Queensland English Syllabus 2001: p. 1)

Since talk comes before writing, oracy – the ability to use spoken language effectively – is one of the basics, indeed more basic than the basics. It is the basic that goes without saying . . . and so, unfortunately, often goes without doing; the forgotten basic that some educational systems assume happens by osmosis, and so they spend no precious curriculum space on it at all. Most culpable of those systems is contemporary teacher education.

As a host of famous philosophers, educationists, psychologists and linguists tell us – from Wittgenstein to Bruner, from Vygotsky to Halliday – language is crucial to ideation, to making meaning, and to symbolic thought. And since humans are social animals, that means making language with each other. All of those Olympian scholars referenced above seem to be, and in three cases explicitly are, pointing the way towards the use of drama, or methods derived from dramatic play. Michael Fleming (2001:126–134) helpfully shows how Ludwig Wittgenstein's philosophical proposition of language as a form of life 'with blurred edges' usefully provides a foundation for exploring reality, illusion and the ambiguities of meaning-making through improvised drama. Jerome Bruner explores both the centrality of spoken language to children's development, and its relationship to dramatic play, linking them to the development of symbolic understanding in a number of his writings. Michael Halliday, best known as the founder of systemic linguistics, put his expertise to the analysis of what he identified as the seven functions of the language of young children, and how they use language to express their needs, create action and make sense of the world. In conversations with one of the authors, he has indicated his interest in drama and support for its use in developing the children's mastery over these functions. Lev Vygotsky goes much further, and his analyses of symbolic dramatic play and its impact on language development have made him unquestionably the dominant philosophical influence in the emerging pedagogy of drama. This is not Vygotsky's only contribution to drama education theory.

Vygotsky's (1965) key concept that links drama education to language development is his notion of the 'zone of proximal development', where children in social, motivated and supported contexts are capable of moving to levels of symbolic and abstract thought of which they are not capable by themselves. This explains to drama educators, who have overwhelmingly come towards theory from practice, something they see in almost any class: why children in drama, dramatic play and even grappling with complex given dramatic texts, frequently and easily express and articulate ideas and language that are far beyond the maturation levels that they ought to be at, according to Piaget. Powerful evidence of this is provided in the large-scale study of the language of 9–11-year-old primary children, carried out in Tasmania by Megan Schaffner, Beth Parsons, and Graham Little (1984). This convincingly shows how much richer, more capable of abstraction, and more diverse the language they use in drama is than that they use in most of their other classroom contexts. Among the findings, which mostly but not exclusively relate to spoken language, the researchers noted the following:

- The greatly increased percentage of the lessons given to children's talk rather than teacher talk;
- the significantly greater opportunity given in drama to use language that was expressive;
- the significantly wider range of language purposes – expressive, imaginative and negotiative, besides the more usual informational and directive talk that normally holds almost exclusive sway; and
- the greater levels of reflective and abstract thought encouraged by drama, including more exploration of moral and attitudinal values.

At the other end of the age range is the major study carried out by anthropological linguist Shirley Brice Heath and her associates (Brice Heath et al. 1993) . This showed that disadvantaged postschool adolescents gain more linguistic competencies and, therefore, agency in their lives from engaging in the arts and especially theatre than most other activities. That study turned Brice Heath from an arts-neutral scholar into a passionate advocate and researcher of the effects of curricular drama in the classroom.

Somewhere between these lies the research carried out by John Carroll and Dorothy Heathcote, *The Treatment of Dr Lister* (Carroll 1980), some of which is recorded on film. Carroll used a linguistics frame to analyse the quality and kinds of language happening in an extended piece of dramatic teaching by Heathcote using a historical context and her techniques of the 'mantle of the expert' and 'teacher-in-role', in which he was also positioned as a participant. (He was Dr Lister, the teacher-in-role.) This research actually predated both the previous studies, and strongly foreshadowed the general results of the Tasmanian study.

These studies are among the more helpful of a plethora of research that has been carried out on the effects of dramatic play and drama on children's speech. Most of the early work happened in the United States and Canada, and is both collected and usefully critiqued in Betty-Jane Wagner's (1998) *Educational Drama and Language Arts: What Research Shows* – particularly usefully, because Wagner is herself an expert in both the fields. She notes that much, but by no means all, of the research points to the significant effect of drama and kindred activities on language, especially in the early years. She also notes shrewdly that most of this early research has been quantitative and quasi-experimental, and that this may often not be the most productive form of research, since particularly as children grow older, there are so many variables that it is impossible to ascribe what verbal capacities have been developed in a few short episodes of drama. More recent research has tended towards qualitative data-gathering (such as that used in the Tasmanian study) or mixed methods. There is a lot to be gained from just engaging in and observing the practice. Any good drama teacher will be full of anecdotes of noticeable change of linguistic habits at least as changes of language observable in school settings, and evidence of far richer reserves of linguistic knowledge and skill than is usually sought or encouraged in classroom settings. The vivid and sophisticated argumentation of the 10-year-old townspeople led by Elijah confronting Ahab in the improvised biblical epic in Dorothy Heathcote's (1971) classic film *Three Looms Waiting* or the 7-year-olds patiently explaining to a lost and frightened dinosaur (their teacher) the intricacies of their school lives and the reasons for his own extinction (transcribed in O'Toole 1991: 12–14) are among the many memorable examples of the genre.

Promoting drama as a method of developing oracy goes back a long way – to the nineteenth century at least. We might pick up the story with a 1905 *Handbook of Suggestions for the Consideration of Teachers and others Concerned in the Work of Public Elementary Schools*, unearthed by Tim Cox (Bolton 1984: 17), which recommended that 'drama could be employed as a method in practising speech with infants'. Cox detects even in this publication that almost universal educational ambivalence about drama on which we have already commented at length, in the warning contained in the Handbook: '... exaggerated emphasis, declamation and gesture are quite unnecessary; the pieces chosen are to be read with feeling and intelligence, but they are not to be acted.' One might also wonder what the dramatic 'pieces chosen' to be read but not acted by infants were. However, it could be that in this particular case, Cox's suspicion is a bit paranoid, as the language of that warning is remarkably reminiscent of Hamlet's injunctions to the Players

> ... suit the action to the word, and the word to the action; with this special observance, that you o'erstep not the modesty of nature; for anything so overdone is from the purpose of playing.

It is also an excellent advice for any drama teacher, especially of infants, and almost exactly contemporary with what Harriet Finlay-Johnson observed and fostered in her village school drama lessons:

> One effect of the play – more particularly the original play – on the scholars would necessarily be a great improvement in their speech and diction. They naturally learned to speak freely, to enunciate clearly and to avoid mumbling or gabbling. They learned to choose their phrases carefully and to clothe their thoughts in appropriate words. (1907: 100)

Ten years later, this theme of using dramatic pieces from plays to improve children's language through active learning, and some of the same techniques used by Miss Finlay-Johnson, were being implemented by another teacher of English at the other end of the class and age spectrum. Henry Caldwell Cook was a secondary English teacher at the exclusive Perse School in Cambridge, England, and called his method the *Play Way*. However, as he constantly, balefully and defiantly pointed out, he was very much going against orthodox English teaching of his time, which, as far as he was concerned, had no understanding of the usefulness of drama. Rather than making common cause with his colleagues, he excoriated them (and in the process gave a vivid picture of what conventional English teachers were teaching):

> Do but observe what our English teachers are doing. . .. The fact that boys of a secondary school have already a considerable familiarity with their mother tongue should be seized upon by the teacher of English as a great opportunity to be rid of subject limitations. He should be able immediately to read the classics of English literature with the boys. Boys of twelve in a secondary school know enough English to understand all that is needful for a due appreciation of many of the English classics. But does the teacher of English use this advantage? Not he. As a conventional schoolmaster he has it so stuck in his mind that everything in a school is a *subject to be learned* that he apes the teachers of more difficult

and unfamiliar subjects, vies with the Latin master in teaching grammar; affects to believe
that English still has cases, a subjunctive mood and the other effete paraphernalia of parsing;
and when all else fails, and the boys really have come at the content, he makes them translate
the sense out of that glorious medium which makes it literature into journalese or current
schoolmaster. (Cook 1917: 359–60).

Though the essence of *the play way* certainly promotes a thoroughly active
approach to learning through drama, Cook's main interest is not in language, but in
promotion of the art form. However, like Finlay-Johnson, he frequently underlines
a respect for language, and is particularly concerned that his students develop an
understanding of linguistic style and appropriateness of register and address:

Style is to be learnt, if at all, by example and experiment rather than by rule and prescription.
In the study of style by imitation a *daily* exercise gives excellent practice, even if it has to
be very short because only a few minutes can be spared for it. But of course there must also
be long exercise done, and lessons devoted to the study.

However, here as throughout the book, his concern is less for the language
learning of his students than:

All the reading, and the literary study, and the dramatic craftsmanship, and the sensible
composition, and the lively acting are knit into a whole by their being the different parts of
one concern – the play.

At least, that is certainly the impression gained by his book. His practice, however, might have been quite another matter. A visitor to the school in 1926, John
Lester, defined Cook's main aim as language development:

Cook's object, like ours, is two-fold: first, to habituate the boy to express his thoughts fitly
in spoken or written words; second, to lead him through his natural interests to nourish his
emotional nature with the great literature of the mother tongue. (Lester 1926: 444)

Lester glowingly describes two lessons, with language a strong feature of both. In
the first, the students themselves fiercely police the grammatical and lexical correctness of their colleagues making public speeches, and in the other, Lester comments
on the students' mastery of Shakespeare's text and their articulacy in debate about
its meaning and the characters. Christopher Parry, a distinguished English teacher
at the forefront of the UK movement in the 1960s and 1970s promoting the use
of drama in English teaching, and himself an ex-student of Cook's, admiringly
described Cook's English lessons as 'a happening in which we were all involved'
(1972: 3). However, if we are talking ambivalence towards drama, few attracted,
and perhaps courted it, like Cook. Another contemporary, perhaps suspicious of
Cook's charismatic individualism, or perhaps still smarting from Cook's withering
dismissal of his contemporaries, wrote tartly:

. . . it would be very dangerous for teachers to be encouraged to visit the School with the
idea that they will find there something that they might and should imitate (Tomkinson
1921:46).

Progress with Progressive Education

The vastly influential UK Hadow (1931) report on *The Primary School*, regarded as something of a manifesto for progressive education, makes interesting critical reading. One of the key recommendations is that:

> Language training should be regarded as fundamentally important. It should be based upon well-planned and systematic training in oral expression (No. 33).

It is as a part of this language training that drama gets its only entry into the formal curriculum, under the heading of English (and right near the foot of the long section, thereby rather belying its enthusiastic tone):

> The value of dramatic work has long been recognised. It makes school studies enjoyable, and the writing and production of class plays is an aid to creative work. Dramatisation of poetry and other forms of literature should have a prominent place in the primary school. Even among the younger children, simple play production with criticism by the class of the interpretation given by different groups of players, will develop the beginning of critical and interpretative power, and will provide a more complete and intensive experience than reading only. Suitably easy plays or scenes may be selected, and natural play acting will be connected with literature, music, dancing, and handicraft (Chapter 12).

Drama is mentioned briefly elsewhere in the Hadow report as contributing to the development of perception and feeling. There is also this shrewd observation:

> [Junior children] were also actors and artists taking intense pleasure in dramatic work, and keenly interested in shape, form and colour. This type of activity was probably the natural complement of the fact that they were keen observers. Reproduction in some form, whether in speech or imitative action, or colour and line, was the natural stimulus of their power of observation (Chapter 7).

However, neither that 'development of perception and feeling' nor this perspicacious observation about the aesthetic capabilities of young children makes it into the curriculum recommendations. In the following recommendation:

> The cultivation of the children's aesthetic sensibility through drawing, craftwork, and music, and the development of their manual skill should receive careful attention (No 34).

drama is yet again conspicuous by its absence.

Over the next 30 years in the UK and its colonies, there was a slow but distinct consolidation of drama, especially within secondary school English programs, particularly in the 1950s. This was accompanied in the UK and Australia by a parallel rise in co-curricular school plays and drama clubs. It was further complemented by two linked developments, the growth of Speech and Drama, and the beginnings of a distinct pedagogy of improvised drama, focussed mainly on young children. There was not always a smooth correspondence. In fact, a polarisation was beginning there, which was to reverberate destructively through the history of drama, particularly in the UK, for the next half century.

Some of the proponents of improvised drama did recognise the value of drama in providing a basis for some language training:

Finally, a word on drama in its relationship to the speech of the child. From the imitated actions, especially rhythmic movements, such as hammering, skipping, beating on a drum . . . you may proceed to the Activity Rhymes. The action comes first, then the speech (Burton 1955:30–31).

On the other hand, they were loth for drama to be traduced into merely serving that purpose:

Note . . . coaching speech in infant dramatic work is of doubtful value. What is gained in distinctness of utterance is balanced by loss of spontaneity and fluency (Ibid).

Then in the 1960s came a swift and major change within and around English and language teaching in England; in Australia, Canada, and the USA mostly a decade later. There was a strong progressivist philosophy underlying this change, and a move away from that concentration on the mechanics of language and literal comprehension so pilloried by Caldwell Cook. This is redolent in the titles of the most influential books. *English for Maturity* (Holbrook 1967) hints at the personal and social development agenda being accepted by progressive English teachers. *The Disappearing Dais* (Whitehead 1966) and *Team Teaching and the Teaching of English* (Adams 1970) both signal the major changes in pedagogy and classroom practice. *Topics in English* and *The Creative Word* (Summerfield 1965 and 1973) point to the contemporary move towards thematic and integrated teaching rather than subject- or component-based structures. Classroom textbooks with titles like *Voices* (Summerfield 1968), *Happenings* (Wollman & Grugeon 1964) and *Reflections* (Clements et al. 1963) succinctly underline the drive for student engagement and active student participation in the learning. Within this movement, drama gained considerable momentum, backed up by some of the strongest and most articulate scholars – a momentum stronger than at any time before or since. Douglas Barnes, James Moffett, Arthur Eastman, and Benjamin de Mott were among the giants of the new English movement who met in 1966 for a conference on Drama and English, which turned into a manifesto to which Barnes put his name as the author. He (they) declared:

Drama is not an educational frill, an applied ornament that can be dispensed with. It is not merely an extra activity for those students whose high intellectual abilities leave them time and energy for lightweight amusements. Nor is it merely an innocuous way of busying those incapable of more abstract intellectual activities. Drama is an essential part of a democratic education. (Barnes 1968: vii).

They cast their net wide, and spent considerable time on the effects of drama on language inside and outside the classroom:

All recognise dialogue as an essential characteristic of drama, and all adults know its importance in thinking and communicating. As teachers, however, we have not always made full use of it. Dialogue in its various aspects is the factor all learning experiences have in common . . .. The intellectual development of a child may well depend not so much upon what has been presented to him in formal instruction, but upon the dialogues in which he has taken an active part. The child whose experience of dialogue is limited in kind or extent is likely also to be limited in the intellectual strategies at his disposal. It must be through language that the processes of dialogue are internalised to become the processes of thought, dialogue becoming dialectic (10–11).

They finally asserted in a challenge that would still today gladden the hearts of all advocates of drama in the school curriculum:

> What we are recommending... is not only that drama activities be part of all English teaching, but that all English teaching approach the condition of drama (52).

At just the same time as Barnes and his colleagues were writing these trenchant words, the next comprehensive UK report on primary education after Hadow, *The Plowden Report* (1965), arrived with an underlying philosophy that was a rallying call for progressive education:

> We attempted to illustrate that children could be creative, could handle worthwhile books and materials, so that we might encourage teachers in a wider range of authorities to move towards meeting children's learning needs more effectively. We wrote that we 'endorsed the trend towards individual and active learning and "learning by acquaintance" and that we should like many more schools to be influenced by it' (Plowden 1987).

This report also affirms the value of drama for its possibilities for developing children's language, though this recommendation's placement is fairly low down among the priorities of English. The grasp of drama itself, though critical, is very limited, especially compared to the sophisticated understanding of Barnes and other contemporaries:

> In practice, drama bridges English and movement. This is apparent from the dramatic play of children in the infant school. They rely mainly on movement yet, even at the stage when play is largely individual and a group may contain three heroes and only one unwilling villain, words will force a way in as part of the movement. We have been much impressed by the dramatic work which has developed in junior schools in some parts of the country. Children re-enact and reshape experiences of everyday life and those derived from literary, Biblical and historical sources. Unscripted speech plays a part but if it is emphasised too much it may cramp movement and kill action. As children become more accustomed to this way of working, improvisations can be discussed, revised and rehearsed until they grow into coherent plays from which children begin to understand something of the problems and strengths of dramatic form. When the amount of dialogue increases, some children may want to polish their plays by putting words on paper (Plowden 1967: Paragraph 600).

Many of the textbooks whose titles we have canvassed earlier also argued articulately for the incorporation of drama for an eclectic variety of reasons, including 'creativity' and 'personal development' and of course learning about the art-form itself, and even:

> It [Drama] is also a means to comprehend and deal with life at all as a sentient, conscious being (Holbrook: 203).
>
> It is ... a vital imaginative experience; and the value of it goes deep for the child because essentially, acting is the child's natural way of enlarging his understanding of other human beings – and therefore his understanding of the nature and conditions of human life itself (Whitehead: 123)

Ironically, in these affirmations of the value of drama in English, it is sometimes hard to spot the supposed effects on language itself – but that's the point, of course. These writers are convinced of the need for a holistic approach to language and literature as part of personal and social development, and so they write that way, and acknowledge the difficulties of ready assessment of such organic effects:

> The practising teacher with his eye upon the children rather than upon the mark-sheets will know well enough that the benefits which accrue from drama lessons are by no means marginal, even if they are not always readily or accurately measurable. Can these intuitions be given the rational and cogent formulation which is needed to rout the sceptics? (Whitehead: 122).

That last enquiry effectively preempts much of that painstaking quantitative research into drama and language referred to earlier and reported by Wagner (1998) – and provides a challenge that foreshadows her own scepticism about the limitations of such methodologies.

One of the most authoritative of this genre of English textbooks is the report of the UK Schools Council Programme in Linguistics and English Teaching, *Language in Use* (Doughty et Al. 1971), which has a very functionalist agenda. At first sight, drama is entirely absent from its index and even its pages. Closer reading shows that even in this report on how to teach the mechanics of language, dramatic exercises and activities are embedded so integrally that they are not even labelled as drama. However, in this as in some other contemporary texts, the drama activities are at such a low level that they incur the wrath of the more discriminating of the drama-in-English advocates, for their dramatic and linguistic vapidity or artificiality:

> If we regard drama thus as an important art experience, particularly in the growth of the child, we shall see that much of the work which is done in the name of drama in schools today is useless. We must have standards of speech and movement ... [but not] the kind of vocal gymnastics called elocution .... Good speech comes from an understanding of the words spoken and the desire to convey them to an audience (Holbrook: 208).

It would seem that even with such emphatic and articulate support, in the 1960s and 1970s English classes were a long way from the state where 'all English teaching approach the condition of drama'.

> Of our sample of 939 teachers working with twelve year olds, a mere 21 would regard themselves as trained drama specialists (Bullock: 160).

This statistic comes from the last of the major British national educational reports that could be described as 'progressive' for the next 20 years or more: *A Language for Life*, usually known as the Bullock Report (1975). This is a survey of the teaching of English in over 2000 schools in Britain (including the one where John was teaching at the time). Although its comments on drama are brief, they are authoritative and detailed, and the report gives support to drama that is strong, tempered with realism:

> Drama has an obvious and substantial contribution to make to the development of children's language and its possibilities in this respect have yet to be fully explored (156).

The report helpfully identifies language areas where drama can make a specific contribution:

> There are countless occasions when written words – not just those in a play – are illuminated by being placed in a real context, which drama can help to realise. In its turn, improvisation can be enriched by the written word (157).

It is partial yet fair in its treatment of the debate on the educational merit of theatre versus improvised forms that was just gathering steam and rancour at the time:

> What is so often lacking in improvisation is stimulus and subject matter of quality, and literature is an unequalled source of this . . .. Nevertheless, quite apart from its other qualities, it is improvisation, involving the complicated relationships between the written and the spoken word, which seems to us to have particular value for language development (157–8).
>
> An important aspect of the creativity of speech as distinct from writing is the inexhaustible fund of grammatical forms and idioms available to children from an early age . . .. If, as Chomsky argues 'the normal use of language is innovative' [Chomsky, N. (1968) *Language and Mind*. London: Harcourt, Brace & Ward.] it becomes a vital principle that the teacher should create opportunities most likely to produce innovation and generate 'natural' language in all its forms (158).
>
> An increasing number of teachers. . . would add that it helps to establish confidence in social intercourse, as well as familiarity with a variety of speech forms (158).

With the Progressives in Retreat

That was the last report of its kind in Britain, because at the time the forces of recidivism were gathering strongly, demanding a return to 'the basics' (literacy and numeracy, rather than oracy, of course), a metrical approach to assessment and constant and rigorous 'testing', an authoritative, centralised 'National' curriculum and 'standards' applied from the top down (and the reintroduction of corporal punishment, too). Plowden in particular, and all the 'progressive' forces of 'child-centred', 'process-driven', 'experiential', 'negotiated' and 'democratic' curriculum, came under vitriolic and sustained attack. In less than a decade, the new conservative government of Margaret Thatcher had given this push its head, and all of the demands apart from corporal punishment were in place, and to remain virtually unchallenged since. Drama suffered like any marginal citizens caught up in other people's battles, and entered a period of turmoil – but has now actually ended up with a closer relationship than ever to English, at least in the UK.

Elsewhere, those cataclysmic events did not happen, at least at the time, and then not so savagely. In Canada, in the 1980s, the Ontario Ministry of Education, for instance, developed its *TALK* oracy project (Booth & Thornley-Hall 1991) with a very strong input from drama, particularly from David Booth, who had established a high reputation in orthodox educational circles for the wizardry of his practice, and other key drama educators such as Norah Morgan and Juliana Saxton. Through the 1980s and 1990s, like Australia, they kept importing the cream of Britain's drama and English specialists to work with teachers and in university summer schools.

Australasia did not suffer from that seismic reversal either. Here, the progressives held sway for longer, and with them the connection between English and drama stayed strong. The movement towards a more student-centred curriculum still had impetus. Particularly influential was Garth Boomer. Boomer is best remembered for his radical challenge to all curriculum: *Negotiating the Curriculum* (1982). He had influence in systemic education via his role as Director of Curriculum in South Australia and also in English education, as President of the Australian Association of Teachers of English. He was a passionate, informed and benevolently critical advocate for drama within English and language teaching, and in his own work and influence perhaps Barnes's vision 'that all English teaching approach the condition of drama' came closest to realization, before Boomer's premature death intervened in 1993.

By this time, Australia was experiencing two more subtle shifts or repositionings, one of English and one of drama, which were eventually to put considerably more distance between the disciplines. Before Boomer's advocacy could really take effect, English was being colonised and appropriated by various branches of applied linguistics, as natural leaders (at least of theory) in the push for 'literacy', which became the new basic. Phrases like *genre theory* and *critical literacy* gripped Australian English syllabuses, and have not let go since. There is nothing intrinsically inimical to the incorporation of drama about linguistics or any of its new 'key concepts'. As Barnes and his colleagues pointed out, drama is a very good way of providing real or realistic and motivated contexts for both speaking and writing in specific genres:

> e.g. For those adolescents who are deprived of a wide range of social experience, dramatic recreation of realistic situations may be an important way of developing control of a range of registers (Barnes: 18).

Further, 'critical literacy' is only another way of understanding subtext, which is one of the central characteristics of dramatic dialogue, and can often best be made manifest in the language, gesture and paralanguage of drama. However, virtually none of the applied linguists have had time to get familiar either with drama or dramatic pedagogy, and so their pedagogy and the structures of their curricula almost invariably exclude it. During the same period, too, literature was sidelined, and has become a battleground of its own between the 'classical canon' and the 'common culture' adherents, a polarisation that the drama community has mostly chosen to leave well alone.

In any case, drama in Australia was busy separating itself from English, into a quite different 'Key Learning Area' of *the Arts*, along with Music, Visual Arts, Dance and sometimes Media, but not Literature. Drama still has a place within the English curriculum (at least where that still includes literature), and there is of course now a plethora of textbooks, manuals and other teaching resources, printed and web-based, produced for English teaching by the teachers and scholars of drama education (e.g., Byron 1986; Haseman & O'Toole 1990; Ackroyd, Neelands, Supple, & Trowsdale 1998; and Anderson, Hughes, & Manuel 2008 – the book from which the quotation that started this chapter was taken). However, there is little preservice or in-service training in any form of drama for most English teachers, secondary or primary. There is also little positive evidence that the majority of teachers involved in English teaching ever access that burgeoning resource literature. There are, as there always have been, brilliant and naturally dramatic teachers, but the practices excoriated by Caldwell Cook at the beginning of the twentieth century, and David Holbrook in the middle of it, are alive and ill in contemporary classrooms.

Speech and Drama

The explicit link between *speech* and *drama* goes right back to the beginning of the twentieth century, or earlier – a study of speech and drama in Dallas, Texas, was recorded in 1884 (Rumbley 1971). In England in 1906, shortly after Sir Henry Beerbohm Tree opened what became the Royal Academy of Dramatic Art, Elsie Fogarty was the founding Director of the Central School of Speech and Drama. While this was, like Tree's academy, primarily aimed at the training of professional actors, it did claim to provide:

> an academically integrated form of training in drama and speech for young actors *and other students* ... offering specialist education to *a broad range of communities* ... committed to a broad range of training systems for vocal and dramatic performance [italics added] (Central School of Speech and Drama 2007).

though it is not clear who those *other students* and *communities* might have been.

In British-influenced school systems, drama has been explicitly present ever since, through the movement that was originally often known as *elocution* and has continued to be known as *speech and drama*. However, the drama component often existed in rather compromised forms, quite early becoming subsidiary to agendas that had more to do with preserving a notional 'correct' English and often with social class distinction than with basic functional oracy. It is unfortunate that Speech and Drama has not really had its due in terms of recognition for its long and sustained contribution to drama's assault on the gates of curriculum, particularly in the British literature. Speech and Drama has often been positioned in opposition to the drama education movement (and with good reason) in the internal wars which are described in Chapter 6. However, many of the pioneers of drama education had some speech and drama in their backgrounds or their careers, such as both Peter Slade and Gavin Bolton, whose contributions will be recognised in detail in later chapters, and many others of the British local drama advisers who were being sporadically appointed all over England during the middle years of the century. Slade's famous Rea Street Centre in Birmingham was still the Speech and Drama Centre when John visited it in the mid 1970s. It was natural that education systems, looking tentatively for leaders to implement those odd but exciting ideas promoted by the likes of the Hadow Report and Douglas Barnes, should look for the nearest thing available, especially if it appeared to offer a bonus for the English teachers. The British class war is largely to blame for that neglect of this worthy contribution.

Although presumably the phrase 'Speech and Drama' was designed to imply the close connection between the two words, perversely it emphasises their distinction. There is already a divided agenda, which has been variously interpreted and addressed over the years. The movement has encompassed speech *through* drama, speech *for* drama, speech *within* drama, drama *within* speech, drama *for* speech and drama *as* speech. And that's before we begin investigating the words themselves.

This whole book wrestles with what the word *drama* actually means, and most of its manifestations in Chapters 3–6 have been represented within Speech and Drama: the 'drama' has of course been largely concerned with language, but it has certainly taken on the aims of personal development and development of social skills (Chapter 4's focus), pedagogical purposes and values education (Chapter 5) and education in the art form and training for dramatic artists (Chapter 7).

The word *speech* is another portmanteau of diverse meanings. It embraces at least four quite different domains of perspective and even world-view – though they all have their roots in the first:

- There is 'simple' oracy – the ability to communicate efficiently and appropriately with others primarily through the spoken word.
- A component of oracy is the specific capacities and uses of verbal and vocal articulation – as in 'speech training', 'speech therapy'. This is often treated separately and now more frequently labelled 'voice' in contexts of education and training. Here, there can of course be an explicit link to drama, since the voice is one of an actor's basic instruments – in British and American classic theatre, the primary one.
- Then there is speech as in *a* speech – a particular public manifestation of speaking usually as a monologue. This leads into a whole long associated tradition of education to do with 'rhetoric' and a plethora of books on communication – with a focus on speech-giving and 'public-speaking' skills. And let's not forget debating and competitive clubs such as Toastmasters.
- The fourth dimension is where the class war comes in, especially if 'speech' has an evaluative adjective like 'good' in front of it: namely the forms and kinds of spoken address used by people, particularly their accents and dialects, which are used universally as one of the most significant markers of both identity and culture – i.e., ways of interpreting, classifying and/or judging who people are, their status and their origins.

The last of these is the dimension that has shaped the history of speech and drama in schools in Britain and its former colonies, a legacy they are all still working hard to shake off. Indubitably through the nineteenth and the first two-thirds of the twentieth century, education has been linked not only to the notion of getting on, but also getting (or staying) up.

Among the strongest markers of social class have been accent and dialect, combining two status measures. The first of these was based on the traditional British mixture of socioeconomic conditions and traditional station in life; the second was geographical. The speaker was judged against a notional 'standard English', constructed closely to be identified with an upper-middle-class accent and dialect common to most of London and urban South East England, and perpetuated in the high-status grammar and public (i.e., private) schools, not least because it was shared by most of the teachers. It was often called 'King's (or Queen's) English', though in fact the British royal family used to speak with a distinctly different accent, otherwise limited to the British upper classes and a handful of the highest status English private schools. There was also a modified form of King's English called 'BBC English' (affected, one might now say, listening to its artificial tones on old recordings). Radio and early television announcers had to conform to this, from the fiat of the first Director-General, Lord Reith. Several generations of English people and middle-class ex-British colonials took their lead from it in vocal artic-ulation, as they took their time from the BBC's broadcast of the 'pips' and Big Ben – it was the BBC and it had to be right. This form has finally ended up being called 'received pronunciation' (RP), which pretty well sums it up. Technically, this way of speaking is characterised by a wider range of vocabulary and tighter grammatical constructions, but a much narrower range of intonation and syntactical flexibility than, say, the dialects of some English-speaking Aboriginal Australians, or working-class Geordies from Tyneside UK. In terms of the functional construc-tion of meaning, it is not better English, though because of the factors outlined above it does travel exceedingly well. Only in the last part of the century, however, since the rise of the meritocracy and since it has become acceptable and even cool to be working class, has RP lost its tyranny.

The second of these status measures was regional differentiation, i.e., the dis-tance from the commercial and social metropolis – middle-class London. National pride ensured that there was no social taint in speaking with a strong Scottish or Welsh accent – though Britain's relationship with the various Irish accents are much more problematic. However, anywhere in England itself, and especially some of its colonies like Australia, India and South Africa, the 'thickness' of a regional dialect and accent (i.e., its diversity from RP) was an inverse measure of both social class and 'being educated'. Rural accents became 'quaint'; industrial ones, especially from 'North of the Trent' a river that divides England approximately into 'South' and 'North', more offensive to the sensitive ears of the upward-mobile, London-based arbiters of acceptability. These arbiters of course tended to include not only the majority of teachers, schooled with the same assumptions, but potential employers too. (For more detail on this particular tower of Babel, see, for exam-ple, the writings of Peter Trudgill, e.g., Hughes & Trudgill 1979.) It all seems a curiosity now, but these assumptions were for years taken for granted and rarely questioned. John's mother was born, of Geordie parents, in the English Midlands (respectively far to the North and just North of the Trent), but through family and schooling learned to speak 'standard English', and maintained to the end of her life that, therefore, she did not have *any* accent at all.

The use of drama to assist in the task of standardising young people's voices into employability and social acceptance seems to have begun in the nineteenth century. That was part of the purpose of including drama in the curriculum or co-curriculum of the prestigious private schools of nineteenth-century Australia, as much as of twentieth-century England. To speak the language of Shakespeare and the English poets was to speak the best English, and of course actors who spoke it professionally in public were the language models to be followed. So the speech trainers brought in drama, with dramatic monologues being particularly favoured. However, they also recognised that effective speech is a concomitant of effective use of the body (or that 'correct speech' goes with 'correct posture', which today we might not see as quite the same thing). The students were encouraged to get up, move around and engage in dialogue – quite a radical and welcome departure from the rows of desks screwed to the floor that characterised a 'normal' classroom. Drama was liberating, drama was fun, and drama would help us get on in the world, as it helped us to speak better. The grim picture of girls balancing books on their heads as they minced round the room reciting Hamlet is a snapshot of the worst practices, rather than the norm.

Partly because Speech and Drama was so well established in the private schools system in Australia, it had a very important part to play in the establishment of drama in all systems in Australia, a more egalitarian society than the UK. In Tasmania, it was actually established in the public (i.e., state) schools in the 1960s. In Queensland, private school speech and drama amalgamated quite peacefully and fairly painlessly with drama and theatre in the 1970s and 1980s to become established within the official curriculum, and continues to provide a co-curricular service to those seeking social advancement for their children, as well as personal and social development. It did have an enormous role to play in teacher training, and *that* played a seminal part in establishing drama in schools in Australia and elsewhere.

Speech and drama is alive and well in many schools today, though the language it uses to promote itself, and its aims, have both changed to cater for an assertively egalitarian present. The colonial connection is still there, and Trinity Guildhall, the largest British speech and drama training and assessment organisation, operates beyond the British Isles in seventeen countries, including seven ex-colonies (Trinity 2007). Interestingly, it prefers to use the phrase 'drama and speech' rather than 'speech and drama'. Australia's AMEB – originally a Music Examining Board – now offers, in this order in its 2007 advertising, syllabuses in 'drama and performance', 'voice and communication' (note the change of terminology), and 'theory'. Perhaps significantly, AMEB's 'Theory of speech and drama' syllabus was withdrawn in 2004. *Vale* speech and drama, old style.

Drama for Second- and Other-Language Learning

Conversation.
Listen and practice:

Julia:	*I'm so excited! We have two weeks off!*
	What are you going to do?
Nancy:	*I'm not sure. I guess I'll just stay home.*
	Maybe I'll catch up on my reading.
	What about you? Any plans?
Julia:	*Well, my parents have rented a condominium*
	in Florida. I'm going to take long walks along
	the beach every day and do lots of swimming.

Nancy: *Sounds great!*
Julia: *Say, why don't you come with us?*
            We have plenty of rooms.
Nancy: *Do you mean it? I'd love to!*

This dramatic epic is taken from a contemporary Taiwanese textbook on the teaching of English, and is quite representative of its genre. As scripted dialogue, it does at least make minimal gestures towards characters with whom the students might potentially empathise, and towards colloquial grammar. However, it makes none towards the kind of allusive and flexible colloquiality, meaningful gaps and pauses, augmented by much bodily paralanguage, which characterises real speech between friends. Nor do the speakers

> get all mixed up while they are speaking, forget what they wanted to say, hesitate, make grammatical mistakes, argue erratically or illogically, use words vaguely, get interrupted, talk at the same time, switch speech styles, manipulate the rules of the language to suit themselves, or fail to understand. In a word, they are not real (Crystal 1975: 3).

So it is likely only to be of minimal benefit when young Taiwanese actually find themselves talking about holidays to their American friends. It's hard to see this conversation going anywhere much, either – when asked to 'continue' such interchanges, students are invariably reluctant, and usually dry up after a couple of sentences. That's of course because although it has the form of dramatic dialogue, it has no drama. There's no tension, let alone background, scene-setting, character-isation or ongoing narrative, to grab the reader/speakers and engage their attention or emotions. Of course, there could be . . . but there very, very rarely is. And in fact, many teachers who use this kind of proto-dramatic exchange for teaching foreign languages actually shy away or discourage such flights, since they inevitably take away from the prescribed vocabulary and wholesome concentration on learning the correct linguistic structures, besides encouraging loose and incorrect usage driven by something as uncontrollable as emotion.

On the other hand, it would be unwise to be too superior about this extract, as the young woman who lent us this book learned English from it herself, and her English is excellent. She did mention, however, that these kinds of conversational episodes were not very popular in the class, and her classmates were actually quite resistant to any 'live' or active approaches to learning language, where they had to open their mouths in public, and no doubt part of that was a cultural question. However, for any students, as Stephen Krashen points out (1981: 103ff), learning language is different from learning other subjects because it *requires* public practice. Krashen suggests that an individual's emotions can either interfere or assist in the learning of a new language –which suggestion he labels in edu-speak jargon his *affective filter hypothesis*. Certainly, speaking out in a new language can result in anxiety, embarrassment or anger, and these emotions can create a kind of filter that blocks the learner's ability to process new or difficult words. As every drama teacher or student knows, drama in any classroom situation handled ineptly can be exposing and certainly increase 'anxiety, embarrassment or anger'. Equally, it can provide a classroom environment that is engaging and nonthreatening, a safe space for learning and the use of language purposefully to make meaning, and thus enhance a student's ability to learn through scaffolded language activities by increasing motivation and encouraging risk-taking. Many language acquisition theorists endorse another of Krashen's grandiosely titled speculations, his *comprehensible input hypothesis*, which suggests that learners acquire language by 'in-taking' language that is a 'little beyond their current level of competence'. Come in Vygotsky with your zone of proximal development.

First, however, we should look through the eyes of the second language teachers, or at least glimpse through the different lenses of their distinct and warring theorists. (Every discipline has its Chapter 6, not just drama.)

Behaviourist theorists support modelling, practice and reinforcement from a language-user proficient in the target language (such as a native speaker), and rely on teaching practices based on imitation and habit formation. Grammar and vocabulary are taught explicitly. Drama activities used in this approach need to demonstrate 'correct usage' and so really cannot get much further than Julia and Nancy, who embody this approach.

Innatist theorists, following Noam Chomsky, believe in an innate mental capacity for language learning and a universal grammar (UG). A child is born with a blueprint for language and 'exposure to, or input from, a particular language sets the specific rules of a child's language' (Goh & Silver 2006:45). Innatists support *immersion* and similar 'natural' approaches to language learning. If the aim is for 'natural' language, in theory all drama is available for use, particularly improvised role-play,to provide live models of language in naturalistic contexts. However, if all instruction, interaction and activities are in the target language, which is what immersion means, in practice, the language use has to be limited to what the students are capable, or nearly capable, of using with some degree of fluency. This of course restricts the topics of conversation and the possible dramatic contexts, besides the degree of 'authentic' emotion that can be generated, at least until the students are both fluent and confident. Drama activities used in this approach often go little further than the same reading of scripts and language games. However, it is possible to begin to structure improvised situations that are based on fictional contexts that have the potential to engage and motivate the students, providing there is a hook for their interest, and enough dramatic tension to keep them talking.

Interactionist theorists propose that language is acquired through social interactions, and that it requires diverse opportunities for language input, negotiation and output as essential processes for language acquisition. Interactionists often use what are known as communicative language teaching approaches – or, switching from jargon to acronym, CLTAs (Goh & Silver 2006:58). CLTAs are learner-centred rather than teacher-centred classes, and include the contextualised teaching of vocabulary and grammar, meaningful interactions through pair and group work, and an emphasis on language for communication. Here are real opportunities for structured and unstructured improvisations and process drama.

Studies of student participation in language classrooms have shown that teachers normally do about 70% of the talking and perform twice as many interactive acts as the students, as has been pointed out by Kao Shin-Mei and Cecily O'Neill, in one of the most substantial offerings in this field by drama specialists (1998:41). In these teacher-dominated classrooms, students

1 seldom address questions to the teacher,
2 almost never address questions to other students and
3 seldom react.

Drama can provide a context for much more genuinely two-way, and multiway communication. Drama offers a framework for the learning that is fictional but, inside the fiction, both purposeful and meaningful, so allowing connection to the real world context. Drama provides intrinsic motivation when students have something to say and a reason for saying it. The 'as if' world of drama offers opportunities to practise and rehearse language in a way that mirrors the unpredictability of language use in the real world. It allows for multiple right answers and many opportunities to refine the 'rightness' of communicating those answers. It supports imagination, and requires the students to apply knowledge acquired through more formal classroom practices in new and creative ways. Through the convention of 'teacher-in-role', drama can even suspend and alter the status relationship between teacher and students. Students are involved physically as well as intellectually and emotionally in the learning process, which leads to greater retention of learning in the long term (Marzano 2003).

This approach is supported by a growing body of research, including Kao and O'Neill's (1998) investigation into the use of process drama for English teaching in Taiwan, and newer writings, such as Liu's (2002) *Process Drama in Second- and Foreign-Language Classrooms.* In fact, Madonna has completed two recent research studies, with results that give differently revealing insights into the theme of this book, into why drama is both welcomed and rejected by schools and teachers.

In Singapore, English is the language of instruction in schools, and the official lingua franca. However, for most of the students, especially in the academically lower streamed schools, it is their second or even third. For the first 'DOL' experiment (Drama and Oral Language), four schools took part in the study, all from the lowest stream, each providing a class of approximately 40 16-year-old students for the drama intervention, and two of the schools providing two control classes at the same level and stream, who were taught as normal by their English teachers, for pre- and post-test comparison. The research consisted of the four classes participating in 10 hours of process drama devised by the researchers, and taught by local drama-trained teachers. All four dramas had a strong focus on oral communication and included embedded activities aimed at encouraging students to become more confident in speaking English. The hypothesis being tested was that involving students in the negotiating and co-constructing of a process drama allows them insights into the relationship between context and language, and enables them to link the language they are learning with their own lives and with the world around them. All six classes were pre- and post-tested using the standard Ministry of Education oral communication examination. All tests were recorded and independently cross-marked by three researchers. The results showed a reliable improvement in exam results for all four drama classes, while the students in the control classes showed no change. In the post-test, the drama classes performed consistently better in each of the criteria of *clarity*, *vocabulary*, *relevance to the topic*, *interaction with the examiner* and *need for prompting*. In addition to the test results, the students and teachers reported that they noted increased confidence in spoken English communication, greater enjoyment of lessons, and improved racial relationships within the class. Match score: Drama Raiders 6 v. Curriculum United 0. For more detail, see Stinson & Freebody 2006; Stinson 2008.

So far so good. The researchers tried to develop the experiment, the following year, in order to work towards sustainability. In one school this time, instead of using drama-trained teachers, the research used teachers who were not drama-trained, but were given some brief in-service in their classes, and asked to teach the drama that had been prepared for them. This is where the school system, or rather the contingencies and miscommunication that comprise so much of systemic school organisation, took over. The Principal supported the experiment. Unfortunately, the 10 teachers chosen were not, as they were supposed to be, volunteers, but very reluctant teachers who had been ordered to do this work, which none had ever encountered before, and several of them actively opposed! In addition, while the Head of the English Department publicly supported the Principal and researchers, it emerged during and after the project that she was less than supportive of the participant teachers. In spite of this, Madonna persevered with the experiment, and not surprisingly, the improvements were far less spectacular. Match score this time: Curriculum United 10 v. Drama Raiders . . . well, about $4^1/_2$ in the end. Surprisingly, there was some improvement evident in some classes, and several of the teachers had been converted to a belief that drama might be a valuable method, and even enjoyable! These were the teachers where the most improvement was noticeable. However, it must be said that for a few of the teachers, the whole experiment was a pretty unhappy one, and for some of their students too.

The moral of these two stories is that to work properly as a medium for teaching a foreign language, drama must be an invited and genuinely welcome immigrant into Curriculum Land, and must itself learn to speak the language of its hosts. The stories also point to another and rather disquieting moral. One of the major provisional findings of Anne Bamford in her UNESCO compendium of arts education research (2006) is that while the arts, well-taught, have plenty to offer schools and young people, when badly taught, they are worse than no arts at all. Since the mode of drama used in this manifestation, process drama, is a genre that has been developed primarily in schools, and as a way of addressing content across the curriculum, this will give us at least food for thought as we look at the third of the three major strands of purpose, which is the application of drama and theatre to teaching.

References

Ackroyd, J., Neelands, J., Supple, M. & Trowsdale, J. (1998) Key Shakespeare: English and Drama Activities for Teaching Shakespeare to 10–14 Year Olds. London: Hodder Murray.
Adams, A. (1970) *Team teaching and the teaching of English* London: Pergamon Press.

AMEB (Australian Music Examinations Board). *Website homepage*. Retrieved from: http://www.ameb. edu.au/ June 2007.

Anderson, M., Hughes, J., & Manuel, J. (eds.) (2008). *Drama in English Teaching: imagination, action and engagement*. Melbourne: Oxford University Press.

Bamford, A. (2006). *The WOW Factor – global research compendium of the impact of arts in education*. Munster: Waxmann.

Barnes, D. (1968) *Drama in the English Classroom*. Champaign, Ill: National Association for Teachers of English.

Booth, D. & Thornley-Hall, C. (Eds.) (1991). *The TALK curriculum*. Markham, Ontario: Pembroke Publishers.

Brice Heath, S. & McLaughlin, M. (1993). *Identity and inner-city youth : beyond ethnicity and gender*. New York: Teachers College Press.

Bullock, A. (Ed.) (1975). *A language for life*. London: H.M.S.O.

Byron, K. (1986) *Drama in the English Classroom*. London: Methuen.

Carroll, J. (1980). *The treatment of Dr Lister*. Bathurst, NSW: Charles Sturt University.

Central School of Speech and Drama (2007) *History* http://www.cssd.ac.uk/pages/history.html and *About Central*. http://www.cssd.ac.uk/pages/about_central.html. Accessed 22 May 2007.

Clements, S. Dixon, J. & Stratta,, L. (1963). *Reflections: an English* course. London: Oxford University Press.

Cook, C. (1917). *The Play Way*. New York: Frederick Stokes.

Cox, T. (1970). 'The development of drama in education 1902–1944'. M. Ed. Thesis, the University of Durham. Quoted in Bolton, G. (1984). *Drama as education*. London: Longmans.

Crystal, D. (1975). *Advanced Conversational English*. London: Longman.

Doughty, P., Pearce, J., & Thornton, G. (1971) *Language in use: Schools programme in linguistics and English teaching*. London: Edward Arnold.

Fleming, M. (2001). *Teaching drama in primary and secondary schools*. London: Fulton.

Goh, C. C. M. and Silver, R. E. (2006). *Language Learning: Home, School and Society*. Singapore: Pearson Educational.

Hadow, W. et.al. (1931). *The Hadow report: The Primary school*. London: H.M.S.O. Retrieved from: http://www.dg.dial.pipex.com/documents/hadow/31.shtml 7 June 2007.

Haseman, B. & O'Toole, J. (1990) *Communicate Live!* Melbourne: Heinemann.

Heathcote, D. (1971) *Three looms waiting*. Directed Richard Eyre. London: BBC Films. The section referred to in the text has been transcribed in O'Toole, J. (1992). *The process of drama*. London: Routledge, pp 206–209.

Holbrook, D. (1967) *English for maturity: English in the secondary school*. Cambridge UK: Cambridge University Press.

Hughes, A. & Trudgill, P. (1979) *English accents and dialects : an introduction to social and regional varieties of British English*. London: Edward Arnold.

Kao, S. M. and O'Neill, C. (1998). *Words into Worlds: Learning a Second Language through Process Drama*. Stanford: Ablex.

Krashen, S. (1981). *Second Language Acquisition and Second Language Learning*. New York: Pergamon Press.

Lester, J. A. (1926). The Active English Class: A Visit to Caldwell Cook's "Mummery" at the Perse School, in Cambridge, England. *The English Journal*., Vol 15, No 6. 443–449.

Liu, J. (2002). Process Drama in Second- and Foreign-Language Classrooms. In G. Brauer, (ed.), *Body and Language: Intercultural Learning Through Drama*. Westport CT: Greenwood. pp. 51–70.

Marzano, R. (2003). *What Works in Schools: Translating Research into Action*. Alexandria: Virginia Association for Supervision and Curriculum Development.

O'Toole, J. (1991) *Oracy: the forgotten basic*. Brisbane: Ministerial Consultative Council on Curriculum.

Plowden, B. (1967). *The Plowden Report: children and their primary schools*. London: HMSO. Retrieved from: http://www.dg.dial.pipex.com/documents/plowden17c.shtml 28 June 2007.

Plowden, B. (1987). The Plowden Report: twenty years on. *Oxford Review of Education Vol. 13 No. 1*. Retrieved from: http://www.dg.dial.pipex.com/documents/plowdenore09.shtml 20 May 2007.

Queensland English Syllabus Years 1–10. (2006). Brisbane: Queensland Studies Authority.

Rumbley, R. (1971). The history of speech and drama education in the Dallas Public Schools (1884–1970). Ph.D. Dissertation. Dallas: North Texas State University.

Schaffner, M., Parsons, B., Little, G. & Felton, H. (1984) *Drama, language and learning: NADIE Working Paper No 1*. Hobart: National Association for Drama in Education

Stinson, M., & Freebody, K. (2006). The DOL project: an investigation into the contribution of Process Drama to improved results in English oral communication. *Youth Theatre Journal, 20*, 27–41.

Stinson, M. (2008). 'Drama, Process Drama, and TESOL' in Michael Anderson, John Hughes and Jackie Manuel (eds.). *Drama in English Teaching: imagination, action and engagement*. Melbourne: Oxford University Press. (pp. 193–212)

Summerfield, G. (1965). *Topics in English*. London: Batsford.

Summerfield, G. (1968). *Voices & Junior Voices*. Harmondsworth: Penguin.

Summerfield, G. & J. (1973). *The creative word*. New York: Random House.

Tomkinson, W.S. (1921) The Teaching of English Oxford University Press (p. 46). Quoted in Gavin Bolton (2007). A History of Drama Education – a Search for Substance. In: Liora Bresler (Ed.) *Handbook of Research in Arts Education*. Amsterdam: Springer.

Trinity College Website: http://www.trinitycollege.co.uk/site/?id= 622 Accessed 25 May 2007.

Vygotsky, L. (1965) *Thought and language*. Edited and translated by Eugenia Hanfmann and Gertrude Vakar. Cambridge : M.I.T. Press.

Wagner, B-J. (1998) *Educational drama and language arts: what research shows*. Portsmouth NH: Heinemann.

Whitehead, F. (1966) *The Disappearing Dais: a study of the principles and practice of English teaching*. London: Chatto & Windus

Wollman, M. & Grugeon, D. (1964). *Happenings*. London: Harrap.

Chapter 4
Drama for Development and Expression

John O'Toole

Child's Play Again

This chapter explores our second Paradigm of Purpose, the *expressive/develop-mental*: the many-faceted claims and the often-implicit assumptions that drama can be used as an instrument of personal and social development, and the expression of 'self' or 'selves'. This entails going back to early childhood. The first chapter of this book started with a brief exploration of dramatic play. The idea that dramatic play is important to the development of particularly the young child is accepted virtually without argument by psychologists, educationalists and of course drama educators. Maisie Cobby was a 1950s British drama adviser and passionate advocate of the idea that teaching drama is making plays – namely formal theatre (a contested notion that we shall hear much more of). However, she is clear about what is important at the start:

> [The child's] make-believe play and his desire to investigate are at their height when he reaches school age. He wants to unravel situations which puzzle and interest him, to know more about the world and the people and strange places and things he sees in picture books. Above all, he needs to understand the relationship which exists between himself and these activities . . .. Always it should be remembered that dramatic play and not dramatic performance is the intention throughout (1954: 4).

Brian Sutton-Smith (1984) and Diana Kelly Byrne (1989), who like Piaget studied her own child, are among the many writers to have identified the structures and networks of personal and social learning through dramatic play. Others, such as Holly Giffin (1990) and Julie Dunn (1995 and 2003), have mapped the communicative and artistic components.

Surprisingly few scholars and writers have pursued dramatic play into later years, though in the 1950s Johan Huizinga identified play as one of humankind's common characteristics: the title of his classic, *Homo Ludens* (1955), roughly translates as 'Humans, the playing species'. Conventional thinking of the last 50 years has focussed entirely on early childhood play, with the assumption that the instinct for spontaneous social dramatic play metamorphoses into other forms in later childhood, such as rule-based games, as Piaget (1932) identified in his famous essay on marbles, or 'proper' drama and theatre making, and dies out naturally in later

J. O'Toole et al., *Drama and Curriculum,* Landscapes: the Arts, Aesthetics, and Education 6, DOI 10.1007/978-1-4020-9370-8_5,
© Springer Science+Business Media B.V. 2009

childhood. It certainly becomes hidden from grown-ups and very difficult to see or observe. Suspecting from clues given by her own and friends' children that this latter was the case, Dunn (2002), already an acute analyst of early childhood play, managed to construct a context where she could observe older children (11- and 12-year-old girls) as they played freely and at great length – a single play narrative might typically last for between 1 and 3 hours. From these observations, she was able to demonstrate the sophistication of their management of dramatic form, including the skills of instantaneous and socially negotiated playwrighting, and of metacommunication and conservation of the illusion, characteristics previously identified in younger children by Giffin.

Adults do engage in forms of dramatic play, too, though they would rarely call it that. Intrigued by what scholars like Dunn were revealing about child's play, Lucy Voss Price from South Africa shrewdly observed her own grown-up brother and a friend engaging in what appeared to be spontaneous dramatic play, and spent 3 years mapping the phenomenon as it occurs in the context of medieval re-enactment groups, and the very complex sets of permissions and rationales that adults construct to allow them to freely engage in a world of spontaneous dramatic and theatrical make-believe (Voss Price 2000). Voss Price also explored the phenomenon of how adults 'conserve the illusion', through what she analyses as 'operative' and 'non-operative' frames of perception, which work in spontaneous parallel. This is effectively the same phenomenon that Coleridge famously dubbed as 'the voluntary suspension of disbelief', one of the building blocks of all dramatic activity. It is also a reworking of what the educational psychologist Lev Vygotsky called 'the dual affect', which in fact goes some way to explain how Coleridge's phrase works to permit participants to identify with what they know to be a fiction. The dual affect – further elaborated by drama theorists such as Gavin Bolton (1979: 20) – acknowledges that children can intellectually and emotionally exist simultaneously and effectually in two worlds: one real but suspended as far as necessary, and one that is fictional but is the 'operational' world of the drama. This is an absolutely necessary concept for drama teachers working in distracting environments. We have already discussed the importance of Vygotsky's theory of the Zone of Proximal Development (1978). As well as explaining the increase in abstract language and high-level thinking demonstrated by primary children in the Tasmanian study referred to in Chapter 3 (Shaffner, Parsons, Little, & Felton 1984), it also makes comprehensible the astonishing depth of response of children to Dorothy Heathcote's teaching, captured many times on film and video (e.g., 1971, 1975, 1976). The challenges she sets, and the freedom provided by the dual affect, combined with the support that she, the other participants and the fictional setting provide to the child, together scaffold the child's understanding to provide a much more sophisticated and complex behaviour than the child could manage alone.

Creative Dramatics and Creative Drama

It is, therefore, hardly surprising that many claims have been made for drama's efficacy in a range of areas of personal and social development. Two of the most influential movements of the twentieth century, attempting to ground drama in the curriculum – one in the USA and one in the UK – have been based on just these claims, and in particular the 'progressive education' notion that drama provides an opportunity for 'creative expression' (or similar phrases). One of the most thoroughly articulated of these sets of claims was made in the USA by the pioneer Winifred Ward in 1947. The form of drama that she used was mainly known as 'creative dramatics' or 'playmaking' – she used the terms interchangeably in her seminal book *Playmaking with Children* (1947) – a developed version of the theories and practices she used in the public schools of Evanston, Illinois, first described in *Creative Dramatics* (1930). Ward is widely regarded as the founder of the American movement, though she cedes the credit to her own mentors. In the UK, the impetus was Peter Slade's *Child Drama* (1956). These two authors are very different, but they may be usefully compared, as both set their national curricular tone for the next 20 years. Both were confident and skilled practitioners, their practice informed by a clearly stated theory of child-centred and developmental education. They both unequivocally articulated ideals of the expressive and creative power of drama. Both took as their starting point children's natural dramatic play, not dramatic text but improvisation, acting out stories and various forms of role-play.

All of Ward's set of aims for drama were firmly grounded in developmental philosophy, and she laid out her creative and expressive curricular objectives quite clearly:

1. To provide for a controlled emotional outlet
2. To provide each child with an avenue of self-expression in one of the arts
3. To encourage and guide the child's creative imagination
4. To give young people opportunities to grow in social understanding and co-operation
5. To give children experience in thinking on their feet and expressing ideas fearlessly.
   (1957: 3–9).

Ward believed that 'The arts add immeasurably to the richness and enjoyment of living' (1957: 5). She was deeply influenced by the philosopher Hughes Mearns and his books on creativity (e.g., *Creative Power* 1929). Her developmental plan was specifically designed for and addressed to the formal education systems – the book's subtitle is *From Kindergarten Through Junior High School*, and the final chapter discusses the teacher's role in playmaking. It is full of vivid anecdotes and practical advice that can be (and has been) lifted straight into the classroom.

From its inception, there was a strong research base to the creative dramatics movement, as others took up Ward's baton. As early as 1961, pioneer sisters in the field, Geraldine Brain Siks and Hazel Brain Dunnington, brought together the research and scholarship in the new field in *Children's Theatre and Creative Dramatics*. The chapters are all based on formal research or practitioner experience and cover a wide range of uses of creative dramatics at the time, heavily developmental, including values education, exceptional children, religious education, correctional institutions, community programs, recreational programs – by distinguished practitioners such as Barbara McIntyre and Nellie McCaslin. The latter wrote many books herself, as her own practice expanded beyond the original aims of creative dramatics and morphed more into drama for specific learning objectives. This territory is also covered in the writings of Siks who is moreover significantly concerned with drama's role in language development (1977: 23, 149ff). The writings of these quite eclectic authors are a very clear example of the kind of porousness that characterises the unreliable categorisations demarcated in this book. One of McCaslin's most lasting oeuvres is the three-edition classic *Children and Drama*, the diverse editions of which contain essays by many of the giants of both creative dramatics and of drama-in-education. In the last edition (1999), Siks, McCaslin, Mary Flory Kelly and Judith Kase-Polisini meet and fraternise courteously with Dorothy Heathcote, Gavin Bolton, John Hodgson, David Booth and Cecily O'Neill (denizens of the realm of drama pedagogy), and the book gives a strong sense of collective wisdom, and no sense at all of factions, impenetrable categories or special pleading – except for drama itself – in a converging range of manifestations. Fittingly, this book contains the swansong of Winifred Ward, written just before she died, deploring the rout of progressive education, still preferring the term 'creative dramatics', still admiringly quoting Hughes Mearns. The chapter is filled with anecdotes of children's and teachers' personal achievements that showed her heart was still fixed firmly on her developmental sleeve.

In the UK, the midyears of the century were likewise the heyday of progressive education, and local education authorities were busy appointing drama advisers. By no means the first but certainly the most influential of these was Peter Slade. He almost single-handedly founded the Child Drama movement (Slade loved emphatic capital letters), whose aims and educational trajectory were actually quite similar to Ward's, but whose focus and manner of expression were both quite different. Although he spent many years as a schools drama adviser, and then head of a team of drama advisers, neither his book nor his practice have ever fitted comfortably into conventional school curricula – which has caused his many followers much grief.

Slade started his professional life in the 1920s in experimental and arena theatre, and then as a director of children's theatre companies. Ward, too, founded a Children's theatre in the 1920s, but with very firmly pedagogical aims for actors: 'to train University, secondary and junior high students in the production and performance of drama, while providing the children of Evanston with rich theatre experiences' (Evanston 2007). By contrast, as he amusingly describes, Slade caused half of his children's theatre company to resign by demanding that they completely retrain themselves in what he then called 'acting in the round'. He was asking them to do exactly the opposite of what Ward was trying to do with her company, to remake themselves with 'a quality of expression and creation which the child seems to me to do naturally' (1966: 3). This natural expression and creation was what then fascinated him and he embarked on a process of informal research, which led to his theory and practice of Child Drama, expounded at length in his eponymous book on the subject (1954). This grounded his theory of teaching in what he observed as two forms of Dramatic Play: Personal and Projected, mixed with liberal doses of Jung, which together demonstrated that children possess a natural Artistry (there are all those cap.s again) – expressing mythic themes from their collective unconscious.

He developed this mix of observation and theory into a kind of loose performative pedagogy, based on dramatic play, dance drama and what he called 'polished impro- visation', and the gradual incorporation of conventions of performance taken from orthodox theatre and rehearsal.

The book is free-wheeling, opinionated and passionate, wholeheartedly centred on his revolutionary discovery: that Child Drama has a life of its own, and exists as an art form in its own right, with intrinsic purposes, control of form, and outcomes that are self-contained artworks. Slade's book is brilliant – if uncontrolled – practical educational research, crammed with detailed examination and analysis of children's play and classroom drama, with transcript, photographs and diagrams laying out for the reader the mechanics of the creative processes he observed. Slade acknowledges that the dramatic forms, skills and conventions change and grow as the Child devel- ops, but not that they 'improve' – the product of each age-range is sufficient unto itself.

> The period [age 5–7] is one of increasing skill, of great enchantment, and the extra sen- sitivity that is developed brings the Child to the threshold of the most wonderful years of dramatic fulfilment. We find exquisite moments in their new Drama creations from now on, in which deep soul experiences and ice-cold logic walk hand in hand (1954: 51).

Curriculum planners do not know what to do with this kind of artistic outpouring either from children or their theorists – is it even 'learning'? And how can you assess deep soul experiences walking hand in hand with ice-cold logic?

Like Ward, Slade worked developmentally, but with much less regard for the formal educational systems into which his disciples would spend the next decades trying to fit his principles. He had plenty of disciples. He was a charismatic teacher (John saw that for himself on a visit in the 1970s) and a very charming, articulate, persuasive speaker, and throughout the 1950s to the 1980s at least, acolytes flocked from round the world to watch him, study him, or just listen, including numbers from Australia. What many of them then found to be a problem was that his way of working was actually quite hard for others to replicate, as it was really completely unsystematised, and they were trying to establish it in contexts like schools that were entirely systematised. Without his personal charisma, lesson-scaffolding skills, and razor-sharp theatrical instincts in the classroom, other dynamics quickly took over. When teachers better known to their children as ordinary classroom pedagogues invited the children to clear the desks, demonstrate their artistry, and come up with some natural mythic themes, instead of the Absorption which was the correct and expected reaction, the classroom often descended within minutes into mayhem. Children were as unused to this kind of freedom as their teachers. Some teachers regretfully turned from Slade's kind of Child Drama, while many others recoiled contemptuously from their colleagues' maladroit attempts to replicate it. Still others soldiered on, like his Rea Street Advisory Centre, with Sylvia and Phyllis and the rest of his team of loyal followers. His last book, *Child Play: Its Importance for Human Development,* was published in 1995, and its very title still shows his pas- sionate interest in dramatic play, and his flag firmly nailed to the mast of personal development: 'It is intended to be a help to parents, teachers, social workers, police,

Home Office, JPs, priests and therapists. It might make some children more happy too. That's why I wrote it' (1995: preface).

The influence of Slade is still felt, particularly in what we believe to be his most lasting achievement. That was to get adults to recognise and respect the potential artistry of children, and their ability, both individually and in group-planning, to manage artistic form – and at least their right to be consulted and involved in the planning of their drama. Slade was, after all, the keenest of observers of children's dramatic play, and he was the pioneer who started to implement in classrooms what the play theorists have taken another 30 years or so to thoroughly establish even existed. This caused the beginning of a sea-change in the way teachers thought about drama in schools, and, we contend, was an often overlooked factor in the development of what are two of the most widespread and significant contemporary genres of dramatic work in schools: process drama and group-devised theatre.

Progressive teachers of the 1960s and 1970s in places like the UK, Canada, and Australia were attracted to drama, inspired by the human developmental vision of Slade, excited by his notions of improvisation and 'natural' drama based on play, but perplexed about how to go about achieving it. Help was at hand, in the form of a book by Slade's most illustrious collaborator, Brian Way. *Development Through Drama* (1967) was embraced by a generation of tentative teachers with little idea of improvised drama or how to go about developing people through it, and must surely be the best-selling drama textbook of all time: in the 1970s and 1980s, Way's book was often the only drama book found in schools, particularly in countries distantly influenced by Slade, such as Canada and Australia. In Queensland in the 1970s, one copy dwelt in every primary and secondary school. It is still found frequently on school shelves and college reading lists. Blessed by the needy of his time, then – as is often the way – this book has been roundly cursed by the more knowledgeable of the following generation, for reasons that Way even presaged himself: 'By the same token, a book like this can be a positive menace!' (1967:8). How? Read on.

Way was quite explicitly aiming for 'the development of people' through drama; specifically, the development of 'individuals; drama is concerned with the individuality of individuals, with the uniqueness of each human essence' (1967:3). And like Slade, he was concerned with using drama's holistic and experiential nature to develop all aspects of those individuals: 'If education is concerned with preparing young people for living rather than for a job in life, then it must concern itself with the whole person . . .. In this sense, a basic definition of drama might be simply "to practise living"' (6). For this grandiose phrase, he received a tart rebuke from John Allen, the UK's former Senior Inspector for Drama: 'I find it difficult to accept the general premise of a book which equates drama with life' (Allen 1979: 95). On the other hand, Way was not alone, nor even original in this notion. Ten years earlier, an anonymous drama adviser is quoted as observing of the dance drama work of Alan Garrard, a British secondary teacher:

> Through it they have 'discovered' themselves, have become sensitive to music and the visual arts, have learned to communicate their ideas and feelings with ease and fluency and to become aware of the needs of others. . ... The experience they have received has led them

towards a deeper understanding of the art of living – and this surely is the purpose of any of
the arts in education. (Wiles 1957:13).

The optimistic vision of life-improvement offered by Garrard and Way was
shared or accepted by thousands of teachers, who fell on Way's book not for the
detailed philosophical argument, but for its practicality – in short, its exercises.
Teachers who were used to the pedagogy of reading, writing, sums and vocabulary
warmed to a method that recognized that 'the thirty or forty minute lesson may
be considered as an important factor in academic study', and were thrilled to hear
that 'in drama a five minute lesson can be as important as the longer one . . .' and
even '. . . a few minutes active drama can do much for tired, strained and possibly
bored minds. So drama need never interfere with a crowded curriculum' (7). Just
what the doctor ordered, and philosophically you could apparently have your cake
and eat it: you could do all those wonderful things for developing the whole person, while not even taking time out from the more important things on the normal
curriculum. Better than that, even: 'A few exercises, for a short space and time,
regularly [his italics], brings eventual results. Keep in mind that the progression is
within each person, each at his or her own rate; the point on the circle is there for
the whole of life' (16).
Now what's this 'circle' (a good Sladean and Jungian concept)? Way's book
is as neat and systematic in its theorising as in its drama method. He conceives
drama's role in human development as a series of four concentric circles, radiating
outward from the hub of 'The Person' (with nicely Sladean capital letters), representing developmental stages: in turn, 'discovery of resources', 'personal release
and mastery of resources', 'sensitivity to others within discovery of environment',
and 'enrichment of other influences both within and outside personal environment' –
with each circle's title getting longer, presumably in synch, with the increasing mastery of The Person. Neatly cutting up this pie into equal slices are radii labelled with
the carefully numbered elements of *1. Concentration; 2. The senses; 3. Imagination;
4. Physical self; 5. Speech; 6. Emotion;* and *7. Intellect.* And, more or less in that
order, he sets out to develop them. Teachers (and students) in the 1970s loved the
sections on stimulation of the imagination and the senses through the use of objects
(Can we bring out the feelie-bags, today, Miss?). Way's exercises cover the field –
or in his terms virtually fill all the segments of all the circles. Like Winifred Ward,
he gives a myriad of useful and thoroughly well-organised suggestions, examples,
anecdotes and starting places. To be fair (and in the spirit of Peter Slade), many of
his exercises are quite open-ended, with lots of opportunity for students' input. But
above all, they are controllable.
Virtually none of Way's exercises was new. Many of them were derived from
books of drama exercises by earlier writers such as Bishop E.J. Burton, who were
themselves developmentally inclined: 'EXPERIENCE: Growing from a seed into
a great tree (with sound); a great wind comes and blows down the tree' . . . with
accompanying narration helpfully provided (Way: 194); it's close to a rewrite of
Burton (1955:33). Although there came to be a great gulf especially in the UK
between the practitioners of theatre and those of improvised drama (particularly

exacerbated by Slade himself), most of the rest of Way's exercises are effectively derivations of acting exercises – as of course were many of Burton's and the earlier drama advisers and writers: the theatre is where they got their ideas from. It is no accident that Way remained steadfastly a theatre practitioner, founding the long-lived and still flourishing Theatre Centre, and a long tradition of participatory theatre for young people.

Turning to theatre to provide useful exercise forms was closely paralleled in America. Creative dramatics and creative drama practitioners alike in both the countries turned to books like Viola Spolin's (1963) *Improvisation for the Theatre*, and dozens of other books offering titles such as *101 + ideas for Drama* (Scher & Verrall 1975) and *Gamesters' Handbook: 140 Games for Teachers and Group Leaders* (Brandes & Phillips 1979). One very popular contemporary descendant is the cheerful exercise-based theatricality of Keith Johnstone's *Theatresports* (1979), which belongs within this creative/expressive paradigm. The updated edition of this book (1999) has caused quite a flutter in the dovecotes of the drama communities, as the word Theatresports has had a[TM] (trademark) slapped on to it, backed up by an 'official' training and certification system. This, to the outrage of many teachers and theatre workers who have been doing this kind of fairly low-risk stuff for years in the common domain, means you're not supposed to do 'Theatresports' unless you have undergone that special training. This is a rare example in our field of territorialising for commercial purposes.

Then from the 1970s onward, came the gathering avalanche of drama for learning, or drama-in-education, with its much greater emphasis on the social impact and significance of drama and on its particular role in the curriculum. This eventually rendered the concentration on ordered developmental exercises in creativity and expression – the way of Winifred Ward and Brian Way – obsolete. Like Peter Slade, it has left its mark on many contemporary syllabuses and drama textbooks that concentrate on developmental structure. In America – and some other Anglophone societies like Canada and Australia – the transition from creative dramatics has been natural and organic, with the most influential of its practitioners, like Nellie McCaslin, David Booth, and the Swortzells (Nancy and Lowell), moving seamlessly from one to the other, and remembering and honouring their roots. In England, with its more fractured and fractious drama community, the transition has often been accompanied with acrimony and recrimination.

Creativity Worldwide

And then again, in other parts of the world, it hasn't really happened like that, and developmental drama is undergoing a rebirth, in more ways than one. Most East Asian countries are currently in the process of discovering drama – along with the other Arts – as a possible inclusion in the curriculum, and the education systems are negotiating it into their curricula. They have all been driven with varying degrees of explicitness by the magically reborn word 'Creativity'. Many of these countries, which Western economists like to dub with backhanded admiration the 'Tiger economies', have for years been putting all their educational energies into producing assembly lines of well-informed engineers, bureaucrats, and business managers. For this, the old colonial mechanistic curriculum structures fitted quite nicely and relatively cheaply: intensive, teacher-based learning of given information in large classes, backed up by regular testing. For the Chinese-based cultures, this also tied in neatly with the ancient Confucian/Imperial principles of respectful absorption of given wisdom and regular doses of examinations. Suddenly, the twenty-first century hove in view with new and quite unpredictable factors like chaos theory and fuzzy logic, information redundancy, a rash of new and startling sciences, the renaissance of human services, explosions of all sorts of new media . . . and – of all people – big corporations like Microsoft demanding creators, innovators, and team-workers instead of carefully trained and competitive operatives. Where in the world of curriculum could governments suddenly find *them*? And so the tigers are tiptoeing into the arts, mostly timidly.

Taiwan was about the first to embrace the concept wholeheartedly, and in 1997 announced that the arts – including drama – were a *key learning area*, and started investing in teacher training to support them. The pioneers were already out there[1] and from the 1980s, had been studying overseas, initially in America with people like Nellie McCaslin and Lin Wright, and later in the UK. They brought back quite eclectically the ideas of creative dramatics, creative drama and the somewhat different philosophy of drama as a pedagogy. As in other South Eastern Asian nations, there was a simultaneous rediscovery of traditional theatre forms, to which the younger generation might usefully be introduced to provide not only creative input, but also a patriotic sense of their cultural heritage.

In Hong Kong, 3 years after its return to China, a radical new curriculum policy plan *Learning to Learn* (Cheng 2000) demanded both creativity and critical thinking, and also made space for the arts. As in Taiwan, there was an energetic and enterprising theatre community already heading off to UK, USA and Australia to develop its expertise, and drama was already quite well-established in many of the plethora of international private schools, which cater for Hong Kong's cosmopolitan population. Since then, an economic downturn and some much less bold educational administrators than in Taiwan have blown first hot then cold on drama, starting several research projects on drama education, of which at the time of writing only one has been released, although the interest in drama continues to rise (and Hong Kong hosted the 7th IDEA World Congress in 2007). So drama hovers around or edges erratically into the curriculum. Other countries like Korea, Japan, Singapore and mainland China have found it less stressful so far to spend the money (considerable money, in Korea's case) on developing Music and Visual Arts (Kim 2005: 5), which, as ever, have always had a role, though marginal, in the curriculum, leaving the small communities of hopeful drama pioneers still on the outer edge, though

---

[1] People like Chang Hsiao-hua, Lin Mei-Chun, and Chen Ren-Fu

there are hopeful signs in Singapore and Hong Kong at the time of writing with drama becoming a recognised curriculum subject in a small number of secondary schools.

In two other quarters of the globe, within the last couple of decades, there has been a very considerable awakening of interest in bringing creative drama into schools, in the hispanophone countries of Spain, Portugal and South America (especially Brazil and Peru), and some francophone communities. Brazil's Augusto Boal, the most famous Latin-American exponent of drama for educational purposes, though highly creative, does not belong here at all, but in the field of dramatic pedagogy. Some, like the writer of Spain's first real drama textbook, Barta-Martinez (1995), another alumnus of the New Yorkers, hedge their bets with a foot in creativity and one in pedagogy.

For many Latin people, creativity and personal development are once again the keynotes. The movement has tended to have rather different cultural roots from England and America. Drama educators have tended to take their inspiration directly from the concept that the actor (not the playwright or director) is the prime mover of theatre, and that the main purpose of the theatre is to move people emotionally. The concomitant of that in schools is to start with developing children's emotional and creative capabilities like those of an actor. This was a very strong message conveyed to this author by the ambiences of two important 'first' conferences in the 1990s, the first IDEA World Congress in Porto, Portugal in 1992, and the 1st Encuentro for Education and Youth Theatre in Lima in 1994. Influential Peruvian drama educator Liliana Galván starts her book on drama and dance education, *Creativity for Change: Innovation for Life and Work* by directly comparing creativity with procreation and birth . . . and the creative development bus rolls on from there: 'The first objective is to create'; other sections concentrate on 'discovering creative potential', 'sensual knowledge', 'creative development', 'conquering space' and even 'creative potential and power in business' (2001: 14, 22 – our translation). Not much ambiguity about aims there.

As may be appearing more and more evident, in writing this chapter it is getting progressively harder to separate 'drama for personal and social development' from the territory of 'drama for learning', particularly as so many of the key practitioners and writers either (a) make no distinction themselves; or (b) do, but quite expressly aim to engage in activities that are clearly for 'personal and social development' *and* 'drama-for-learning'. The word 'creativity' obviously belongs just as much there as here. It may be helpful to resolve some of the more obviously overlapping areas using Ward's five aims for creative dramatics, which encapsulate quite a few separate developmental claims that have been widely used for drama, and resonate very strongly with her British counterparts. We will add *movement*, which is usually conceptualised by drama writers in expressive/developmental terms, and *drama for healing* (dramatherapy and psychodrama). The use of drama for motivating students, and the role of drama in the development and/or problematisation of moral values might equally be said to belong here, and they do . . . but they also belong in the next chapter, which is where you will find them.

Revisiting Developmental Claims

1. Emotional Development: 'To provide for a controlled emotional outlet'

Educating the emotions is a very popular claim for drama, but rather a double-edged sword, as far as orthodox curriculum is concerned, as has been seen in the first two chapters. Ward shrewdly makes a good case for the *safe* incorporation of emotion in the classroom: 'Better than any other school experience, the arts offer opportunities for channelling emotions into constructive uses' (1947: 4) and backs it up with a nice biblical example of learning about forgiveness. Slade is more forthright, as usual:

> Now what I'm really pleading for then is a very serious, calculated, scientific form of emotional education, based upon – dare I say it now? – something like thirty or forty years of very careful observation (1966: 18).

Nice disingenuous challenge, using the word *scientific* in this particular context, particularly given the free-wheeling nature of his science.

What 'emotional education' actually means is not clear from the writings of most of this generation, and less clear still from the classroom activities they specify. Even Ward has to assert without a shred of evidence that 'playing the part of Joseph in that dramatic scene in which he forgives his brothers . . . makes a far deeper impression on a child than merely reading about Joseph'. John Wiles did use long-term observation of Alan Garrard's teaching as a basis for asserting that drama can at least 'award [the child] with a new and happy emotional experience' (34), which is rather less sweeping. Brian Way's educational concern, like Ward's, is with *controlling* the emotions:

> As has been constantly reiterated, drama is as concerned with exploring and *mastering* [our italics] the emotional self as it is concerned with discovering and mastering the physical self (219).

And in trying to explain this dramatically, he becomes positively cyclic:

> Mood and atmosphere cannot exist without people, and atmosphere is created by the mood of people. Mood is created by feelings, which are all rooted in emotions (219).

Which leaves us where?

Valiantly, teachers have tried down the years to educate, train or help children to establish mastery over emotions using drama, mainly resorting to acting exercises. After all, actors have to depict emotion, but only recently have teachers started to read Stanislavski or Michael Chekhov, who for years had been explaining to professional actors how to work internally. Instead, teachers did (and many still do) spend a great deal of time getting children externally – on command – to 'show' emotions, especially nice big ones, like *fear, happy, sad*, etc. This approach to emotion Gavin Bolton has called 'adjectival . . . safely descriptive' rather than 'verbal', or in other words actually experienced.

> In the early days of my teaching ... I trained my seven year old class ... to look sad, happy, murderous, or even surprised .... When I ... switched to ... creative drama, one of the things it required me to do was to narrate exciting stories (a tambourine in my hand for sound effects) while children switched on their 'scared' look. 'Plucking up courage (their courageous look) they entered the cave slowly, their eyes peering into the dark (some of them are not peering), their eyes *peering* into the dark ...' (1985: 100–101).

Bolton is the wisest writer on *real* emotion and its place in drama, and this wickedly accurate parody – worth reading the whole paragraph – is a very useful cautionary tale, and acts as a prelude to his real message, which is that '*experiencing* is the key to the dramatic educational process' (101). In another essay, he pointedly observed that 'the sad position is that in its own way, drama has become yet another subject that trains children to avoid their feelings' (1985: 99). In the course of four thematically connected essays, Bolton not only defined what emotion in drama is and means, considerably more satisfactorily than Brian Way, but also mapped out in complex but clear terms the roles that the careful management of authentic emotion in drama actually plays in *learning*. In the course of this, naturally, he touched on the education of the emotions, and emphasised that for emotional learning to occur, the emotional *engagement* in the drama has to be authentic. It must also be carefully managed in terms of adequate protections, but tough, too. As he pointed out when discussing children watching theatre: 'if a show guarantees that children's emotional level remains at low ebb in the name of safety, they might as well have stayed at home' (1973: 24).

Bolton's deeply reasoned understandings resonate quite closely with, and complement, the much more recent findings of neurologists such as Antonio Damasio that the brain, body, and emotions are intricately and integrally linked:

> The mysterious first-person perspective of consciousness consists of newly-minted knowledge, information if you will, expressed as feeling ... the 'looks' of emotions can be simulated, but what feelings feel like cannot be duplicated ... unless flesh is duplicated, unless the brain's actions on flesh are duplicated, unless the brain's sensing of flesh after it has been acted upon has been duplicated (Damasio 1999: 313–315).

Buried in there is quite a powerful argument for the development of what Damasio carefully defines as consciousness through the use of embodied action expressing cognitive and emotional expression – through drama no less. Elsewhere, Damasio demonstrates that neuroscience affirms the strong links between cognition, the emotions, and performance in all the arts.

2. Self-Expression and Self-Esteem: 'To provide each child with an avenue of self-expression in one of the arts'

One of the earliest drama textsbooks, also a treasure of sustained empirical observation, was Harriet Finlay-Johnson's *The Dramatic Method of Teaching* (1907). She had no doubt of the importance of drama as a vehicle for self-expression:

> The crowd in this play, of soldiers etc., were not drilled or trained to their parts in the orthodox way. In fact they never acted the play twice alike, but just expressed themselves as they felt at the moment. Hence the play always went with a swing and never mechanically. No true educational expert will need to be told that this *self expression* is the very thing we need most to aim at in order properly to exercise and train the children's faculties and get the best results (1907: 103).

Self-expression is a real weasel word, often used, infrequently defined, and as slippery as it is attractive. How do you express self, especially when contemporary psychology and role theory identify multiple selves, displayed in a densely woven tapestry of behaviour ranging from quite involuntary to entirely deliberate manifestations of that self (those selves)? Individual development king Brian Way and his followers buy wholeheartedly into at least the singular version of this claim: 'Consciousness of self is wholly positive, and springs from an intuitive awareness of the uniqueness of individual personality' (1967: 158), and a lot of the exercises of this school of thought set about 'helping each young person to become fully responsible for *control* [our italics] of his own behaviour' – through growing consciousness of that self.

Self-expression is often implicitly linked – perhaps partly because the phrases sound so similar – to the notion of raising self-esteem, on the assumption that expressing at least parts of the self, or selves, helps individuals to acknowledge their identity (or identities) explicitly and, therefore, come to terms with it (them). Drama is certainly invoked for this purpose, and often in therapeutic or clinical rather than strictly curricular settings, which will be dealt with later this chapter. Certainly, to use drama in schools to deal with perceived deficits in self-esteem, especially where there are social factors contributing to those deficits, is an argument that cuts considerable ice with curriculum managers. Elyse Dodgson worked with black adolescent girls in a South London School:

> black and female, belonging as they do to two groups which have been traditionally treated as inferior. It is through drama that I hope my pupils will feel more aware of their own worth, power and potential, and thus become visible. . . . By discovering our own voices, we will begin to find out who we are, what we think and feel, what we know and will need to know. I hope that through my drama my pupils can become confident, articulate and assertive young women (1982: 33).

As Dodgson implies, enterprising teachers of all the arts can and do translate this claim into giving them curriculum space. It is not hard to demonstrate, *qualitatively*. Observing or even reading about those black girls' brave and imaginative work as a result of Dodgson's inspirational teaching is very persuasive. All competent arts teachers can point as commonplace to examples of startling behaviour changes as a result of exposure to the arts, of which their schooling has often starved the neediest children. In their turn, school administrators (and other teachers, more geared up to academic success) are only too glad to hand over the demoralised, the unruly, the pathological specimens and other failures of their system into classes where they may be redeemable, or at least are out of the way. So especially in secondary schools, the drama class sometimes ends up as the hospital ward of the subject electives, and the most conscientious drama teachers long wistfully for an occasional crack at the academically capable, even as they work their restoration jobs on the battered self-esteem of their charges.

Drama is often entrusted with doing this kind of thing on a grander scale altogether, expressing, constructing or restoring a group, community or national identity. This is usually seen as the province of grown-up theatre, and national funding bodies like the British Council and the Australia Council exist, in a sense, to provide funds for doing just that both at national and community level. However, sometimes it can percolate down to the level of schools and children. Europe is currently redolent with festivals of young people's theatre, such as the biennial *European Children's Theatre Encounter (EDERED)*, where groups of young people 'represent' their nations both in showing and sharing their national characteristics (Aaltonen 2006). One of the most ambitious attempts at collective identity building through drama actually in schools in recent years has been happening in Hungary (or was, because we have not had recent news). During the years of Communist rule following the World War II, a whole generation of Hungarian children grew up with no access to the rich heritage of traditional folklore that was an important part of what it meant to be Hungarian; fairytales were banned, apparently. In the post-Communist period, the children of those children were likewise starved of the old traditions, because their parents simply did not know them, and the children were perceived to be growing up not only with inadequate sets of cultural references but consequently impoverished imaginations. So a major reeducation program was instituted, including drama, to teach in schools what the parents no longer could (Gabnai 1996:96–101).

Talking of the imagination:

3. *Creative Imagination:* 'To encourage and guide the child's creative imagination'

Ward was writing during the middle third of the twentieth century, when Dewey-inspired progressive, child-centred and experiential education was central at least to the rhetoric of schooling, and before the word 'creative' went out of fashion. This it did in quite spectacular fashion in the last third of the century, and to our shame many of us who were teaching at the time actively connived at its betrayal and ostracism. Creativity was seen as soft and indefinable, and 'creative drama' had a ring to it that we felt did not appeal to the bosses of the curriculum, where creativity had never been much prized. Along with words like 'informal', 'child-centred' and 'process', in the UK at any rate creativity became a dirty word in what was explicitly a new 'war' declared on progressive education by an alliance of traditionalists and economic rationalists – a series of salvoes, whose titles, *A Black Paper – The Fight for Education* (Cox, Dyson, & Boyson 1969–1975), left no doubt of their bellicosity. Creativity and imagination do not flourish in war zones. The Plowden report was savaged. The antagonists demanded a return to traditional subjects and standards, regular examinations and inspections. Within little more than a decade, virtually all the Black Papers' demands had become reality in the

UK, and drama was a major casualty. This defeat of progressive education was mourned in the USA at the end of her life by Winifred Ward, as we have noted. In Australia and Canada, those forces were on the march, but much less brutal and less successful; however, we were not taking chances on being dismissed as 'new age' and soft. We modelled our drama and theatre rhetoric on language that could be easily justified (defended is perhaps a better word) to mechanists and rationalists. 'Slade? Creative dramatics?' Never heard of them. Like our colleagues in visual arts and music, we even distanced ourselves from 'Creative Arts', fearing – with some justification – that the curriculum guardians might make the phrase a useful label for collapsing all the arts into one composite, thereby saving space on the overcrowded timetable.

Then at the end of the century, it all changed. As we indicated above with specific reference to Asia, worldwide big business and government suddenly decided that creativity is a crucial driver of commercial innovation for the twenty-first century. This immediately spawned a new literature attempting to define it in just those terms, such as Richard Florida's very influential books *The Rise of the Creative Class: and How it's Transforming Work, Leisure, Community and Everyday Life* (2002) and *The Flight of the Creative Class* (2005). Back in Ward's time creativity was generally seen as especially appropriate to children and their appreciation of the arts, not commercial enterprise. As she and her generation found, that was acceptable as a notion, but rather hard to assess or test and, therefore, even harder to interest education systems in. Now it offers a whole new beckoning doorway into the curriculum.

4. *Social Understanding and Cooperation:* 'To give young people opportunities to grow in social understanding and co-operation'

In Brian Way's individualistic firmament, the social aspects of drama were not entirely dismissed, but they were relegated to Chapter 12 of twelve chapters. Others of his predecessors and contemporaries gave them much more prominence, including Ward, and Slade too, who saw the group as the central component of Child Drama. A curious and perhaps significant connection here is that 'sociometry' – the psychological study of groups – was invented by Jacob Moreno, a social psychologist who became a theatre director and whom we will meet later in this book as he also founded both psychodrama and sociodrama. Just as significant is that in live theatre the emphasis has shifted through the century from the individual actor to the ensemble, the company – a move just beginning to be belatedly mirrored in actor-training:

> The objective of the actors' training is to encourage development of individual skills at the highest level and to utilise those skills in contributing unreservedly to the development of the group by actively participating in the content and conditions of its working life (Royal Academy of Dramatic Art 2007).
>
> The graduates of VCA Drama are renowned for their capacity to work creatively and collaboratively, in both traditional and groundbreaking performance contexts (Victorian College of the Arts: Drama 2007).

Bishop Burton (1955: 13) had set the tone quite early for the 'social under-standing' campaign: 'Drama is an activity of the community. Leaders, priests, specialist mimes, may emerge, but drama is a social matter in which everyone is concerned' – though his exceptions are exceedingly odd. Nowadays, this is seen almost as axiomatic, and not really needing to be proved to school sys-tems. A great number of current research papers and dissertations, especially on theatre in secondary schools, too numerous to itemise, focus on drama's social-ising or community-building capacities, and on its development of the skills of social communication, at the level of individuals, classroom, school and com-munity. So do many current textbooks, exemplified in the first-page introduc-tion of a text by one of the authors of this book, Madonna, addressed to the students:

Interpersonal skills and drama:
Cooperation, collaborative planning, working towards shared goals and listening to each other as you offer, and accept, ideas and suggestions are some of the skills you will develop if you make a commitment to learning drama. By working closely with others you learn how to give advice and feedback in supportive and productive ways, and thus operate as a valuable team member (Stinson & Wall, 2003: vii).

While some of the books still stress the development of interpersonal and group skills through drama, many of them are concentrating on the potential of drama to address grander and starker issues of social communication – the publishers' blurbs of two of these both stress this scale of 'growing in social understanding and cooperation':

Drama and diversity: a pluralistic perspective for educational drama offers a pluralistic perspective for the field of educational drama and theater practice, demonstrating how educators can respectfully work across and between differences such as race, social class, gender, sexual orientation, and ability (Grady, 2000).
   The theatre of urban: youth and schooling in dangerous times re-examines familiar 'urban issues' facing these schools, such as racism, classism, (hetero)sexism, and religious fundamentalism in light of the theatre performances of diverse young people and their reflections upon their own creative work together (Gallagher, 2007).

With the same agenda of social activism at the local level, drama and theatre are currently gaining great popularity in a myriad of schemes to help address social issues such as bullying and conflict in schools. One of the largest has now been run-ning for over 10 years in at least three countries (O'Toole, Burton, & Plunkett 2004; Lofgren & Malm 2005). This scheme explicitly ties drama into whole-class peer teaching within the curriculum, to provide both cognitive understanding (through the drama), sufficient to enable the students to manage some of their own conflict and bullying issues; and new social networks (through the peer teaching), to reshape together uneven power and communication patterns within the school and thus the school social ethos. Significantly, one of the barriers to this scheme's efficacy and its wider implementation is the difficulty that some schools and some teachers have in fitting it into their curriculum.

5. *Self-Confidence in Public:* 'To give children experience in thinking on their feet and expressing ideas fearlessly'

This aim actually incorporates two: the ability to think quickly and marshal ideas under pressure; and the self-confidence and/or courage to be able to articulate those ideas when in public, or when otherwise under scrutiny. Again, these are often conflated into 'raising self-confidence' (and that overlaps with 'self-esteem' in 2 above, of course). This is a claim which has very serious curricular traction. It is in fact, of all the claims made for drama in schools, the one that is most frequently affirmed by students and their parents and most easily accepted by school principals. As Brad Haseman's (1990) survey of the growth of secondary drama in Queensland found, self-confidence ranked highest on a list of students' reasons for being attracted to drama, and equal highest of what drama teachers listed as their principals' reasons for supporting drama (equal with drama's benefit for the 'school's image'!).

A century earlier, Harriet Finlay-Johnson very shrewdly backed up her claims of drama's role in developing the self-confidence of her working-class village children (for whom a 'business' career would be the pinnacle of ambition) with a closely reasoned piece of lesson analysis:

> There have been rumours too in other quarters that boys leaving school and beginning work are lacking in initiative and self-reliance – both 'business' qualities needed by boys. I have found my Dramatic Method [she liked capital letters too] forced children to exercise these powers and automatically, as it were, develop them.
>
> The boy who represented Cromwell had to write his own speeches, and therefore on *him* was thrown the responsibility of finding out and putting together material. There was the first step towards developing self-reliance – responsibility of the individual. Probably one book of reference failed him and he developed *perseverance*. All books failed him at some junctures and he had to display *ingenuity*. He had to work in an introduction to the play and its characters and describe the hero indirectly yet gracefully, and to be brief about it. Here came in *resourcefulness*. . .. He had to confer with 'Coke' [a fellow student]. . . And here were two schoolboys analysing history and men!

In mid-century, it was still one of the achievable goals of drama:

> To increase the self-confidence of the child; to improve its resourcefulness and initiative; to develop a sensitivity towards itself and society . . . – these are some of the things his [Garrard's] way stands for (Wiles: 34).

And from then on, developing self-confidence was one of the major aims of Speech and Drama syllabuses. It still is; one of the newest syllabuses states: 'The syllabus is designed to foster an individual's confidence and skill in communication in both everyday life and the professional sector' (AMEB 2007).

Drama's capacity to develop self-confidence among adolescents has received powerful support from outside. We have earlier briefly referred to a 10-year study by Shirley Brice Heath and her associate (Brice Heath et al. 1993) of how American youths at risk might be given more personal agency. Their observations compared young people in three diverse leisure activities: sport, church and institutional youth clubs, and youth theatre. The latter provided by far the most positive results.

Movement and Motor Development

Movement and motor development is an area that is becoming increasingly a priority today among drama teachers, especially in North America, as part of the fight against obesity in children. For some years, it has received relatively scant attention, but 50 years ago was a major concern of almost all drama courses, especially at the early childhood and primary level.

Right back in 1931, the Hadow Report stated

> Drama, both of the less and more formal kinds, for which children, owing to their happy lack of self-consciousness, display such remarkable gifts, offers further good opportunities of developing that power of expression in movement which, if the psychologists are right, is so closely correlated with the development of perception and feeling. (1931: 76).

In the 1967 Plowden Report, the link between drama and movement is made repeatedly – as in the paragraph quoted in Chapter 3 (p. 56), and

> Children have a great capacity to respond to music, stories and ideas, and there is a close link through movement, whether as dance or drama, with other areas of learning and experience – with speech, language, literature and art as well as with music (1967: 704).

and yet again:

> Movement may be concerned with agility, on the ground or on apparatus, with ball or athletic skill, or with expressive movement of dramatic or dance-like quality (706).

Drama is in fact *only* mentioned along with either or both of the words 'movement' and 'dance'. Movement and physical development were absolutely central to the dance-drama of Alan Garrard. For Bishop Burton, too:

> Through drama they may try out movements and action, and gain confidence in the necessary bodily techniques of daily life (1955: 2).

In American creative dramatics, movement and bodily development were equally central, eloquently summed up by Geraldine Siks:

> In drama a main concern is with expressive body movement. Children need to learn how to use and control their physical selves to enable them to use body movement expressively to give form to their impulses and imaginings (1977: 71).

This determination is followed up with the most detailed of analyses of physical movement, locomotor and non-locomotor, direction, effort, etc., and exercises to help develop them, in order to aid the child's expressive capacities.

Through most of the century in the UK, drama teachers and advisers like Stanley Evernden and Maisie Cobby stressed the importance of developing movement and gesture. Movement analysts and teachers, especially Rudolph Laban, were very popular as sources of dramatic movement curriculum. Slade turned himself into one. Nor does Brian Way ignore movement in his comprehensive development plan – (elevated above 'speaking' in the implicit pecking order of his chapter headings). And in the practice of teaching movement, games were central – games and warm-ups.

Since that mid-century heyday, movement has suffered a sharp decline in emphasis, as a consequence, to some extent unintended and ironic, of the rise of drama-in-education. That movement has in fact been quite justifiably attacked for this failing. The concentration of the students became directed to negotiating the dramatic action and meaning; meaning took precedence over action; in experiential role-play, meaning was mainly made manifest in words. Where exploring conflict and dilemma using authentic emotions were the order of the day, teachers could not afford the risks to limbs or furniture of the action being manifested in movement. When the limitations of endless directly experiential role-play became clear, and the more sophisticated forms of process drama emerged in the late 1980s, more theatrical conventions and some games reemerged a little, and, fostered by Cecily O'Neill, Morgan and Saxton, and others, the physical manifestation or symbolization of dramatic moments and meaning once again became part of the vocabulary of the drama lesson.

Contemporary Arts syllabuses such as those in Australasia tend to leave movement to Dance – and of course Physical Education, where in practice dance almost invariably resides, even though Dance is classified in the Arts Key Learning Area, while Physical Education is domiciled elsewhere. There *has* been an increased interest in the physical aspects of theatre among secondary drama teachers in the last decade, mainly owing to the adult theatrical trend towards physical theatre, circus and other highly visceral forms of theatre. This has in turn been something of a revolt against the word-dominated theatre of most of the twentieth century.

Drama for Healing – Therapy and Psychodrama

Hello again. It's Peter Slade speaking. Now all you boys and girls who are working so hard to get drama – or whatever you call it nowadays – established in schools know of me as a pioneer of Child Drama. However, my obituary (a very complimentary one, in the Guardian) led off by calling me a pioneer of drama therapy – 'the first British dramatherapist'. Nice headline, that – if not strictly accurate. However, I did work as hard at dramatherapy as at Child Drama – you can see that my theory of Projected and Personal Play was quite central to both. I was the first person to speak on Dramatherapy at the British Medical Association in 1940. The British Association of Dramatherapists (BADTH) recognised my contribution, noting that through the 1930s and 1940s I 'was refining [my] ideas on the healing power of drama through constant and rigorous touring, workshops and lectures, culminating in the publication, in 1954, of [my] hugely influential book, Child Drama' (BADTH, 2007).

Slade was actually picking up on an idea that had intrigued theatre and drama practitioners for about half a century – or much longer, in one sense, if you consider Aristotle's notions of catharsis: drama purging people of unhealthy excesses of terror and pity. Using drama as a way of teaching personal development inevitably leads towards notions of healing. If we are engaged in developing through drama personal aspects of people who are perceived to have deficits or deficiencies, or we are using drama to repair emotional or intellectual damage, then we are de facto engaged in therapy. In drama we explore, manipulate and control both empathy and emotional distance, and as we have seen, perhaps also map and even have some impact on shaping individual and group identities.

However, it is a concept that has made drama educators other than Slade very nervous. As teachers, we rarely see ourselves as healers, or believe that we have the proper training to either diagnose or treat pathologies in our students. The one exception to this is the area of drama with special needs, as we say today, or 'remedial drama' as we said the day before yesterday, to which we will return after a trip down memory lane.

Adam Blatner has identified 15 real-life uses or experiments with drama for healing from the seventeenth to the nineteenth centuries, reported by witnesses as acute as Goethe and Alexandre Dumas, and starting in 1668:

> Hans Jakob Christoffel von Grimmelshausen in Germany wrote in his *Simplicissimus* (book 2, chapter 13) that doctors used symbolic enactments in the treatment of delusions: e.g. one man 'thought he had already died and wandered around as a ghost, refusing both medicine and food and drink until a clever doctor paid two men to pretend they were ghosts, but ones who loved to drink. They joined the other and persuaded him that modern ghosts were in the habit of eating and drinking, through which he was cured (1988: Appendix A).

There's a gut-wrenching fictional depiction of this very treatment from half a century earlier, by Shakespeare no less (or probably his young collaborator John Fletcher), in *The Two Noble Kinsmen*. The gaoler's daughter has gone mad with unrequited love, and her egregious father persuades an equally egregious suitor to pose as her lost lover Palamon, and make love to her, to restore her sanity. The success of this distasteful treatment is left more ambiguous than Grimmelshausen's example.

It is surely significant that the explicit application of drama to therapy emerged at the turn of the twentieth century, with the early exploration of internal approaches to acting and the development of improvisation in rehearsal. Stanislavsky was apparently the major influence on the foundation of 'Therapeutic Theatre' in Kiev in 1908 by Vladimir Iljine, who went on to write *Improvising Theatre Play in the Treatment of Mood Disorders* (1909), and *Patients Play Theatre: A Way of Healing Body and Mind* (1910) (Blatner, 1988: Appendix A). According to Blatner, Iljine also worked on educational drama.

The most famous figure in the field, Jacob Moreno, who is commonly regarded as the founder of *psychodrama*, started working in Vienna at about the same time in creative drama with children, and a few years later with prostitutes. He fell in with a theatre crowd at the Café Museum, and they brought their expertise together into the *Stegreiftheater* – the Theatre of Spontaneity – an early form of improvised theatre, where actors and director (Moreno) worked spontaneously to create a piece of theatre, inviting the audience to contribute ideas to the unfolding narrative. As well as being an experimental theatre, the Stegreiftheater was instrumental in developing Moreno's 'theory of creative spontaneity', and altogether:

a socio-therapeutic endeavour, in that morals, ideas and values of the community were reflected back to members of the community. Moreno also discovered, during the course of the Stegreiftheater, how to use spontaneity techniques to alleviate emotional disequilibrium, a process which he later developed as *psychodrama* (Nolte 2000: 210).

This, according to Nolte, resulted from his increasingly systematic dealings with a couple of neurotic actors, Barbara and George, who had got married while in the company, but had tempestuous rows at home, which affected their acting. As their director, Moreno started to manage Barbara's tantrums through subtle casting, which in turn increased George's tolerance. Then he invited them, in the spirit of stegreifteater, to play out their home life on stage, which apparently affected the audiences greatly. From these thoroughly theatrical roots came the theory of Psychodrama.

Moreno moved to the USA, and there was a steady growth over the next 30 years, when Slade was getting going in Britain too, where 'many occupational therapists discovered the benefits of using drama with their clients' (BADTH 2007). The fashion really took off all over the world in the 1960s (when else!). Fritz Perls dabbled in *Gestalt theatre* on the back of his *gestalt therapy*, most publicly at the Big Sur Folk Festival held near his Esalen Institute in 1967. Eric Berne's *transactional analysis* led to *transactional psychodrama*. France cashed in with *Expression scenique*. And of course, the 1960s was the period when a plethora of quasi-real, quasi-psychotherapeutic, quasi-mystical and quasi-dramatic encounter groups had their day. Some of these were organised and driven by careful and research-driven practice; some driven by passion and imagination; and some driven by mountebanks and charlatans.

The nervousness of educators about the value and appropriateness of psychodrama in our own hands has been reciprocated since the 1960s by drama therapists, and there has been a two-way standoff until recent years. As Slade pointed out,

> In dramatherapy it has been recognised by some doctors and psychiatrists that the Personal Play part of Drama is of value and importance in the treatment of patients (1972: 5).

'Some doctors and psychiatrists'. Even more than in schools, drama has found it hard to breach the doors of the medical curriculum. By the 1960s, the 'real' psychodrama practitioners and drama therapists had seen with alarm the proliferation of groups with variable agendas, credentials, and training, and had responded by 'medicalising' themselves. Partly to establish respectability and partly to ensure quality control, systems of clinical accreditation were set up and rigidly policed. Pyschodrama was formally a part of psychotherapy and 'amateurs' like drama educators were not even acknowledged, let alone spoken to.

The word *dramatherapy*, however, was still rather more open than *psychodrama* to general usage (although there are also accredited drama therapy courses, and some client systems still insist on clinically approved practitioners – in Australia, for example, in some hospitals and special needs education). There have always been some drama educators who were game to approach the field of therapy. This they did initially from education's territory of 'remediation'. Sue Jennings, the most influential British drama therapist of recent times, boldly titled her first book *Remedial*

Drama: A Handbook for Teachers and Therapists (1973) and since then has moved wholeheartedly into the field of dramatherapy, with many other books and her own consultancy company. Dorothy Heathcote, too, made regular visits to institutions of people with disabilities, and featured her own therapeutic work on several films, such as *Who's Handicapped?* (1972).

Some psychodrama and drama therapy practitioners and theorists were becoming uneasy, too, at the rigid academic and clinical demarcation (so different from the eclectic approaches of Moreno and Iljine, to say nothing of Slade).

> Because it was originated by a psychiatrist, and he developed it largely within the setting of a mental hospital, psychodrama is widely thought of as 'a method of psychotherapy'. This is misleading at best, and has had a strong negative influence upon the non-clinical applications of the method. It is more accurate to describe psychodrama as a method or system of communication, and psychotherapy as one of its functions or uses (Nolte: 211).

Leading US authority on drama therapy Robert Landy of New York University discovered with admiration the work of drama educators Dorothy Heathcote and Gavin Bolton, and acknowledged the convergences and common purposes in a number of essays and a book: *Essays in Drama Therapy: The Double Life* (1996), to which Bolton wrote a foreword. Blatner (2007) is another leading US psychodrama practitioner who has during his career become interested also in educational process of drama, and has gravitated from writing books like *The Foundations of Psychodrama* (1988) to collecting a very eclectic anthology of work in applied theatre: *Interactive And Improvisational Drama.*

Peter Slade would be relieved and gratified. By the 1990s, work in drama education particularly in adult and out-of-school contexts was segueing more and more into areas of therapy, often under the new term *applied theatre*. The rise of applied theatre has seen many techniques from theatre and educational drama used for explicitly therapeutic purposes. Recent initiatives include numerous projects in mental health and with survivors of child abuse (e.g., O'Connor 2003; Goode & Dobson 2000; Bundy & Burton 2007), and many more devoted to the rehabilitation of prisoners, including a UK theatre company, *Geese Theatre* and several books (e.g., Thompson 1998; Balfour 2004).

However, this convergence raises two interesting and problematic issues. The first is the question of original purpose. Effective drama practice may achieve therapeutic outcomes as a side effect – the story of 'Tracey' in *Cooling Conflict* is a moving example of this, though the program's aim was just to teach her class something useful about how to manage conflict (O'Toole et al. 2005: 51–60). It may of course do the opposite, and we are much less willing to scrutinise our practice for examples of harm resulting from our drama-work. Explicit drama therapists have different purposes, and must be accountable for their results in terms of whether or not any healing has in fact occurred – any learning is for them a side effect.

The second and even more urgent problematic is the question of the two sets of skills and knowledge bases that are necessary for working simultaneously in drama and therapy – and the extent to which they are easily compatible. Few people are trained in both the areas, and many of the most responsible practitioners acknowledge this, and ensure that whichever set of skills they lack are nonetheless provided. South Africa's Dramaide project was directed by a theatre education company, and employed two nurses. Bundy & Burton's project was set up from the start as an equal partnership of therapeutic counsellors and drama educators. So too were both O'Connor's and Goode's, but both of their accounts candidly show some of the tensions and pitfalls which beset the application of artistic stimuli and structures to people with psychological needs and problems. The robust application of role-play and performance to subjects such as mental health, substance abuse or suicide, particularly with teenagers, causes many health professionals extreme concern. Conversely too, the authors of this book are not the only drama educators concerned that social workers and therapists are sometimes overeager to snatch at the enticing possibilities of applied theatre, especially if they have seen a well-applied example, but without really understanding the specialised and sophisticated management of the elements of drama necessary to apply it to their clients – with dire effects (or no effects) on either the clients or the art.

Artist–therapist partnerships are often fraught with difficulties because both sets of professionals are working in a quite different paradigm, with different underlying assumptions. Medical professionals are mostly driven by a sense of care for their 'patients' who 'depend' on their 'treatment' in order for them to 'get better'. It is quite difficult for them to really communicate with artists who view their 'participants' as 'independent decision-makers' capable of 'artistic expression' and 'risk-taking'.

Perhaps for the reasons implicit in the above paragraphs, it would be true to say that drama therapy has not penetrated very far through the doorway of the psychomedical systems, nor really into schools at all. Furthermore, those reasons would seem to imply a serious need for more and better training of the professionals who aim to span both the fields. However, in the last year, the two established Australian university courses in drama therapy have been cut – not because of any quality indicators, nor because they were lacking takers (both were oversubscribed), but because they didn't fit the changing profile of their university. Once more, plus ça change.

References

Aaltonen, H. (2006). *Intercultural bridges in teenagers' theatrical events: performing self and constructing cultural identity through a creative drama process in the 10th European Children's Theatre Encounter*. Unpublished Ph.D Thesis. Vaasa, Finland: Åbo Akademi.

AMEB (Australian Music Education Board). (2007). *Voice and Communication Syllabus.* http://www. ameb.edu.au/speech/syllabus/index.html Retrieved 28 June 2007.

Barta-Martinez, F. (1995) *En escena*. Madrid: Alhambra Longman.

Blatner, A. (1988). *The foundations of psychodrama*. New York: Springer.

Blatner, A. (Ed.). (2007). *Interactive and Improvisational Drama: Varieties of Applied Theatre and Performance*. New York: i-Universe.

Bolton, G. (1973). Moral responsibility in children's theatre. *Outlook (Annual Journal of the British Children's Theatre Association)*. Vol. 5.

Bolton, G. (1979) *Towards and theory of drama in education*. London: Longmans.

Bolton, G. (1985) Emotion in the dramatic process: is it an adjective or a verb? In: D. Davis & C. Lawrence (Eds.) *Gavin Bolton: Selected Writings* (100–107). London: Longmans

Bolton, G. (1975/1986) Drama and emotion: some uses and abuses. In: D. Davis & C. Lawrence (Eds.) *Gavin Bolton: Selected Writings*. (89–99) London: Longmans

Bolton, G. (1986) Emotion in drama. In: D. Davis & C. Lawrence (Eds.) *Gavin Bolton: Selected Writings*. (108–132) London: Longmans

Bolton G. (1980) Theatre form in drama teaching. In: D. Davis & C. Lawrence (Eds.) *Gavin Bolton: Selected Writings*. (164–179) London: Longmans

Brandes, D. & Phillips, H. (1979). *Gamesters' handbook : 140 games for teachers and group leaders*. London: Hutchinson.

Brice Heath, S. & McLaughlin, M. (1993). *Identity and inner-city youth: beyond ethnicity and gender*. New York: Teachers College Press.

British Association of Dramatherapists. (2007). *A brief history of drama therapyand its development in the United Kingdom*. http://www.badth.org.uk/Dth/therapy.htm. retrieved 30 June 2007.

Burton, E.J. (1955). *Drama in schools*. London: Herbert Jenkins.

Cheng, K-M. (2000). *Learning to learn*. Hong Kong Education Commission.

Cobby, M. (1954). *We play and grow: teacher's handbook*. London: Pitman.

Cox, C., Dyson, A., & Boyson, R. (1969–1975) *The Black papers: the fight for education*. London: Dent.

Dodgson, E. (1982) Working in a South London School. In M. Wootton (Ed.). *new directions in drama teaching: studies in secondary school practice*. London: Heinemann.

Dunn, J. (1995). *Who's pretending? : a study of the dramatic play of primary school children*. Unpublished MA Thesis. Queensland University of Technology.

Dunn, J. (2002) *Imagined worlds in play*. Unpublished PhD thesis. Bribane: Griffith University.

Dunn, J. (2003). Linking drama education and dramatic play in the early years. In Susan Wright (Ed.) *Children, meaning-making and the arts*. Frenchs Forest: Pearson Educational.

Evanston (2007) – Archives of the Children's Theatre of Evanston, 1929–1986. Evanston, Ill: Northwestern University. http://www.library.northwestern.edu/archives/findingaids/childrens_theatre.pdf Retrieved 25 June 2007

Florida, R. (2002) *The rise of the creative class : and how it's transforming work, leisure, community and everyday life*. New York: Basic Books.

Florida, R. (2005) *The flight of the creative class*. New York: Harper Business.

Gabnai, K. (1996). Making encounters meaningful. In J. O'Toole & K. Donelan (Eds.) *Drama, culture and empowerment: the IDEA Dialogues*. Brisbane: IDEA Publications.

Gallagher, K. (2007). *The theatre of urban: youth and schooling in dangerous times*. Toronto: University of Toronto Press.

Galván, L. (2001) *Creatividad para el cambio: innovación para la vida y la impresa*. Lima: UPC. [Translation by J. O'T]

Giffin, H. (1990).To say and not to say: skills of dramatic play. *Youth Theatre Journal*, Vol 5 No 2. 14–20.

Goode, T. & Dobson, W. (2000). Knowing who we are (and that we are not alone). In John O'Toole, & Margret Lepp (Ed.s) *Drama for life: stories of adult learning and empowerment*. Brisbane: Playlab Press.

Grady, S. (2000) *Drama and diversity: a pluralistic perspective for educational drama*. Portsmouth, NH: Heinemann.

Hadow W. (1931) *The Hadow Report: the primary school*. London: HMSO. http://www.dg.dial.pipex.com/documents/hadow/3107.shtml Retrieved 28 June 2007.

Haseman, B. (1990). Working out!: a survey of drama in Queensland secondary schools. *NADIE Journal 14*(2), 34–41.

Heathcote, D. (1971) *Three Looms Waiting*. Directed by Richard Eyre. London: BBC Films.

Heathcote, D. (1972) *Who's handicapped?* Newcastle upon Tyne: Sideline Productions.

Heathcote, D. (1975) *Building Belief*. Chicago: North Western University.

Huizinga, J. (1955). *Homo ludens: a study of the play element in culture*. Boston: Beacon Press.

Jennings, S. (1973) *Remedial drama: a handbook for teachers and therapists*. London: Pitman.

Johnstone, K. (1979). *Impro: Improvisation and the theatre*. New York: Routledge.

Johnstone, K. (1999). *Impro for storytellers: theatresports and the art of making things happen*. London: Faber and Faber.

Kelly-Byrne, D. (1989). *A child's play life: an ethnographic study*. New York: Teachers' College Press.

Kim, J-H. (2005). *Arts Education: International arts education symposium proceedings*. Seoul: Korean Arts and Cultural Education Services.

Landy, R. (1996). *Essays in drama therapy: the double life*. London: Jessica Kingsley.

Lofgren, H., & Malm, B. (2005) *DRACON InternationalI bridging the fields of drama and conflict management*. Malmö: Malmö School of Education

McCaslin, N. (Ed.) (1999). *Children & Drama*. Third edition. Los Angeles: Players Press.

Nolte, N. (2000). The uses of psychodrama. In John O'Toole, & Margret Lepp (Ed.s). *Drama for life: stories of adult learning and empowerment*. Brisbane: Playlab Press.

O'Connor, P. (2003). *Reflection and refraction: the dimpled mirror of process drama: how process drama assists people to reflect on their attitudes and behaviours associated with mental illness*. Ph.D. Thesis. Brisbane: Griffith University.

O'Toole, J., Burton, B. & Plunkett, A. (2004) *Cooling Conflict*. Frenchs Forest: Pearson Educational.

Piaget, J. (1932). *The moral judgment of the child*. London: Routledge & Kegan Paul.

Plowden, B. (1967). *The Plowden Report: children and their primary schools*. London: HMSO.

http://www.dg.dial.pipex.com/documents/plowden17c.shtml Retrieved 28 June 2007.

Scher, A. & Verrall, C. (1975). *101 + ideas for drama*. London: Heinemann Educational.

Shaffner, M., Parsons, B., Little, G. & Felton, H. (1984) *Drama, language and learning: NADIE Working Paper No 1*. Hobart: National Association for Drama in Education.

Siks, G. & Dunnington, H. (1961). *Children's theatre and creative dramatics*. Seattle: University of Washington Press.

Siks, G. (1977). *Drama with children*. New York: Harper & Row.

Slade, P. (1954). *Child Drama*. London: London University Press.

Slade, P. (1995). *Child Play: Its Importance for Human Development*

Slade, P. (1966) *Child drama and its value in education*. Birmingham: Educational Drama Association.

Slade, P. (1972). *New trends*. Birmingham: Educational Drama Association.

Spolin, V. (1963). *Improvisation for the theater : a handbook of teaching and directing techniques*. Evanston, Ill: Northwestern University Press.

Stinson, M. & Wall, D. (2003). *Dramactive: Book 1*. Sydney: McGraw Hill.

Thompson, J. (Ed.) (1998). *Prison theatre: perspectives and practices*. London: Jessica Kingsley.

Balfour, M. (Ed.) (2004) Theatre in prison : theory and practice. Bristol: Intellect Books.

Voss Price, L. (2000). The chivalrous art of opening doors: dramatic play with adult learners. In J. O'Toole & M. Lepp (Eds.) *Drama for life: stories of adult learning and empowerment*. Brisbane: Playlab Press.

Vygotsky, L.S. (1978). *Mind and society: The development of higher psychological processes*. Cambridge, MA: Harvard University Press.

Ward, W. (1947). *Playmaking with children from kindergarten to high school*. New York: Appleton-Century Crofts.

Ward, W. (1930). *Creative dramatics*. New York: Appleton.

Way, B. (1967). *Development through drama*. London: Longmans.

Chapter 5
Drama as Pedagogy

John O'Toole

The copious references in the last chapter to the next strand in our Paradigms of Purpose, that we have named the *social/pedagogical*: drama for learning, have already underlined that there is an organic connection rather than the hiatus between them that the page break implies. This chapter picks up, for instance, on drama's motivating power, on the significance or utility of drama in the education of values and ethics and on the big and open questions of its role in behaviour-change and attitude-change and, therefore, social agency, at levels from the school classroom to the geopolitical agendas of Theatre for Development and Theatre of the Oppressed. The chapter deals, besides, in the more utilitarian or instrumental functions of drama's uses in learning the kinds of knowledge and skills that currently comprise the formal curriculum of schooling.

Marvellous Miss Johnson

Moving along from Aristotle and the mysteries – dramatic or otherwise – of the middle ages, and the hopeful hyperboles of Jan Comenius (remember – all the world's knowledge in eight plays?), we can usefully pick up the story of drama for *learning* at the beginning of the twentieth century with that redoubtable English country schoolmarm Harriet Finlay-Johnson. As a primary school principal with the responsibility of educating her charges for a still-stable and socially stratified workforce and social existence, she was principally concerned with utilising drama within the formal curriculum that she was given to teach.

> The first aid which I invoked was Nature Study, mainly from its aesthetic standpoint, and from the first I realised that to be of any value, it must be Nature *really studied by the child itself* [her italics] (1907: 16).

This quote is particularly revealing in that it not only shows the humanistic and child-centred foundations of her teaching philosophy, but also the primary value and stress that she put upon the aesthetic element of drama. This is important, as those teachers who have used drama for primarily instrumental or personal growth purposes have throughout the following century been a target for the other teachers who

J. O'Toole et al., *Drama and Curriculum,* Landscapes: the Arts, Aesthetics, and Education 6, DOI 10.1007/978-1-4020-9370-8_6,
© Springer Science+Business Media B.V. 2009

have seen themselves as defenders of the art form; the instrumentalists' supposed lack of concern for the art forms a stick to beat them with.

Finlay-Johnson's book was unequivocally titled *The Dramatic Method of Teaching*. Besides Nature Study (in her curriculum, the precursor to what we now term the natural sciences), separate chapters in her book dealt with Arithmetic and Composition (a pairing highly unlikely to be seen together today), Literature (including a healthy dose of Shakespeare for these rural working class elementary school children), History, Geography, and Manual Work (gardening and manual arts for the boys; needlecraft and cookery for the girls). In addition, there was extensive discussion of drama's value in language teaching, developing practical skills, reading competence, etc., and even in the postschool world of the adult community.

> Our first attempt at Drama as a legitimate school subject was concerned with History (34).

Drama as a way of teaching history remained the cornerstone of her work. From the start, she managed to incorporate both, in exemplary fashion, within the confines of her given timetable – one much more rigid than is customary today in primary and middle schools:

> The time occupied by History *plays* proper consisted of that set apart for History *lessons* [her italics]; because we considered our play in the light of a lesson. We had two of these each week, one of a half-hour's duration, and one of one hour. Preparation had to occupy the scholars' own leisure time and odd minutes in school, many of which would otherwise have been wasted, while for the making of notes an occasional writing lesson was set apart. Once a week we had what we termed a 'library morning' when scholars were allowed each to take a book from off the library shelf and read it silently in the desks. Questions might be asked and answered, and little discussions were permitted, so long as only one person spoke at a time and the general order and peace of the class was not upset too much. Then it was that the most valuable discoveries were made for possible 'plays' and a good deal of the preparation done (69).

Throughout the book, she used the term 'scholars' for her children, gently underlining the respect that she gave to them and demanded as well for learning. It is hard to better her rationale for the children learning history at all or her advocacy for drama:

> Under this most graphic kind of teaching, historical characters like those of Richard II and Wat Tyler are no longer unreal figures with curious names, tiresome acts and elusive dates. Certainly not only are they real (and children love the concrete, we know!) but it is impossible that any scholar should be dull or that his brain should be inactive during such a lesson . . . . All the same, my scholars *do* remember an enormous amount of detailed history and fact – not to mention such things as genealogical tables, dates and statistics – which they have absorbed unconsciously during their plays and the preparation of plays (134: 31).

Contemporary teachers of history take note, as well as those politicians who would make schools the battleground for reshaping it towards their agendas.

Finlay-Johnson identified the importance of drama as a motivating factor to help children engage in curriculum.

> When our scholars began to dramatize their lessons, they at once developed a keen desire to know many things which hitherto had been matters of pure indifference to them (36).

> What struck me most forcibly always was the fact that nothing – the amount of prepa-
> ration, the arrangement of multitudinous details, the memorising of long, long parts or the
> making of copious notes – ever seemed to be looked upon as the least trouble. The truth
> was all these things constituted healthy brain and bodily activity for normal children, and
> developed them equally in all directions. And even adults never confess to weariness when
> they 'want' to do anything; the pleasure outbalances the other sensations (205).
>
> Arithmetic may become a delightful subject when taught largely by means of plays (224).

This latter point she illustrates with many examples of selling flowers and setting
up shops to help teach tables and give practice in mathematical calculation and
money management. She goes on to analyse this motivational factor in terms of
what we would now call dramatic tension.

> The scholars would not have been real children if they had not been desperately anxious to
> catch the cashier giving wrong change (232).

What did her drama consist of? Not the sophisticated drama pedagogy of today's
'process drama', based on an intricate mix of complex role-play techniques and theatrical conventions mainly derived from the rehearsal room; nor yet Slade's Personal
and Projected Play; but formal play-making with and by the children.

> Why not continue the principle of the kindergarten game in the school for older scholars? I
> did so, but with this difference: instead of letting the teacher originate or conduct the play,
> I demanded that, just as the individual must study nature and not have it studied for him,
> the play must be the child's own . . . It would fitly express the stage of development arrived
> at by the child's mind, and would therefore be valuable to him as a vehicle of expression
> and assimilation, . . . rather than a finished product pleasing to the more cultivated mind of
> an adult (19).

As this passage shows, she anticipated Slade in identifying the roots of the activity in children's own play, games and dramatic instincts. She used the term 'game'
a lot to describe the many informal and improvisational activities that she and they
employed as precursors to her plays, though her main practice remained anchored
in the literary western tradition of making a scripted play for acting to a public
audience. This was sometimes the parents and village community, but mostly just
for their own amusement – playing to themselves. However, the learning and the
satisfaction were, as she described in detail that was intricately analysed, primarily
located in the playmaking itself, the process and not the performance. She gave
many examples of the children's playscripts, some of which – read cursorily, and
without taking note of her caveat above – can look lame to a contemporary eye. If
you read sensitively and critically, their careful aesthetic shaping becomes evident,
as does their youthful energy, and above all the meticulous respect for the learning
they are embodying.

Furthermore, Finlay-Johnson identified the many-layered and multiple learning
effects of her Dramatic Method, including its ability to bring together disparate
disciplines. Study of *A Midsummer Night's Dream* led firstly to understanding of the
poetic figure of speech *alliteration*, then discoveries in *design*, and the *properties of
paint*. That in turn led to an *arithmetic* game devised in the yard by the children
themselves . . . and a great deal more, as Miss Finlay-Johnson asserted, with gentle
but irresistible triumph:

And all this was their own initiative, and ... with how little trouble on the part of either teacher or child! Certainly it gave no more trouble or exertion in the preparation than an ordinary game; yet at the end what a splendid harvest of lasting results in the wider outlook, the closer study of humanity, the enriched and strengthened memory, the greater knowledge of the beauties of our language... and all of this lasting treasure absorbed from and through a game in school! (141).

Finally, like all the best drama teachers, she knew her place in the pecking order:

The nearest approach to the tolling of a funeral bell which they could manage in school was produced by striking a spoon against the side of a basin, and this I was deputed to do (86).

This book was to be the most coherent and thorough analysis of drama as a method of *learning and teaching* for nearly 70 years, when there was a rash of them. It would seem that other paradigms took precedence for most of the century. Advocates of drama for *development and expression* did certainly also acknowledge its learning possibilities. Bishop Burton was just as admiring and sanguine, if less precise than Finlay-Johnson:

First, there is the general place of dramatic activity within education, its value for individual moral and social qualities, and its application as a method of teaching in various subjects – Scripture, English, the visual arts, geography, history and physical education. At the earliest stage nearly all education is dramatic in basis (1955: 21).

Like Finlay-Johnson, he identified the connection between dramatic play and learning, but he didn't get as far as Arithmetic, Nature Study and Manual Work, however, and his book is more concerned with grander concerns:

Through imaginative play they are readjusted to daily life, and are helped to develop the hearing ear and the seeing eye (5).

Winifred Ward, on the other hand, was quite nervous of the expressive art form being traduced into instrumental uses, and warned that 'Drama is an art, not a tool for making learning easy'. Nevertheless, she then went on to describe her own action research projects in history, natural science, art and creative writing, and stressed drama's potential to help integrate learning in the primary school (1957, pp.154ff).

By contrast, those in the first half of the twentieth century primarily concerned with drama as art-form and literature, like Caldwell Cook and Maisie Cobby, barely give the notion of drama as pedagogy a mention. The idea must have taken root, however, as this quotation shows from John Allen, a staunch opponent of both instrumental and developmental drama on the grounds that either dilutes or demeans the power of the art-form:

Attempting then to establish unassailable credentials, drama teachers went off on a new tack, claiming that drama was a tool for teaching other subjects. This view has wide support. It was being propounded all over Australia when I visited the continent in 1959 (75).

We confess to finding this revelation entirely startling, since we have been unable to find any direct verification of it in Australia, and only little evidence of this kind of focus from the sources we have accessed from the 1950s onwards. The idea that anything of the sort was happening at the time 'all over Australia' is cheering news but underscores, therefore, the uphill slog that drama as pedagogy faced in getting any further for 30 years . . . and also that all the vision, effort and enthusiasm propounding it all over 1950s Australia seems to have left not a wrack behind!

Wind of Change: Hurricane Heathcote

Then in the 1960s, the game changed, and the name most usually associated with this change is Dorothy Heathcote. Down-to-earth daughter of an industrial working class village, trained above her station in postwar England at Esme Church's Theatre School, she was deeply grounded in both working class, no-nonsense common sense and in the practice of theatre (a point sometimes lost on her occasional but virulent and persistent detractors). She burst like a cyclone on the great City of Curriculum, startling not just the denizens of drama classrooms but also the city burghers. Drama would never be the same again in schools – or rather, there is now no excuse if it is the same again. In Curriculum City, her presence has inspired great interest and admiration, and she has been called the Best Teacher in Britain, . . . in the World, In a Class of Her Own, and featured in popular radio and television documentaries. Forty years on, a Commissioner of Police in faraway New Zealand, taken by Peter O'Connor to watch his applied theatre team engaged in some process drama on domestic violence, leaned over and whispered admiringly that he had once seen something like this by a woman named Mrs Heathcote, and did Peter know of her? Mind you, admiration does not translate into visible action in Curriculum City. Her work *has* probably helped change that stubborn metropolis's leaders' attitudes towards drama, attitudes that Heathcote was not especially concerned about (though for those of us fighting to get through the gate it's been immensely valuable). Perhaps her work has been a factor in changing their attitude to how children learn, and to power relations in teaching (about which Heathcote has always been passionately committed), and the respective curricular roles of content, context, processes and relationships.

Within the community of drama teachers and workers, this cyclone blew drama for learning right back to the centre of attention, not just in the UK. From the 1960s, she travelled widely, and soon she had scores of admirers, acolytes and disciples flocking from round the world to her unassuming rooms in Newcastle upon Tyne – where the University's education gatekeepers steadfastly refused to acknowledge her distinction until decades later. The geography is important, as just down the road at Durham University a parallel course was run by her most devoted admirer and biographer, Gavin Bolton, who was in his own way just as influential. Together they set the standards and the parameters for the movement that came to be defined as *drama-in-education* (D-i-E) – with hyphens, invariably, if you were both British and territorial. Their teaching and influence ensured that the UK would for two decades be the almost unchallenged world leader of *drama as a learning medium*, the form of words used by Betty-Jane Wagner in the first book documenting Heathcote's practice (1976), or *learning through drama*, as it was termed in the 1977 UK Schools Council report (McGregor, Tate, & Robinson 1977). By 1985, the work was sufficiently coherent and the authority of Heathcote and Bolton sufficiently acknowledged for both to have their collected writings on drama for learning anthologised (Johnson and O'Neill 1984; Davis & Lawrence 1985), and for the process of guru-isation to be galloping ahead, a beatification not encouraged by them, and resented and savagely attacked by later would-be authorities.

Like any startling climatic event, Cyclone Dorothy did not arrive out of nowhere, unheralded and alone. There were other omens in the skies, other gifted pioneers guided by the same philosophical orientation and trying out some of the same techniques. The groundwork had already been laid in educational circles, as we have indicated, by the pioneers of improvised drama based on dramatic play and role-play – by Slade and Ward and Bishop Burton and Jacob Moreno. From another direction, the theatre, came the influence of the improvised rehearsal techniques of Stanislavski and the educational ideas of Walter Benjamin and Bertolt Brecht. Benjamin actually described in 1928 his *ideas* for a fusion of theatre and education, based on a 'director' crafting the authenticity of children's play and improvisation into symbolic and significant embodied meaning (1928/1973: 28–32), which Heathcote was to provide in concrete form 40 years later. Brecht was a major influence on Heathcote's work, particularly in her use of distancing and framing techniques, as she and a number of her commentators have noted.

TIE/DIE in the Swinging Sixties

Improvisation was very much in vogue in the 1960s, both in education and in the theatre, as exemplified in John Hodgson and Ernest Richards's influential *Improvisation* (1966). Several theatre groups in Chicago claim that this city 'invented' improvisation, in the form they call 'long-form improv.' (see numerous promotional websites). That would come as news both to Commedia dell' Arte troupes, which have been plying the form since medieval times, and to Julie Dunn's pre-teens with their spontaneous 3-hour dramatic play episodes. Chicago was, however, influential through another figure already encountered in Chapter 4, Viola Spolin, the author most famously of *Improvisation for the Theater* (1963) and other similar compendia (e.g., *Theater Games for the Classroom*, 1986). With her son Paul Sills in the late 1950s, she founded the groundbreaking *Second City Company* specialising in improvised theatre, mostly for comedy. Soon after, the *San Francisco Mime Troupe* was founded to provide improvised satirical theatre, whose purposes became more explicitly political and activist through the 1960s and 1970s.

Throughout North America and Europe, radical and fringe theatre were playing not only with improvisation, but also with the fusing of actor and audience through participatory techniques. From the early 1960s, Brian Way had begun to use peripheral forms of audience interaction in his educational theatre company *Theatre Centre*, involving secondary students as extras in crowd scenes in *Vanity Fair* or asking primary students to help the North Wind blow. Exactly contemporary with Heathcote, and influenced by exactly the same precursors, *Coventry Belgrade*

Theatre started experimenting with integral participation in plays performed in schools by their team of adult actors, and then a host of other regional theatre companies and Education Authority-funded groups, bringing all of their juvenile audiences right into the drama itself, as characters who could affect the dramatic action. The companies started devising work for small audiences, particularly single classes in their own schoolrooms, led by the actors, who soon became termed 'actor-teachers'. This phenomenon was from the start closely allied with the drama-in-education movement, and was quickly labelled as theatre-in-education (again, often territorially hyphenated). T-i-E was a new departure in two ways: 'new objectives for theatre – new techniques in education' as the first book on the phenomenon observed in its subtitle (O'Toole 1977). T-i-E shared a common philosophy and the parallel development of some key techniques with D-i-E (as well as the hyphens) such as *teacher-in-role*. The continuing close relationship between D-i-E and T-i-E has been thoroughly chronicled by Tony Jackson (1980, 1993, 2008).

Teacher-in-role, whose potentially radical implications for curriculum will be dealt with next, is usually considered to be one of Heathcote's most famous 'inventions'; it emerged spontaneously in her teaching, and she is certainly a masterly exponent of it. However, the late distinguished Canadian drama educator Norah Morgan described to John a series of lessons in the late 1940s with young Canadian Air Force officers, using a teaching technique that was clearly classic *teacher-in-role*. It is effectively the same technique as that devised and employed by the actor-teachers in T-i-E. More humbly, thousands of early childhood teachers have naturally, unwittingly, used this convention – that makes many secondary teachers giddily anxious to contemplate – joining in their children's dramatic play episodes as a co-player, or teaching maths by setting up shops and playing a swindling shop-assistant like Miss Finlay-Johnson.

Heathcote and Bolton attracted many followers, often gifted teachers and researchers themselves, who theorized their work and tailored the practice to be more easily developed into the curriculum. Following Wagner's enthusiastic and mainly descriptive first analysis of Heathcote's work, Bolton (1979) started to give it a theoretical basis, and a basis in curriculum. His first essay at this was his very cautiously titled *Towards a Theory of Drama in Education* (unusually, without the hyphens). He followed the success of this with the much more boldly titled *Drama as Education: An Argument for Placing Drama at the Centre of the Curriculum* (1984), and a number of later books, distinguished for their clarity and depth, including one with Heathcote herself on her signature strategy of the 'mantle of the expert' (1995). Heathcote's own practice, generously demonstrated and widely filmed, was so uncompromising, so innovative and so clearly the work of a master teacher that its effect was often dazzling and even off-putting to 'ordinary' teachers. It was Bolton who first made her work more accessible, through his own meticulous and rather less charismatic practice, and those limpid writings.

The Schools Council report gave drama-in-education a level of respectability and even authoritativeness.Cecily O'Neill (1982), along with a growing number of other teacher-writers (e.g., Wootton 1982; Nixon 1982), continued to nail down the essentials and make the practice eminently manageable in classrooms with ordinary teachers. O'Neill's contribution is justifiably lauded; her practice managed to be artful, poetic and still easily managed, and she produced among the earliest recipe books, *Drama Guidelines* (1977) and *Drama Structures* (1982), whose combined sales must by now rival Brian Way's. She took the practice of process drama further in her own venture into theorising the practice, *Dramaworlds* (1995), bringing in more distanced techniques and theatre forms, and clarifying as she went. Another whose contribution has been sustained, articulate and very accessible has been Jonothan Neelands (e.g. 1984) who has also persistently stressed, not shrilly but very determinedly, the social imperatives and responsibilities of drama. Like O'Neill, a gifted and beguiling teacher, and an even more dedicated globetrotter, his demonstrations of practice have been as influential as his books in drawing people to drama. He has also stuck at the task of persuading the orthodox schools systems to accept drama – witness the title of his latest book *Improve Your Primary School Through Drama* (2006). These and a host of other practitioner-theorists (among many others Bowell & Heap 2001; Bunyan & Rainer 1995; Burton 1991; Manley & O'Neill 1998; Haseman & O'Toole 1988; Taylor 1996, 1998) have developed Heathcote's instinctual tour-de-force into manageable pedagogy.

Interest and initiative in Britain's former colonies was not far behind, and Heathcote's influence travelled the globe, as she did herself, and as hundreds of disciples and would-be students did in the opposite direction, to sit at her feet. However, they found there was not much sitting, as they were invariably co-opted full-on as coplanners and teaching auxiliaries into her ferocious schedule of experiment and demonstration in schools, prisons and hospitals.

The best of them took her ideas in new directions. One of Heathcote's earliest students was the distinguished Canadian educator and equally spellbinding teacher David Booth, who focused the structures and techniques he learned from Heathcote on enriching narrative and storytelling across the curriculum, to create *Story Drama*. Norah Morgan was swept into Heathcote's net, and with Juliana Saxton produced a thoroughly theorized book for ordinary teachers *Teaching Drama: A Mind of Many Wonders* (1987: the subtitle culled from the Tasmanian Language Project mentioned in Chapter 3). These two also realised the enormous implications that this drama had for changing the whole curricular game of teachers' questioning of students. They wrote a book artfully entitled *Teaching, Questioning and Learning*, later retitled as *Asking Better Questions* (1991, 1994), both titles disguising for teachers who might be put off by the very word 'drama' the thoroughly dramatic nature of their pedagogy. In Australia, Pam Gaudry and Roma Burgess (1985) anchored their work on Heathcote's philosophy, but broadened it out into a full and eclectic program for drama in the secondary school.

Process Drama and the Curriculum

The British drama-in-education movement and their followers overseas took a quantum leap forward in curriculum. The dramatic process, as for Finlay-Johnson, is where the learning happens. However, the immediate roots are not in performing plays as actors, like they were for Finlay-Johnson, but in improvised dramatic play, following Slade and Ward. Performance, if it occurs at all, is incorporated as just a part of the process, and is frequently informal, described as 'demonstrating' or 'reenacting'. The dominant form of drama as a learning medium is often now referred to as 'process drama'. Wagner describes its goal as 'to create an experience through which students may come to understand human interactions, empathize with other people, and internalize other points of view' (1998: 5). It provided the tools for using drama as a teaching method across the whole curriculum to produce deep understanding and higher order thinking, learning that is holistic and experiential, not just cognitive – in Gavin Bolton's words 'change in a participant's understanding of the world' (1984: 148).

Process drama quite naturally embodies two mighty steps in curriculum and classroom management, both of which are also a divergence from traditional Western theatre practice. First, all the students are effectively engaged all the time within the dramatic action, usually as characters within the fictional context, and never as just a passive audience, or listeners. Second, though the overall structure is usually created and controlled by the teacher, the genre demands that the participants are not only given a degree of freedom in how they interpret their roles and functions, but they are usually invited at certain points to help or even take a lead in planning the drama itself. The bold and experienced teacher may even start the work by asking 'What shall we make a play about today?', and work from the children's ideas to structure a drama that is both dramatically enjoyable for them – 'the play for the children' as Geoff Gillham (1974) memorably entitled it – and a valid learning experience within the formal curriculum – 'the play for the teacher'.

Process drama's characteristics include that the drama is always improvised, involving the creation and enactment of realistic models of human behaviour in specific fictional contexts. It creates the learning context on the spot in the classroom, with the learners all involved as participants in making the drama and as characters within it. The dramatic action unfolds as it goes along, rarely complete, and never entirely preordained. Therefore the drama is episodic, the improvised scenes frequently stopping for replanning or shifting the dramatic action, often negotiated among all the participants. What Heathcote called 'living-through role-play' (1984: 48) is still usually the central dramatic technique used. Since its development into the more sophisticated genre of 'process drama', a range of other improvisational and theatrical techniques, now usually known as 'conventions', are employed to shift the point of view or the dramatic distance of the participants, who are also the characters in the drama. The degree of empathy and distance of the participants in their relationship to their characters, and the types of dramatic tension that drive the drama and maintain their interest, are controlled by the careful management of focus and framing techniques to construct and deconstruct the narrative, which is never linear and rarely central.

There is no external audience – the participants are engaged in the moment, which exists for their own experiential learning, not to communicate to others. Accordingly, reflection is usually built-in within the action, or through discussion. The drama thus always incorporates the students' ideas and suggestions, sometimes changing its original objectives and goals if a productive idea is suggested. This of course also means that in the best tradition of constructivist learning, it builds on what the students already know and can contribute. The purpose of the drama is never just to enact, but to problematise, and to make the students ask questions and interrogate the learning context. The teacher takes part actively – not only structuring the dramatic action as playwright and director, but through the key technique of teacher-in-role, as an actor/character in the unfolding drama.

Most important of all, in terms of the structures of status and power that underlie and drive curriculum in real school contexts, process drama has a quite exceptional potential to allow these structures to be suspended, altered and renegotiated, just for the purposes of the students' learning, and bounded by those purposes alone, by three of its key characteristics. The first of these is uncommon enough: *negotiating the lesson*. The need to cater for the 'children's play' as well as the 'teacher's play' means that the students, outside the drama itself but in the lesson planning, have the opportunity to make suggestions, veto teacher's ideas and collaboratively negotiate the drama/lesson plan stage by stage, as both playwrights and curriculum planners. The other two, the conventions of *mantle of the expert* and *teacher-in-role*, are unique characteristics that only drama can provide in the classroom.

The basic precondition of drama is that all the participants must voluntarily and together suspend their disbelief, and agree to enter a shared fictional world. This world is constructed and managed within the classroom or teaching space. For the time of the drama, that space with its inhabitants becomes a medieval castle, directors' boardroom, space station, etc., and while the fictional world is operating, most of the normal rules of the classroom are suspended. This includes the status patterns, which usually dictate that the teacher is the one who knows and helps, instructs, or controls, and the children are the ones who do not know and receive help, instructions or control. In the convention of *mantle of the expert*, the students as dramatis personae are put in the position of people with the expertise necessary to solve the problem which provides the central tension of the drama – as scientists, archaeologists, priests, for example. If the convention is operated as thoroughly as Heathcote and Bolton conceive it, they must actually master a substantial amount of the recondite knowledge before the plot or problem can be resolved, through the effective joint operation of their knowledge.

Teacher-in-role is even more subversive of the infrastructure of teacher authority and student dependence. By becoming a character in the drama, the teacher can choose a different status relationship to the participants, and also an unfamiliar role, in functional classroom terms, where in 'real life' the teacher has a built-in higher status in terms of authority, age, knowledge and usually size. Especially when working together with the mantle of the expert, the teacher can choose to intervene as a character who *needs* help or information, such as a stranger from an alien land or a supplicant seeking help from 'you expert physicists'; somebody who has information but low status, such as a messenger, or a tour guide; or a provocateur, sent to challenge the prevailing attitudes or assumptions (in real life or the drama), such as a rebellious subject or the mother of a terrorist. This convention is actually a lot safer than it sounds to nervous teachers. As the students know from years of dramatic playing, but adult teachers have often forgotten, the 'dual affect' works smoothly to control the interaction. As long as all the participants have agreed to voluntarily suspend their disbelief and enter the fictional world, the life of the fiction is operative in the foreground, and the 'real world' is effectively inoperative – but never entirely forgotten, nor entirely suspended and it can be reinstated in a moment. Students tend to have much more confidence in drama than their teachers, and expertise in metacommunication and conservation of the illusion. They understand which real-life taboos can be broken within the dramatic fiction and which cannot. A teacher can actually guide the dramatic progress and the learning more effectively and less obtrusively by well-timed intervention in role than by stopping the drama to discuss or negotiate.

These potentially far-reaching curricular implications have been well researched in many studies of drama curriculum and teaching (e.g., Flynn 1995; Nixon 1982; O'Mara 2004; Scheurer 1995; Taylor 1998; Warner 1997). Not only can drama be used to teach standard subjects in a first-hand, experiential way, but the students themselves can have a say in negotiating the dramatic action and the themes explored, and the social or personal use that will be made of the 'change of understanding' that is the outcome. This gives real meaning to Garth Boomer's phrase 'negotiating the curriculum' (1982). As Richard Courtney, the doyen of drama curriculum, writes, 'In the classroom . . . the teacher is working with living immediacy. Curriculum results from this encounter' (1980: 67). Central to Courtney's philosophy, curriculum develops within the context of a classroom, not imposed from without.

However, this fact is barely acknowledged by mainstream educational theorists, who, 30 years on, still just don't know about process drama. For instance, drama figures nowhere in Australia's influential model of curriculum development: 'New Basics and Productive Pedagogies', neither in the substance nor in the many examples. Moreover, the characteristics of process drama noted above demand a range of skills from teachers that are outside their experience and training, and run counter to both. Few teachers have themselves encountered much drama in their own schooling, fewer still sufficient to give them the artistic understanding to select and shape dramatic narrative, focus and conventions. Even more significantly, teachers usually operate more as they themselves were taught – as purveyors of content rather than as facilitators of learning, in large institutions driven by hierarchical structures of power and status, and imperatives of discipline and control. Teaching through dramatic process entails suspending teachers' status, relinquishing some of their sovereignty over knowledge, even putting themselves in the hands of the students-in-role. This is daunting to many teachers.

Cosmetic in-servicing in the new pedagogy has been shown not to work for most, though there are now readily available drama education resources in most school systems in English-speaking Western countries and on the web. Most primary generalists and secondary history, science and English teachers have neither the time nor the motivation for what they don't know they might need, even if the financial and skills resources were available. On the other hand, there are many teachers who do use drama as a pedagogy for a number of purposes. The first of these is the simply functional one of teaching standard school subjects such as history, or approaching curricular material such as stories or science. This is sometimes known as 'drama across the curriculum'.

Drama, Values and Social Change

Knowledge and learning are of course never objective nor value-neutral, much though ultraconservative groups and politicians might wish them to be seen as such. Drama depicts human behaviour and attitudes and, therefore, deals in exploring and challenging the values and judgments, which attach to the behaviour and attitudes, and offering a range of points of view and perspectives to scrutinize them. This slippery negotiability of drama with respect to educating values tends to polarise orthodox educators. In the 1970s, an ultraconservative Christian fundamentalist group in Queensland, with the ear of the autocratic premier, rather hysterically sought to ban the tiny manifestations of drama just beginning to occur in classrooms as 'social engineering' – shades of Plato, really. Even in the 1980s, a local T-i-E team was barred from using either of the phrases 'social change' or 'multicultural-ism' in their program or program notes (and even though Australia was officially a multicultural society) on the grounds that both were too charged with political values.

On the other hand, and in other places, some equally conservative observers had welcomed drama:

> With the present moral decline of adult values, it is now more necessary than ever that we give our young people a solid foundation on which to construct their lives – a positive education in every possible sense of the phrase, both inside and outside the classroom (Wiles & Garrard 1957: 11)

Since the 1950s and 1970s, the educational climate has shifted a number of times, and many educational systems (though not always their own political masters) have recognised that education is never neutral, and that if encouraged rather than repressed, the education of values and attitudes could be both valuable and to a degree controllable. This is not just in the 'West': contemporary Taiwan and Hong Kong are notable examples of systems starting to use words like 'independent and critical thinking' and 'education for change' in their manifestos (e.g., Cheng 2000). Some cautious testing and questioning of values, positions and attitudes – moral, political and social – is often encouraged in schools, and drama is making quite frequent appearances in this process, within subjects called 'citizenship education', 'liberal studies' and 'civics'. Drama classes themselves have always been a hotbed of values exploration, and most of the writers on drama pedagogy have made no bones about it. Joe Winston very deftly uses the didactic sounding phrase 'moral education' in two books, a theoretical study of drama education and a practical text-book for primary children (1998, 2000), which encourage students to confront and question moral challenges. By definition, drama also explicitly explores difference and 'otherness' – to use the useful cant phrase. By 'stepping into somebody else's shoes', a participant in drama (as actor or audience) will discover by empathy, some-times also by distanced reflection, what 'self' and 'other' have in common, or just how 'other' the other is. This is often used to conscript drama into exploring issues of culture and cultural difference (e.g., O'Farrell 1996; Grady 2000), though as wise teachers in multicultural classrooms know, it is an area of curriculum where fools are wont to rush in, and angels need considerable skills in managing the art form in order to tread carefully enough to create new understanding of cultural issues.

From the early days of drama-in-education and particularly in the UK, drama has also had a very strong social, and socialist, imperative, as an agent of change. Here, overwhelmingly the major influence has been from the theatre rather than education, in the gigantic influence of Bertolt Brecht, and his successors such as Edward Bond and Albert Hunt (even more strongly felt in theatre-in-education). Marxist thinking has been a potent force, with inspiring writer-practitioners like David Davis taking up the work of Heathcote and Bolton and explicitly adding to Bolton's 'drama for change of understanding . . .' the idea '. . . and means of aiding action on the world' (Roper & Davis 2000: 228). Some radical curriculum theorists, most notably Paolo Freire, and some of the 'de-schooling society' theorists, have also been significant in the last three decades. They have brought a broader liberatory pedagogy to the work of drama educators worldwide, especially as the UK's trenchant drama for social change agenda imploded in competing dichotomies and infighting. Freire's particular influence, through the work of his own theatrical disciple Augusto Boal, will be dealt with separately later in this chapter, though to an increasing extent it is becoming melded in the work of drama education.

Theatre-in-education has always had a particularly strong radical orientation, perhaps because its mission has been to visit schools and stimulate (stir up) the students, then get out again, rather than to deliver an ongoing curriculum acceptable to the school's funders and gatekeepers. Theatre companies have provided a very important input of well-researched and confronting dramatic curriculum, on all sorts of social issues, some of which have had a significant impact on broader public opin-ion and understanding of social issues, just as the companies had hoped. An early, famous and frequently revived environmental program from Coventry Belgrade, *This Rare Earth* (1973–1974), was one of the main whistle-blowers for the British public on Japanese mercury poisoning and the despoilation of the environment, well before environmental concern became common currency. In Australia, *Annie's Coming Out* (on physical disablement) and *The Heartbreak Kid* (on multicultural issues in adolescence) were commercially successful and award-winning films that started life as T-i-E programs – the latter via a popular TV series, *Heartbreak High*. The current offerings of *Zeal Theatre* include confronting and very popular programs on vandalism (*The Stones*), long-term effects of bullying (*The Apology*), community violence (*The Forwards*) and a society dependent on medication (*Side Effects*).

On the other hand, this political and social activism has not always escaped the scrutiny of the educational gatekeepers, and throughout the 1980s and 1990s, numerous UK T-i-E companies got themselves barred from schools or disbanded. In Australia, too, State Arts Councils and such bodies have policed the travelling players, and companies like the Brecht- and Albert Hunt-inspired Popular Theatre Troupe suffered a similar fate.

Adult Drama for Learning

Meanwhile, two movements using drama as pedagogy, with quite separate origins from drama-in-education, have become established in the curriculum of adult education. The first of these was invented and named 'socio-drama' by the founder of Psychodrama, Jacob Moreno and his associates, and it refers mainly to the application of psychodrama techniques to groups, community and organisations and hence, its incorporation into adult and organisational training. Unfortunately it is more often referred to nowadays as 'role-play training' or 'simulation' – unfortunately, because this mutated form has very deliberately distanced itself from its dramatic origins:

> A casual visitor looking at creative drama sessions could well mistake them for a role-play simulation in progress (van Ments 1983:158).

Not if van Ments and his colleagues have their way. In the copious literature and practice of this first cousin of process drama, the word drama is rarely, if ever, mentioned. Its main purpose is to use role-play to teach and assess procedural knowledge in adult training contexts. It can entail small-scale role-plays, sometimes scripted or semiscripted, to an audience given the task of assessing the role-players for the correctness of their procedures. Alternatively, role-play training can be in the form of large-group simulation exercises – from fictional office dilemmas exploring ethics in decision-making (Chalmers 1993), to whole battalions of troops and warships on strategic exercises, which in the end, are all just make-believe, subject to the conditions that make for good or bad drama. And that is where the pedagogical problem lies, which a few simulation specialists such as Chalmers are beginning to acknowledge. The structures of role-play developed by Moreno and his associates were from the start embraced by behaviouristic trainers seeking 'authentic' and embodied training. However, to ensure that they were teaching and assessing with precision, the trainers needed to exclude – iron out – those residual effects of drama that make it unpredictable, namely the human, emotional component, and particularly the improvisational and playful component. That way they could control the whole procedure. For very simple tasks and procedures, like correctly waiting at table, the simplistic imitation that this reduces the activity to is quite useful, up to a point . . . (until a waiter has to deal in real life with an angry or bloody-minded patron). At the same time, the trainers and writers of manuals of simulation instruction, with titles like *Instructional Design Library: Role-playing* rather illogically believed that the fictional aspect of the simulation made it motivating and kept it consequence-free.

It is no surprise to drama educators that instructional and drama-free role-play is neither as efficient a form of training as they believe, nor as popular among its recipients. Recent popular satires on it such as the famous role-play training episode of the TV comedy *The Office* are no more excruciating than the real-life manifestation in Evelyn Taylor's description of cruel and inept role-play training of corrective services officers (2000). As Heather Smigiel conclusively shows (1996, 2000), the reason for its shortcomings is the very fact that the dramatic and artistic components of role-play have been left out. In any human interaction, the emotional dimension is a significant element, and dramatic artistry allows this to be managed much *more* authentically than simply seeking to exclude it. The better the management of the art, the better the learning. This has been analysed in detail elsewhere (O'Toole & Lepp 2000: Chapter 2). Some role-play trainers are beginning to understand this and co-opt drama educators to bring back drama, for example, in training of magistrates and judges (O'Connor 2000 and Donelan & O'Brien 2008), nurses (Lepp 2000), medics (Cahill 2005), police (O'Toole 2000; Bates & Stevenson 2000), and teachers themselves (K. Taylor 2000).

Simulation and role-play are being enthusiastically embraced by Internet educators, who are beginning to use the technology to create conditions of interactivity very akin to the process drama classroom (see Wills 2007; Ip & Linser 2005; Vincent 2005), though it is rarely called drama in this context either. In fact the first of these references, a project submission for a complex design of role-play training, quite spectacularly manages to avoid the word drama altogether in 18 closely argued pages with a host of internal references. The drama educators are beginning to fight back against this unwitting obliteration (e.g., Carroll 2005; Carroll, Anderson, & Cameron 2006; Davis 2006), and making our own Internet pedagogy, with allies in the new technology like game designers, bloggers and scholars in digital narrative, who come from a less mechanistic orientation than the instructional designers. The dramatic and educational possibilities of the Internet have been recognized by some of the foremost curriculum scholars of the new technology, such as Brenda Laurel (*Computers as Theatre* 1993), and James Gee (*What Video Games Have to Teach us About Learning and Literacy* 2003) – though he doesn't use the word drama much, either, come to think of it.

Theatre for Development and Liberation

The second of these movements, theatre for development, is a way of consciousness-raising in economically developing countries, mainly among poor, traditional communities. Theatre seems a naturally attractive way of communicating with remote people with high illiteracy rates and little access to television, radio and computers; or to propagate modern sanitation and health, environmental management, avoidance of HIV-AIDS or the basics of democratic elections. Many governments and nongovernmental organisations like UNICEF have generously funded it, for nearly 30 years (for a good introduction, see Kerr 1995 or Mumma, Mwangi, & Odhiambo 1998). This was originally in the form of small groups of players touring the communities, sometimes on foot or bicycle, with western-style plays-with-a-message, sometimes engaging the audiences in discussion (e.g., Pattanaik 2000). Where communities might be resistant, as for instance to sexual or sanitation practices that contravene traditional mores, subtler techniques have been used (e.g., Dugga 2002), such as touring the schools and engaging the children, assisting them to create theatre themselves to convince their parents (Dalrymple 1996) or using the community elders as actors for the audience literally to *Listen to your Mothers* (Nyangore 2000).

Another model has been to work with communities where there is already a Western theatre tradition, such as a school theatre festival (e.g., Mangeni 2000). However, local resistance to being given gratuitous advice by outsiders, especially in alien artistic forms, can be severe and even hostile, and to prevent the experience becoming counter-productive, Theatre for Development is changing. Now more frequently facilitators join communities to discover *their* concerns, and *with* them create theatre on these issues based on their own local traditional performance forms (e.g., Prentki 2003; Chinyowa 2005; Mangeni 2007).

The other side of this community pedagogy is that if theatre can be used by governments and NGOs to question traditional life and practices, it can equally be used by those opposed to governments to challenge the assumptions of the powerful and sow questions and subversion among their subjects. In Western societies, protest demonstrations – themselves a form of theatre – frequently incorporate some form of theatrical performance to catch attention. In the developing world, the revolutionary demand for universal empowerment through literacy via Paolo Freire's *Pedagogy of the Oppressed* (1970) has found expression in *Theatre of the Oppressed*, articulated by the Brazilian educator/theatre artist Augusto Boal and his followers (Boal 1979; Schutzman & Cohen-Cruz 1994). They have harnessed common theatre exercises, games and techniques of audience participation into a system of interactive theatre, usually centred on the convention that Boal dubbed as 'forum theatre.' The form of this convention is both simple and highly participatory. Though it was not new, Boal adopted and refined it for his radical theatre company working with impoverished communities in Brazil, and through his influence it is now found all over the world. A group of actors create a scene of an incident involving some kind of oppression, with the oppressed person as the central protagonist. The scene is usually derived from a true-life story by one of the participants. The scene is performed a number of times, and members of the audience are invited to step into the scene as 'spect-actors', replacing the protagonist at any point where they believe that a change of the protagonist's behaviour might affect or reduce the oppression. This usually provides the basis of very enthusiastic and productive discussion intended to empower the audience with an active – and proactive – understanding of their oppression and how to go about dealing with it. Boal has since gone on to further refine his use of theatre forms like forum theatre to address more personal therapy and oppression-busting, such as dealing with what he has famously dubbed each individual's 'cop-in-the-head' (1995). Having in 1971 been arrested, tortured and exiled for his radical ideas, Boal got to be so world-famous that when the previous military junta was overthrown, he returned home in triumph in 1986, and in 1992 was elected a member, a 'vereador', of Rio's City Council, where he used his forum theatre ideas to generate real-life legislation, described in his book *Legislative Theatre* (1998).

In the last decade or so, forum theatre has become incorporated more and more within drama education. Intellectually, the social activism of Boal's theory, and his preoccupation with countering oppression in any sphere of activity, have rung strong bells for many drama educators, who see daily examples of oppression happening both in their students' lives and in their schools. Theatre-in-education companies have enthusiastically embraced forum theatre. In terms of the practice in classrooms, though forum theatre is structurally not at all like process drama, in that it depends basically on a clear differentiation between playwright/performing group and audience, it is not incompatible, since both acknowledge the importance of active and experiential engagement in the drama by the participants. Many ways have been found to incorporate forum theatre with process drama – using 'hot-seat' role-play for the spect-actors to interrogate the characters of a forum scene before intervening, or obversely, distancing the dilemma of a process drama by enacting it as a forum.

Oh that theatre art and drama education could always be so seamlessly welded together for educational purposes . . .. But read on.

References

Allen, J. (1979). *Drama in schools: its theory and practice*. London: Heinemann.

Bates, M., & Stevenson, P. (2000) Who's in control: Emotional intelligence and the training of police. In J. O'Toole & M. Lepp (Eds.), *Drama for life: Drama for human learning and empowerment*. Brisbane: Playlab Press.

Benjamin, W. (1928). 'Program for a Proletarian Children's Theater.' Trans. Susan Buck-Morss. *Performance* 1.5 (March/April 1973): 28–32. Trans. from *Über Kinder, Jungend und Erziehung*. Edition Suhrkamp, 391. Frankfurt am Main: Suhrkamp Verlag, 1969.

Boal, A. (1979). *Theatre of the oppressed*. London: Pluto.

Boal, A. (1995). *The rainbow of desire*. London: Routledge.

Boal, A. (1998). *Legislative theatre: Using performance to make politics*. London: Routledge.

Bolton, G. (1979). *Towards a theory of drama in education*. London: Longmans.

Bolton, G. (1984). *Drama as education: an argument for placing drama at the centre of the curriculum*. London: Longmans.

Boomer, G. (1982). *Negotiating the curriculum: educating for the 21st century*. London: Falmer.

Booth, D. (1994). *Story drama: Reading, writing, and role-playing across the curriculum*. Markham, ON: Pembroke.

Bowell, P. & Heap, B. (2001). *Planning process drama*. London: Fulton.

Bunyan, P. & Rainer, J. (1995). *The patchwork quilt: a cross-phase educational drama project*. Sheffield: National Association for the Teaching of English.

Burton, B. (1991). *The act of learning: the drama-theatre continuum in the classroom*. Melbourne: Longman Cheshire.

Burton, E.J. (1955). *Drama in schools – approaches, methods, & activities*. London: Herbert Jenkins.

Cahill, H. (2005). Profound learning: drama partnerships between adolescents and tertiary students of medicine and education. *NJ/Journal of Drama Australia, 29*(2), 59–72.

Carroll, J. (2005). Playing the game, role distance and digital performance. *IDEA Journal/Applied Theatre Researcher Vol 6*. www.griffith.edu.au/centre/cpci/atr

Carroll, J. Anderson, M., & Cameron, D. (2006). *Real players? drama technology and education*. Stoke on Trent: Trentham Books.

Chalmers, F. (1993). *Best person for the job*. Video. Brisbane: Dept. of Education.

Cheng, K.-M. (2000). *Learning to learn*. Hong Kong Education Commission.

Chinyowa, K. (2006). *Manifestations of play as aesthetic in African Theatre for Development.* Unpublished PhD thesis. Brisbane: Griffith University.

Courtney, R. (1980). *The dramatic curriculum.* New York: Drama Books.

Dalrymple, L. (1996). The Dramaide project. In J. O'Toole & K. Donelan (Eds.), *Drama, culture & empowerment* (pp. 33–35). Brisbane: IDEA Publications.

Davis, S. (2006). *Cyberdrama – exploring possibilities. NJ – Journal of Drama Australia, 30*(1). 91–104.

Davis, D., & Lawrence, C. (1985). *Gavin Bolton: Selected writings.* London: Longmans.

Dickinson, R., & Neelands, J. (2006). *Improve your primary school through drama.* London: David Fulton.

Donelan, K., & O'Brien, A. (2008). *Creative interventions for marginalised youth: The Risky Business Project.* Melbourne: Drama Australia Publications.

Dugga, V. (2002). Development agenda versus people's agenda: theatre diplomacy in rural West Nigeria. In B. Rasmussen & A.-L. Østern (Eds.), *Playing betwixt and between: The IDEA Dialogues 2001.* Bergen: IDEA Publications.

Finlay Johnson, H. (1907). *The dramatic method of teaching.* London: Nisbet.

Flynn, R. M. (1995). *Developing and Using Curriculum-Based Creative Drama in Fifth-Grade Reading/Language Arts Instruction: A Drama.* University Microfilms International. Dissertation Services. UMI Number: 9622061.

Freire, P. (1970). *Pedagogy of the oppressed.* New York: Seabury.

Gaudry, P., & Burgess, R. (1985). *Time for drama: A handbook for secondary teachers.* Melbourne: Longman Cheshire.

Gee, J. (2003). *What video games have to teach us about learning and literacy.* New York: Palgrave-Macmillan.

Gillham, G. (1974). *Report on the Condercum Project.* Unpublished. The phrase has been used frequently, particularly by Gavin Bolton, and is now common currency.

Grady, S. (2000). *Drama and diversity : A pluralistic perspective for educational drama.* Portsmouth, NH: Heinemann.

Haseman, B. & O'Toole, J. (1998). *Dramawise.* Melbourne: Heinemann.

Heathcote, D., & Bolton, G. (1995). *Drama for learning : Dorothy Heathcote's mantle of the expert approach to education.* Portsmouth, NH: Heinemann.

Hodgson, J., & Richards, E. (1966). *Improvisation.* London: Methuen.

Ip, A., & Linser, R. (2005). *Fablusi – The online role-play simulation platform.* Retrieved 31 December 2005 from http://www.fablusi.com/

Jackson, T. (Ed.). (1980). *Learning through theatre: Essays and casebooks on theatre in education.* Manchester: Manchester University Press.

Jackson, T. (Ed.). (1993). *Learning through theatre: New perspectives on theatre in education.* London: Routledge.

Jackson, T. (2008). *Theatre, education and the making of meanings: art or instrument?.* Manchester: Manchester University Press.

Johnson, L., & O'Neill, C. (1984). *Dorothy Heathcote: Collected writings on education and drama.* London: Hutchinson.

Kerr, D. (1995). *African popular theatre: From pre-colonial times to the present day.* Portsmouth, NH: Heinemann.

Laurel, B. (1993). *Computers as theatre.* Reading, MA: Addison-Wesley.

Lepp, M. (2000). A thousand mile journey begins with a single step. Advanced learning in Swedish health care education. In J. O'Toole & M. Lepp (Eds.), *Drama for life: drama for human learning and empowerment.* Brisbane: Playlab Press.

Mangeni, P. (2000). One earth one family. In J. O'Toole & M. Lepp (Eds.), *Drama for life* (pp. 103–188). Brisbane: Playlab Press.

Mangeni, P. (2007). *Negotiating gender equity through Theatre for Development.* Unpublished PhD thesis. Brisbane: Griffith University.

Manley, A. & O'Neill, C. (1998). *Dreamseekers: Creative approaches to the African-American heritage.* Portsmouth, NH: Heinemann.

McGregor, L., Tate, M. & Robinson, K. (1977). *Learning through drama: Report of the schools council drama teaching project* (pp. 10–16). London: Heinemann.

Morgan, N., & Saxton, J. (1987). *Teaching drama: A mind of many wonders*. London: Hutchinson.

Morgan, N., & Saxton, J. (1991). *Teaching, questioning, and learning*. London: Routledge.

Morgan, N., & Saxton, J. (1994). *Asking better questions*. Markham, ON: Pembroke.

Mumma, O., Mwangi, E., & Odhiambo, C. (1998). *Orientations of drama, theatre and culture*. Nairobi: KDEA.

Neelands, J. (1984). *Making sense of drama*. Portsmouth NH: Heinemann.

Nixon, J. (1982). *Drama and the whole curriculum*. London: Hutchinson.

Nyangore, V. (2000). Listen to your mothers. In J. O'Toole & M. Lepp (Eds.), *Drama for life* (pp. 77–84). Brisbane: Playlab Press.

O'Connor, P. (2000). Re-thinking race relations: New thinking for judges, priests and journalists. In J. O'Toole & M. Lepp (Eds.), *Drama for life: Drama for human learning and empowerment*. Brisbane: Playlab Press.

O'Farrell, L. (1996). Creating our cultural identity. In J. O'Toole & K. Donelan (Eds.), *Drama, culture and empowerment* (pp. 125–130). Brisbane: IDEA Publications.

O'Mara, J. (2004). At Sunny Bay: Building students' repertoire of literacy practices through process drama' in A. Healy & E. Honan (Eds.), *Text next: New resources for literacy learning*. Newtown, NSW: Primary English Teachers Association.

O'Neill, C. (1977). *Drama guidelines*. London: Heinemann.

O'Neill, C. (1982). *Drama structures*. London: Hutchinson.

O'Neill, C. (1995). *Drama worlds*. Portsmouth, NH: Heinemann.

O'Neill, C. & Lambert, A. (1982). *Drama structures*. London: Hutchinson.

O'Toole, J. (1977). *Theatre in education: New objectives for theatre – new techniques in education*. London: Hodder & Stoughton.

O'Toole, J. (2000). Mickey Mouse and the police constables. In J. O'Toole & M. Lepp (Eds.), *Drama for life: Drama for human learning and empowerment*. Brisbane: Playlab Press.

O'Toole, J., & Lepp, M. (2000). *Drama for life*. Brisbane: Playlab Press.

Pattanaik, S. (2000). Messengers on bicycles. In J. O'Toole & M. Lepp (Eds.), *Drama for life* (pp. 85–92). Brisbane: Playlab Press.

Prentki, T. (2003). Save the children – Save the world. *Research in Drama Education, 8*(1), 39–54.

Roper, W., & Davis, D. (2000). Howard Gardner: Knowledge, learning and development in drama and arts education. *Research in Drama Education, 5*(2), 217–234.

Scheurer, P. (1995). *A Thousand Joans: A Teacher Case Study: Drama in Education. A Process of Discovery* Unpublished PhD Dissertation. Ohio State University. UMI Dissertation Services. No: 963942.

Schutzman, M., & Cohen-Cruz, J. (1994). *Playing Boal: Theatre, therapy, activism*. London: Routledge.

Smigiel, H. (1996). *Educational drama in workplace and vocational training*. Unpublished Ph.D Thesis, University of Tasmania.

Smigiel, H. (2000). Making life work: educational drama in vocational training. In J. O'Toole & M. Lepp (Eds.), *Drama for life: Drama for human learning and empowerment*. Brisbane: Playlab Press.

Spolin, V. (1963). *Improvisation for theater: A handbook of teaching and directing techniques*. Evanston, Ill: Northwestern University Press.

Spolin, V. (1986). *Theater games for the classroom: A teacher's handbook*. Evanston, IL: Northwestern University Press.

Taylor, E. (2000). Role-play without tears. In J. O'Toole & M. Lepp (Eds.), *Drama for life: Drama for human learning and empowerment*. Brisbane: Playlab Press.

Taylor, K. (2000). The teaching art: preparing a drama teacher. In J. O'Toole & M. Lepp (Eds.), *Drama for life: Drama for human learning and empowerment*. Brisbane: Playlab Press.

Taylor, P. (Ed.). (1996). *Researching drama and arts education: New paradigms and possibilities*. London: Falmer.

Taylor, P. (1998). *Redcoats and patriots: Reflective practice in drama and social studies.* Portsmouth, NH: Heinemann.

van Ments, M. (1983). *The effective use of role-play.* London: Kogan Page.

Vincent, A. (2005). *Simulation homepage.* Macquarie University Centre for Middle East and North African Studies. Retrieved 31 December 2005 from http://www.mq.edu.au/mec/sim/index.html

Wagner, B-J. (1976). *Dorothy Heathcote: drama as a learning medium.* Washington: NEA.

Wagner, B-J. (1998). *Educational drama and language arts: What research shows.* Portsmouth NH: Heinemann.

Ward, W. (1957). *Playmaking with children* (2nd ed.). New York: Appleton.

Warner, C. (1997). The edging in of engagement: Exploring the nature of engagement in drama. *Research in drama education, 2*(1), 21–42.

Wills, S. (2007). *Project EnRole.* Melbourne: The Carrick Institute for Learning and Teaching in Higher Education. Retrieved 7 August 2007. http://www.usyd.edu.au/learning/ quality/docs/devonshire_carrick_grant.pdf

Wiles, J., & Garrard, A. (1957). *Leap to life : An experiment in school and youth drama.* London: Chatto & Windus.

Winston, J. (1998). *Drama, narrative and moral education : Exploring traditional tales in the primary years.* London: Falmer Press.

Winston, J. (2000). *Drama, literacy and moral education 5–11.* London: David Fulton.

Wohkling, W., & Gill, P. (1980). *Instructional design library: Role-playing.* Englewood Cliffs, NJ: Educational Technology Publications.

Wootton, M. (Ed.). (1982). *New directions in drama teaching: Studies in secondary school practice.* London: Heinemann.

Chapter 6
Civil Wars

John O'Toole

The Battle of the Paradigms

As this subheading suggests, the porosity that characterises drama's ability simultaneously to permeate a number of learning contexts occasionally gets blocked. The good oil stops oozing smoothly, and congeals – or to be more accurate metaphorically if not chemically – turns into acid.

This has happened painfully and damagingly, mainly between on the one hand the notion of drama as an art form (a fairly obvious notion, and our focus in the next chapter) and on the other the concept of drama as a medium either for learning (Chapter 5) or for expressive development and personal growth (Chapter 4). This happened mainly in the UK. Dichotomy became trichotomy (the personal growth mob were then disowned by the learning medium crowd, too) and eventually megaotomy: theatre versus drama; art-form versus instrument; process versus product; subject versus service; improvisation versus script; theatre-in-education versus children's theatre versus theatre for schools . . . let alone the broader battles, drama skills versus dramatic understanding; drama for capability versus drama for life; practice versus theory; progressive versus reactionary; drama for assessment versus drama for experience; drama education versus speech and drama; and most savage of all, Marxist versus poststructuralist. All the Paradigms of Purpose that we have identified ceased for a while to be useful distinctions, and took on the appearance of barricades.

This phenomenon might not be unique to drama, but merely one of the stresses that competing for curriculum space inevitably creates, as Gavin Bolton pointed out sagely in summing up his brief history of the movement:

> Drama, like other subjects qualifying for a place in the school curriculum, has been part of a continual polarisation between two distinct views of education: knowledge-centred and child-centred (1984: 20).

Although the acid was at its most vitriolic and corrosive during the 1980s and early 1990s, it started splashing about much earlier. John Allen, UK Senior Drama Inspector for Schools and later Principal of the Central School of Speech and Drama, noted that in 1949 the English Ministry of Education was

J. O'Toole et al., *Drama and Curriculum,* Landscapes: the Arts, Aesthetics, and Education 6, DOI 10.1007/978-1-4020-9370-8_7,
© Springer Science+Business Media B.V. 2009

concerned about the possibility of professional children's theatre and drama in schools pulling in different directions (Allen 1979; 12)

... concerned enough to set up a working party. Allen continued:

> It was in 1951 I think that a memorable conference on drama in education took place at the Bonnington Hotel, Southampton Row, London. Here, for the first time, I realised with an alarm I can recall to this day, the depths of the split that was developing between concepts of drama in schools and the theatre arts ... [which] appears to exist wherever in the English speaking world new attitudes to drama in schools have taken root (ibid).

He had no hesitation in levelling the blame:

> In those days the protagonist of the educational view of drama was the eloquent and articulate Peter Slade, whose book *Child Drama* was largely responsible for rationalising this unfortunate dichotomy (ibid).

This is very much the pot calling the kettle black, for just as Slade was uncompromising in pursuing his vision of a child-based, play-based drama curriculum, Allen's own passion for theatre, its disciplines and its creative integrity, led him in this very book to continue, in his own words:

> to tend to drive a wedge between more traditional forms of theatrical activity and the work of the new wave of specialists with their enthusiasm for all those aspects of drama which distinguish it from theatre (128).

There is something disingenuous about so much of this debate, viewed with hindsight, as its warriors oversimplified the arguments of their opponents and looked for easy targets, a sophistry that Allen himself is prone to fall into:

> The repeated emphasis on drama as 'learning-by-doing' is to devalue drama until it is virtually unrecognisable as an art (106).

An exasperated Gavin Bolton, a leader of the 'new wave', wrote a riposte, rebuking Allen's oversimplification:

> Wide disagreement among practitioners as to content, purpose or method can be dispelled in seconds by the common understanding they all share that drama [in contrast to traditional school studies] is 'doing'. Nevertheless, I shall argue that this is only partially so, and that it is neglect of the part that is *not* 'doing' that has distorted our understanding of the nature of drama and has caused us to underrate its potential for learning (1981: 255).

As it happened, Bolton and Allen had great respect for each other, less and less evident among the protagonists as the war hotted up.

Easy targets were simple to spot, even within the opposing camps. In the hands of a Caldwell Cook or a John Allen, formal theatrical production work and school plays, study of the classical canon or contemporary avant garde, could be inspiring, accessible to all ages and deeply educational. The authors of this book were welded to drama by teachers arousing a passion for plays, including those by Shakespeare, well-taught and directed. Nevertheless, there was still plenty of dull learning, sterile and fascistic directing, demeaning or incomprehensible scripts and coarse acting practice. On the other side of the barricades, crass, mindless, limp, trivial and disorganised exercises and process work were no less evident as teachers lacking the mastery, organisational flair, child-centred generosity and charisma of Slade, Way or Heathcote struggled to master these new activities and relationships that were so different from the curriculum they were used to. Bolton himself, after a round of visits to his students (including a dire lesson by the author), remarked plaintively that he wondered sometimes whether he would ever see another drama lesson that got past the stage of warm-up games before it disintegrated or the bell went.

The war started hotting up at the beginning of the 1970s, with what was actually a very pertinent and even-handed attack by John Pick on 'five platitudes which seem to me to shelter some of the limper fallacies of children's drama' (1971: 6–11), by which he really meant the process movement. These were

- *We aim to make people better* – Pick wisely reminded us equally that 'drama's powers to do harm are unlimited'.
  - *'Involvement' is desirable* – as he asked: involvement in what? By this he was questioning the unchecked indulgence in raw emotional empathy and expression that was at the time very popular in role-play based drama.
  - *Drama teaches human sympathy . . . [and] . . . creative cooperation* – he extended the above warnings to remind us that distance is as necessary as empathy for any actor portraying a dramatic character . . . and also that the school play and amateur dramatic societies were both renowned for endemic dissension!
  - *Drama must develop apart from 'Theatre'* – he made a plea for not drawing an artificial distinction between 'creative drama' and 'theatre'. However, he was himself, unwittingly, deepening the dividing line, by saying 'there is time for both kinds of work', and providing distinct examples of each.
  - *Drama must come from the child* – this climax of his attack was addressed in the kind of passionate and thinly veiled ad hominem attack that has been so characteristic of and damaging to UK drama education, even though in this case it was accompanied with a backhanded compliment:

    I really believe that more nonsense is talked under this heading than any other. It is even talked by those eminent drama teachers – no names [needed by the cognoscenti] – who have great reputations for working with children and who in fact structure every second of their work and teach almost exclusively by the force of their personalities. 'I believe in total freedom' they announce afterwards.
      And so, in a sense, they do. They are skilled enough to realise that a child is free when he has security, a clear understanding of the possibilities, the technique to exploit them, and a strong person at hand to guide him towards improvement. This is what the best teachers – for all their trendy talk – seem to do. But lesser men will talk as if . . ..

For anyone who had missed the reference, that was one in the eye for Peter Slade. Anyway, Pick's concern was with what 'lesser men' are able to make of drama's potential, including processual forms, with which he was not unsympathetic, and which he wanted to bring into the educational mainstream:

  Our discussions should be those of educationalists everywhere, not those of a charged little coterie plugging its own bag of tricks (11).

A decade later in 1981, as an antidote not just to Pick but the whole faction which he saw as trying to fragment and divide the movement, Bolton did a bit of his own myth-busting (again, five myths). In this, he took head-on the myth that *Drama is anti-theatre*. Here he introduced, as crisply and vividly as always, the concept and diagram that should have put paid to the argument for good.

> If we were to watch a child in a garden being a policeman, we would say he is 'playing'; if we watched an actor on stage being a policeman, we would say he is 'performing'. We might agree that although both are 'pretending' there is a difference in *quality* or *mode* of action .... You will notice I have called them 'playing' and 'performing', apparently avoiding the term 'acting'. At the risk of offending those readers who have a very clearly defined notion of acting as something only an actor does, I intend to use the term as all-embracing, applying it to both the child's and the man's behaviour. This allows me to think in terms of *continuum* of acting behaviour rather than two separate categories:

$$\text{Dramatic Playing} \xleftarrow{\qquad\qquad \text{Acting} \qquad\qquad} \text{Performing}$$
(1985: 264)

It didn't stop the bickering, not in the UK anyway. However, in other locales we picked it up and used it widely to frame our emerging drama curricula, and also quite deliberately to immunise us against the British disease. An elaboration of it appears as a central organising device in Queensland's first Years 1–10 Drama Guidelines (Queensland Department of Education 1991: 3):

Playing mode ⟷ Playmaking mode ⟷ Plays mode

Here 'playing' incorporated not just dramatic play, but the more private and exploratory forms of role-play and improvisation; 'play-making' included both more formalised kinds of improvisation and devised performance, and the rehearsal activities and actors' and directors' exercises which precede the creation of formal theatre, i.e., 'plays'. The model was emphasised as a continuum, not three separate categories.

In addition to Bolton, Heathcote had been stressing for a decade her own theatrical roots, and the commonality between her teaching process and the basic dimensions of all theatre, particularly her consciously theatrical use in her teaching of the physical contrasts between sound/silence, movement/stillness and light/darkness. Her 'way out of the drama/theatre abyss' was to make direct if somewhat obscure parallels between Brecht's definition of a playwright and her own practice as a teacher:

... I am a playwright. I show   *As a teacher I have to be selective*
What I have seen. In mankind's markets   *too, helping people find frames of*
I have seen how humanity is traded. That   *reference, understanding tension*
I show, I, the playwright.   *as an aid to learning*

(Heathcote 1980: 13)

That didn't stop the war either, and in fact some of those most committed to ending it may have exacerbated it by their parts in a conference just as inflammatory as the Bonnington Hotel affair 40 years earlier, the Riverside Conference of 1978.

This was thoroughly documented by Ken Robinson, one of the Schools Council Project leaders (1980). His take on the need for it was that

> the dichotomy between educational drama and theatre has been opened up because of a mistaken emphasis, by educationalists, on self-expression and individuality, and that this has blurred some of the most important functions of the arts in schools (4).

The idea for the conference, which was proposed by the Young People's Theatre Scheme at the Royal Court, a theatre noted for the progressive and 'educational' stance of its adult productions of Brecht, Edward Bond and other socialistic playwrights, seemed a good one at first sight. They brought together the most distinguished drama educators – Heathcote and Bolton, no less – with Royal Court theatre practitioners Bill Gaskill and Nicholas Wright and Youth Director Gerald Chapman, together with groups of children and a group of actors for practical demonstrations of drama teaching and theatre directing by Heathcote, Bolton and Gaskill. However, as Robinson observed:

> Not surprisingly it did not end with a neat set of conclusions and a round of hearty applause. On some issues there was warm agreement, on others heated division. Over all there was a feeling that the debate which the conference had ignited should be kept alive and fuelled by further elaboration from those whose work had been seen (2).

Kept alive and stoked up it was, unfortunately, and mainly by others than those whose work was on display. The conference itself, and the documentation, was full of gems of insight, but also great gulfs of misapprehension. The actors found Heathcote's work with them mystifying and incomprehensible, and from direct participant accounts her response to this was quite uncompromising and to them off-putting. Bolton bravely declared his experience of demonstrating his teaching 'a very happy experience for me – apart from the second of the three lessons, which I handled ineptly', and titled his chapter reflecting on it *Theatre Form in Drama Teaching*. However, he acknowledged that some spectators were 'alarmed' and others 'critical' of his apparent lack of either direction or progress. From personal observations, the authors of this book know that in Bolton's very low-key, meticulous teaching, the theatre form is invariably embedded very deeply and unobtrusively, not easily recognisable by 'outsiders', especially those looking for something 'theatrical'. Although he asserts 'to the question what have drama and theatre in common, my answer is that ... the two forms share the same basic structures', his chapter is really about the pedagogy (73).

A philosophical issue, brought up by one of the key observers, theatre director Nicholas Wright, was Heathcote's and Bolton's rather sweeping use of the term 'universal', criticising the essentialist implications of the term, and pointing out that the argument of a play

> might be true only in the specific set of social, economic and cultural circumstances revealed and implied in the play . . .. It is, if you like, particular. But it is not universal. (104)

Of course this critique is not actually connected to the drama versus theatre debate, in that the same concepts of getting down to the 'universal' are equally applicable – or inapplicable – to all manifestations of both. Moreover, the use of this grand word has actually led to much interesting philosophical discussion and useful clarification of terms down the years. However, the word became something of an albatross round the necks of Heathcote and Bolton, and, to change the metaphor, has been used not only as a stick to beat them with, but an easy and lazy excuse to dismiss their work and approach altogether.

Perhaps the most unfortunate aspect of the Riverside Conference is that the whole event, and the way all the writers discussed it, was framed in terms of the (apparently endemic) dichotomy. Bolton's continuum was still a year or two away, and originally published in America, to boot. One group of key players who might have made an enormous difference, and whose complete absence was, even at the time, as astounding as it was unfortunate, was the theatre-in-education movement. Some of Heathcote and Bolton's strongest admirers and apologists came from this field, and also worked in theatres. The companies of actor-teachers, whose core business was bridging the apparent divide and working equally and simultaneously in a world that comprises and integrates both 'worlds' of theatre and education, could and should have been the catalyst for a real chemical change in understanding at the conference.

Invigorated by the Riverside air, the battle intensified. It was time for a new wave of preemptive assaults on the growing establishment of drama process, this one led by an ambitious young defender of dramatic art, David Hornbrook. Ironically, the only example of his actual practice this author ever saw was a quite competent lesson using process drama, the form he later excoriated and rejected. He picked up the justifiable concerns of Pick and Allen about sloppy and inartistic process work, and basically offered as an alternative a canonical view of drama, where the function of drama education is to

> get better at handling the medium, become more adept at producing and understanding dramas of all kinds. Thus, in the same way that visual art may wish to make judgments of worth between, shall we say, the design of a cornflakes packet and a Rembrandt self-portrait, so dramatic art has its criteria of value, eclectic and contested certainly, but held and understood within the context of cultural. [And there the sentence ends. Cultural what? – Is this a typo, a grammatical error or a semantic muddle?] (Hornbrook 1989: 132)

This is a view of theatre that many supporters of theatre arts teaching would feel was unduly narrow and elitist, but Hornbrook did not stop there. He ruthlessly polarised the debate by a sustained and waspish attack on 'Dorothy, Gavin and the new Muggletonians'. In choosing to attack drama process by directly attacking Heathcote and Bolton, and using the words of their admirers to hang them with, he disingenuously noted that 'the employment of first names, the avuncular familiarity, the selective use of critical judgment make it almost impossible to prise the text from the personality' (20) . . . and then went on to use all those sophistries himself. He was particularly scathing about their emerging status as 'gurus', a process that he reinforced and reified by his very attacks. He constantly picked on the worst examples of process work as exemplars of the medium, and the most unguarded descriptions to attack. In brief, he used all the tricks he condemned, in his attempt to discredit and bury drama process, at first in print (1989, 1991), and then in the very powerful position that his reputation as a defender of traditional values brought him, as Inspector of Drama for Greater London. He took no prisoners.

The effects of this malignant attack were predictably damaging and oddly benign to different parts of the body of drama educators. First, an aspect of process-based drama work that has been insufficiently acknowledged then or since was that it is not at all easy. It involves a particular and complex pedagogy, and also an understanding of drama, which are both quite different from what most people, and certainly the 'general public', think of as either teaching or drama. For teachers of the time, negotiating the curriculum was both new and terrifyingly unpredictable. In drama terms, the public performance to seated audiences of scripted dramatic narratives in recognisable sequences of scenes was replaced by everybody in the room being simultaneously engaged in equally unpredictable inventions and explorations of character, motive, theme or whatever else took the teacher's or students' attention. This meant that to use these new forms entailed *both* mastering a new pedagogy *and* inventing a new kind of artistry. It is no wonder that Hornbrook's swashbuckling call to arms ironically provided a refuge for many teachers who had tried drama process and found that they could not make it work for them, and many more who had only seen it used ineffectually. Add to those adherents of drama who also saw themselves as defending a canon of great work, and Hornbrook had something of a potential army, as well as the polarised situation he had sought, in Britain at any rate.

There was another effect, the most serious of all, of the whole long war in Britain, outside the drama community itself. Drama had generated plenty of goodwill for itself in schools, after so many years of effort to gain curricular access. However, the drama/theatre war, and the passion with which it was waged, confused those who held the responsibility for curriculum in schools: the principals, school and systemic curriculum committees and advisers, examination boards, parents' groups, and, preeminently, politicians. They could not understand what all the shouting was about; they were frequently the subjects of attempts to enlist them on one side or other; and they were still confused, anyway, about what the real purpose of drama in schools should be. Do these drama teachers want our children to learn about plays, do plays or just play about? And why on earth might some of them think that drama should infuse the whole curriculum? This, remember, was at the time when progressive education was in full retreat, scattering before the might of the Black Paper army. As usual, those on the edge were first to be trampled underfoot. Drama lost its place on the National Curriculum, except at Senior examination level, where adherence to the canon kept it alive, and it had to retreat once more under the protective wing of English (which might have been a blessing in disguise).

Hornbrook had very little impact outside the UK. He did visit Australia in 1983 with his message, but apart from a small contingent of personal admirers, his ideas more or less bounced off. There were two reasons for this, which may also have applied elsewhere: the first was that there was a much more unified and eclectic understanding of drama and how it worked in schools. The first major secondary drama textbook, by Roma Burgess and Pamela Gaudry (1985), was grounded in a sound understanding of drama processes and significantly influenced by the work of Heathcote's ex-student John Deverall, but it also moved effortlessly through its own loose and porous categorisations of purposes for drama in schools: for personal development, therapy, as a learning medium and as art form. The other reason was that Australian drama educators were in close touch with their British counterparts, and we saw the Hornbrook phenomenon coming – at least we saw the 'debate' and the dire effect it was having on drama in that country. We took our own preemptive action, turning the acid to good use.

The good effect of the Hornbrook attack was that it stung into more energetic action both the passionate adherents of dramatic process, for instrumental and/or expressive-developmental purposes, and those who saw it and used it as part of that continuum from dramatic playing to performing plays. In a concerted way, all this body of practitioners and writers started to pay much more conscious attention to the art-form in the process. To ask, in fact: What is the artistry in drama process, and can process drama be considered a genre of the art form? Quite quickly a body of work addressing this very question built up. The truth was that many drama educators were getting more adept at the form and the pedagogy. Cecily O'Neill (1995), David Booth (1994) and Jonothan Neelands (Neelands and Goode 1990), whose own practices were self-evidently highly artistic to all but the most jaundiced eye, critically examined that practice, or had it examined for them, and the key artistic elements identified (e.g., *Pre-text and Story Drama: The Artistry of Cecily O'Neill and David Booth*: Taylor 1995). They all wrote books, which demonstrated that drama process could even be to an extent formularised, without destroying it entirely as an aesthetic experience. Burgess and Gaudry (1985), and Brad Haseman and John O'Toole (1987; 1992) analysed drama process in terms of the artistic elements – for the first time actually defining what might be meant by this contentious word 'process'. Coming in from another direction, Augusto Boal and his colleagues have never for a moment doubted that what they do is art:

> The oppressed person himself or herself is the artist that creates images through which to rehearse ways of liberation. That's why we also go into the realm of education, because images convey ideas. Images are a language that the child can create . . .. Using the images of theatre techniques can allow youngsters to speak more profoundly what they want to say. And that is precisely why the Theatre of the Oppressed is a language (1996: 48).

. . . and Boal's own confidence now infuses those who use drama as a learning medium in more routine contexts.

Hornbrook himself seemed unaware of these developments, and disappointingly neither his second book and later writings, nor his actions as Drama Inspector, have acknowledged or addressed any of their arguments, merely reiterating more shrilly and canonically his original theme. Hornbrook's influence receded during the 1990s. The fractured and wounded British drama community has pulled itself together, and once again emerged as a major force in world drama education, eminent if no longer preeminent. There are still some distinguished practitioners who cannot bring themselves to use the phrase 'process drama', even though the genre, and the concept of drama as a learning medium that it represents, are major parts of their normal practice! Like all good drama educators these days, they, and we, are both teachers and artists.

This of course is taking us out from the territory of drama as a learning medium and provides an excellent point to seep into the next Chapter, which deals with our fourth Paradigm of Purpose: drama as art-form.

References

Allen, J. (1979). *Drama in schools: Its theory and practice*. London: Heinemann.

Boal, A. (1996). Politics, education and change. In J. O'Toole & K. Donelan (Eds.), *Drama, culture and empowerment: The IDEA Dialogues*. Brisbane: IDEA Publications.

Bolton, G. (1984). *Drama as education: An argument for placing drama at the centre of the curriculum*. London: Longmans.

Bolton, G. (1985). Drama in education – a re-appraisal. Originally published in Nellie McCaslin, (Ed.), (1981). *Children and drama*. 2nd Edition. New York: Longman. Reprinted in David Davis & Chris Lawrence (Eds.), *Gavin Bolton's selected writings on drama and education*. London: Longman.

Booth, D. (1994). *Story drama: Reading, writing, and role-playing across the curriculum*. Markham, ON: Pembroke.

Burgess, P., & Gaudry, R. (1985). *A time for drama*. Melbourne: Longman Cheshire.

Haseman, B., & O'Toole, J. (1987). *Dramawise – an introduction to the elements of drama*. Melbourne: Heinemann.

Heathcote, D. (1980). From the particular to the universal. In K. Robinson (Ed.), *Exploring theatre and education*. London: Heinemann.

Hornbrook, D. (1989). *Education and dramatic art*. Oxford: Basil Blackwell.

Hornbrook, D. (1991). *Education in drama: Casting the dramatic curriculum*. London: Falmer.

Neelands, J., & Goode, A (1990). *Structuring drama work*. Cambridge: Cambridge University Press.

O'Neill, C. (1995). *Drama worlds*. Portsmouth, NH: Heinemann.

O'Toole, J. (1992). *The process of drama: Negotiating the elements of dramatic form*. London: Routledge.

Pick, J. (1971). Five fallacies in drama. *Young Drama* (Vol. 1, No. 1, pp. 11). London: Heinemann.

Queensland Department of Education. (1991). *Drama makes meaning – Years 1–10 curriculum guide*. Brisbane: Queensland Department of Education.

Taylor, P. (1995). *Pre-text and story drama: The artistry of Cecily O'Neill and David Booth*. Brisbane: National Association for drama in education.

Chapter 7
The Three Pillars of Art

John O'Toole

Drama and Music

This chapter may come as a bit of an anticlimax after the stirring battle-scenes of the last. Moreover, many of its principles have already been canvassed in other chapters. However, this chapter does spell out the fourth Paradigm of Purpose, which we have been alluding to: the *aesthetic/cognitive* – drama as an art-form – and also effectively removes the casus belli. In fact, it offers a complete resolution of the paradigm problem – so that's worth reading on for!

It can be instructive to contrast drama with music. Part of the whole trouble for drama is its protean versatility. In theory, the ability to change shape at will and accomplish a wide diversity of quite different ends is a wonderful and almost magical capacity. But think of it from the point of view of its would-be employer. In a job-interview, having a candidate in front of you who is constantly changing shape and offering something totally different is entirely disconcerting, like a comedy trickster ('Ok, Ok if you think that's good . . . look at this, look at this one . . . see – nothing up my sleeve!. . .). And adult audiences know that magic is just sleight of hand, illusion to confuse and deceive. We, the drama cognoscenti, know that cheap tricks are not the reason why we want to use our world of illusion, of course, but that was Plato's take on drama, and we can't blame those who have succeeded him as Academy chiefs for having the same distrust.

Now consider music. Worldwide, music's place in the school curriculum is very consistent, and one we envy: it has a narrow, marginal but quite stable and deeply embedded position, and it always commands respect. Along with 'art' (i.e., mostly painting), it is what education managers think of as *the arts*. This is in spite of the fact that music is very expensive. (The schools' instrumental music program is one of the Queensland Education Department's most costly outlays, but has continued unchallenged for over 30 years). Even more than drama, music also has an important function in the public life of the school. Yet music doesn't claim to do half the things drama does. As a career path, it's just as unlikely and unpopular with most parents. It's far more demanding of skills from the teacher, while the skill demands on the students, in the hands of unimaginative teachers, often render it a subject unloved and eventually avoided by the students (in the very egalitarian Queensland senior

J. O'Toole et al., *Drama and Curriculum*, Landscapes: the Arts, Aesthetics,   127
and Education 6, DOI 10.1007/978-1-4020-9370-8_8,
© Springer Science+Business Media B.V. 2009

examination system, music manages to attract less than half the students of either drama or visual arts). And really, when you study music, you just study music. It's one of the 'great' and natural art-forms, sufficient unto itself. Like Everest, you do it because it's there.

And that's a measure of its modest but permanent success in the curriculum. Managers know where they are with music. It's not pretending to be any other subject, and so it can be timetabled, assessed, chosen by the talented, the interested or the science leftovers. It offers recognisable and finite skills to learn, a body of knowledge to be absorbed, a history with legendary geniuses to be learned about (well, of course, that's highly contested, but only within the discipline by those pesky populists who think that music is a class act, and those restless students who think that rock and rap are music too). As we saw in Chapter 3, drama apologists loudly promote research indicating that drama increases literacy, and demand attention and inclusion for this capacity. Parallel research is indicating that music-rich teaching has equally beneficial effects on mathematics skills such as counting and sequencing, but music teachers rarely if ever advance that as a reason for having music in the curriculum, and many actively downplay it; that would demean music's role and status.

As the proponents of drama as an art-form in the drama wars pointed out vociferously, drama can make exactly the same claims as music to be one of the world's 'great' and universal art-forms. The current Queensland Senior drama syllabus merely uses that as its starting point as it stakes its claim thus:

> Drama is one of the oldest art forms known. It has its origin in the impulse to imitate, symbolise and ritualise experiences in an attempt to understand and control them. Societies and cultures throughout history have developed enactive ways of making and communicating meaning that involve performers and audiences (Queensland Studies Authority 2001: 1).

For many decades, drama when taught as an art-form has followed music quite closely in both content and the structural elements of the curriculum and especially cocurriculum. One of the twin pillars of this has been that students should be given access to and perhaps experience of this classic art-form as part of their cultural heritage – knowledge of the canon of respectively (Western) music and (Western) dramatic literature as an essential prerequisite for a fully educated adult.

The First Pillar: Appreciating Drama

This is drama's longest continuous establishment in schools, colleges and universities, one already touched on in Chapter 3. Drama has long been a basic component of literature courses, and sometimes still is – in the English-speaking world mainly taught through English and *liberal studies* classes; in Europe, often through a separate branch of pedagogical endeavour, 'theatre science', which sounds even more impressive in German, where in at least one University 'teaterwissenschaft' is taught in the 'Sprach- und Literaturwissenschaftliche' Faculty.

Young people are taught to appreciate drama primarily as consumers, both for its supposed civilizing influence and to generate audiences for adult theatre. As Hornbrook put it:

> all this, together with an understanding of drama's place in a wider culture, amounts to a contextualizing of experience which is an essential and embracing aspect of the dramatic curriculum (1991: 112).

Traditionally, even the practical drama enthusiasts like Bishop Burton acknowledged it as such: 'Children are led towards the appreciation of drama … and the works of the great dramatists, and thus towards the true and full humanity that such an experience brings' (1955: 21). It has of course helped drama's cause no end that England's most famous citizen, and the world's most famous writer, was a common playwright, and the study of Shakespeare has formed the backbone of the study of drama as literature effectively since his own time (Ben Jonson started the cult). For Caldwell Cook, it was so obvious it did not need justifying: 'Provided they are over ten, a Shakespeare play is the most useful beginning' (1917: 186). No buts or maybes: QED.

Cook was savagely contemptuous of how Shakespeare was often taught, however:

> Remember how you were taught Shakespeare at school, the dreary reading of a dull play, the dreary explanation of the meanings of obscure words, the lifeless recitation of speeches … .. When a teacher says that in his treatment of Shakespeare 'the parts are assigned and the play read dramatically', this generally means no more than the boys reading in turns while seated in their desks … [such lessons, as] Disraeli said of public dinners: 'they are meant to be dull' (196).

Newer models of English teaching have emerged in parallel with changes experienced in drama. Ironically, drama as literature has been traditionally taught sitting down, reading theatre as literary text or watching films and visiting schools theatre. Caldwell Cook bravely challenged this sedentary study by moving the desks and encouraging his students to bring Shakespeare to life as actors – a radical act in his own day, and not one to be encouraged by the (then) status quo. Since then, enterprising teachers have done their best with inflexible classrooms and school halls to ensure that their students somehow experience drama as performance. However, given the example of Cook himself, and the plethora of books, teaching demonstrations and learning resources on Shakespeare, to say nothing of the hundreds of films, videos, American musicals, teen movies and ice dance spectaculars based on Shakespeare's plays, which have filled the 90 years since those acid observations, it is depressing that the Royal Shakespeare Company in 2007 still has to set out its (new) vision to help teachers ensure 'that all young people have a positive experience of Shakespeare at school [and] all teaching of Shakespeare should include some theatre-based activities'.

Which is not to say that many thousands of students have not received inspiring teaching of Shakespeare, from Cook's time through to today. Andy Kempe and Helen Nicholson point out in their influential manual for training secondary drama teachers:

English and drama specialists possess complementary skills and subject-knowledge, particularly in the field of dramatic literature, and there has been much productive cooperation in
schools. In England, where all year 9 students must take Standard Attainment Tests which
include a Shakespeare play, many English and drama teachers work together to ensure that
pupils participate in dramatic interpretations of the text (2001: 45).

In Australia, the situation is comparable, since in most states teacher registration for secondary schools requires teachers trained in two subjects, and a large
proportion of the drama students also take English, and bring their practical understanding and pedagogy to the wide range of complex dramatic texts still taught in
English classrooms. However, this is overall a small proportion of the army which
teaches English in schools, the only subject compulsory to all students throughout
schooling.

Shakespeare in particular, along with any other writer who falls into the category
of being canonised (literally) by Harold Bloom, has become caught up in English
teaching's own culture wars. For those who do not follow literature, Bloom, a Yale
Professor, is the most renowned and assertive of those essentialists who believe that
literature can be ranked on a universal scale of importance, and he nailed his colours
to the mast with the publication of *The Western Canon* (1994). Incidentally, both
the earliest book he selected, the Babylonian *Epic of Gilgamesh* and the latest, Tony
Kushner's *Angels in America*, are frequently performed as contemporary theatre
and studied in senior drama classes. Right in the middle is Shakespeare. Bloom's
own bardolatry (thank you for the word George Bernard Shaw) is quite spectacular,
witnessed by even the title of his hagiography *Shakespeare: The Invention of the
Human*. As a not unsympathetic reviewer emphasises:

For Bloom, Shakespeare stands alone not only as the greatest literary genius who ever lived,
but the greatest intellect of all time, so far ahead of anyone who came before or after him
that we can never catch up (Atwan 1999).

Sometimes, your most enthusiastic advocates are not your best friends, and many
of the theatrical classics in Bloom's canon have been right in the line of fire just
because they appear there. It is not the place of this book to map the debates and
conflicts that have taken place in English teaching over the last 30 years, but several
of these have impacted significantly on the place of drama as an art-form in English
and literature courses. One of these has been the challenge to the very notion of
high or heritage art. Bloom represents all the dogmatic certainty that the generation
of cultural and social critics following Raymond Williams abhors. The opposition
nailed its own colours to the mast with concepts such as Paul Willis's theory of
the 'grounded aesthetic' that already exists within the 'common culture' of young
people (1990), labelling the traditional hierarchies of 'literary heritage' or 'classic'
literature as the trappings of privilege and the dominance of an intellectual elite.
This coincided with another dual attack in the form of a pincer movement, on the
one flank from reader response theorists like Wolfgang Iser (1978), questioning the
essentialist idea that the author of a book is any more than partially responsible –
along with the reader – for the meanings that are 'contained' or 'potential' in any
work of literature. On the other flank, the poststructuralists and postmodernists like

Roland Barthes (1977) weighed in with 'the death of the author', their challenge to the very existence, let alone the prestige or sanctity, of the person who merely wrote the words of an engagement with literature in its social context.

The biggest threat of all to the place of literature within school syllabuses has come from a coalition of new functionalists. Since classical, and certainly medieval, times, study of classic literature has formed a major part of the schooling of any 'well-educated person'. As the twentieth century has moved towards the new millennium, modern careers in business and industry have made exponentially increased demands for high levels of literacy and more recently multiliteracies. The successors of Thomas Gradgrind have shifted their demands for 'facts: teach them nothing but facts' to 'basics: teach them nothing but the basics' and the exponents of literacy theory and practice have gleefully seized the territory, in some cases almost to push literature out of English courses entirely (usually conveniently overlooking that both literary study and dramatic pedagogy have a lot to offer in learning to read and write well). And as if all those assaults weren't enough, another joint territorial invading force has come along in the form of Media, Film & TV and New Media Studies.

One net effect of these displacements in Australia at least has been to make it easier and more necessary for drama to detach itself from the hegemony of English and reposition itself within the arts. Indeed, many drama teachers have been ungrateful enough to their literary hosts to form an alliance with the media battalion, and they now live together and slightly uneasily in *The Arts Key Learning Area*. Literature, apparently not an art-form, and nothing like the force it once was, still lives within English, and English teachers continue to teach some drama, usually including Shakespeare, though most of them now get no preservice training in how to do that in ways that include 'some theatre-based activities', as the Royal Shakespeare Company prescribes in its *Stand up for Shakespeare* education program.

The Second Pillar: Performing Drama

This last emphasis on 'theatre-based activities', as well as reminding us of the second pillar of art that drama and music share, *performance*, raises the question of where dramatic artists get their training. For many young children, the urge to perform in public is very strong, sometimes obsessive, and countless professional actors ascribe their start to self-organized epics in the kitchen, the street outside or a corner of the classroom at recess. So the early childhood teachers providing the dress-up box and the corner stage space are in a sense fledgling trainers for theatre, though only a minute fraction of their exhibitionists ever get to write their actors' memoirs.

Many schools provide, and have always provided, opportunities for their students to perform dramatically in cocurricular drama clubs and school performances. Worldwide, this is probably the most common manifestation of drama on school premises. As well as being a useful safety valve for the performative extroverts (as those with an interest in drama are often mistakenly perceived), the public dramatic and/or musical performance can be usefully harnessed to the school's public image. Moreover, in Australia as in many other countries, music and drama are very commonly combined in this context – the school musical is often a feature event of the school year, much more so than the classical play tradition in countries like Greece and the UK – while joint musical and dramatic performances are prepared for public events such as speech and open days. Two further curious local manifestations of this shared recognition of music and drama as performance arts are the traditional district or interschool 'eisteddfod', a competitive recital of individual musical or dramatic 'pieces', and the much more recent and even more curious 'rock and roll eisteddfod', an opportunity for secondary school students to strut their stuff by dancing and miming to taped rock music – often with professional choreographers and expensive effects provided by commercial sponsors. All over the world, schools come together to exhibit their dramatic work in festivals, usually competitive ones. Many schools invest considerable amounts of money and student and staff time to ensure that the performances are of high-quality or at least have high production values.

At their best, theatre productions and festivals establish drama as a high-status and highly valued activity, and its effects seep through the school. This chapter's author's own first experience of drama was not untypical of its period: a role in a junior interhouse drama festival in Karel Kapek's classic *R.U.R.* – something of a fiasco where I had the big entry: 'My God – the manuscript (*long pause*) … it's been stolen!' We didn't win, but it got me cast as Portia in the annual school Shakespeare play. The school, mainly for upwardly mobile working class boys, had grown from a 'technical' school into one determined to show that the young people of common backgrounds could live up academically and culturally to the privileged classes. Costumes for the annual play, which was usually Shakespeare but in one year Sophocles, were hired from London, and a London evening paper critic came down to review the play. The English teachers in the school were at least partly selected for their capacity to direct it – and in doing so make the plays' artistry and their language accessible to the young actors. They would have enthusiastically agreed with Caldwell Cook's dictum that:

> After all, if you can act Shakespeare you can act anything, and if you cannot act even Shakespeare you might as well sit down again (1917: 183).

My Portia didn't live up to the school Rosalind of a few years earlier – some kid called Paul Scofield – but the experience was formative, as it was for many from the school, which scaffolded our enthusiasm with evening play-readings in the teachers' homes, lively English teaching, and annual camps in Stratford on Avon to see the plays.

One notable feature of the anecdote above was the quality of the plays themselves. Thirty years later, the boot on the other foot, the author was adjudicating a similar house drama festival, senior this time, where 9 of the 12 plays presented consisted of comedy sketches, nearly all from British or American sit-coms; two were stock scenes from Shakespeare; the twelfth was student-devised and attempted a serious topic, but with no teacher assistance, it was doomed. After politely deploring the selection of plays, I was not invited back.

An example of a more valuable and contemporary use of the interschool drama festival is one from Uganda, which tied the annual festival into a Theatre for Development agenda. All the plays were workshopped with professionals and dealt with important issues of health, for the edification of all the audiences, including both school and local community (Mangeni 2000).

None of these examples above, good or bad, were primarily formulated to provide career openings (though, incidentally but not coincidentally, my school did produce many distinguished dramatic professionals besides Paul Scofield). Nevertheless, like any artists, actors – and directors and playwrights – must get their basic practice and training somewhere. The provision of specialised opportunities for dramatic artists demands a quite different curriculum from passive and sedentary literary study. Of course this rarely happens in general schooling, since actor training, unlike say drawing or singing, is rarely seen as a necessary skill for the layperson, and professional actors are few and far between. It goes without saying, too, that theatre is rarely viewed as a favourable career choice by parents and schoolteachers – 'Don't put your daughter on the stage, Mrs Worthington'. In recent years, dramatic art as a career has become somewhat more respectable, and some district systems in a number of countries including UK, Australia and Singapore have created performing arts high schools, or special intensive courses for senior students. Besides them, most schools provide those drama clubs and school performances for the wannabe performers.

In both England and the USA, the first professional acting schools were founded in the early years of the twentieth century. Before that, it was apparently socially easier in the USA for an enterprising young person to make a career in the theatre, than in the more closed and class-ridden England. From the middle of the nineteenth century, young Americans would go to teachers of 'elocution', to help them break into the touring repertoire or summer stock theatres – until the word 'elocution' became discredited as the 'pretentious incapacity of its usually self-appointed professors ended in their virtual extinction' (Payne 1952: 298). This opened the way for the burgeoning industry of Academies and University Departments of Theatre Arts, particularly since Hollywood established itself as the world's dominant film centre. In England, Beerbohm Tree's Royal Academy of Dramatic Art (1904) just preceded Elsie Fogerty's Central School of Speech and Drama (1906), and the trend accelerated since the 1950s (when Australia's first, NIDA, was established) until currently, for example, in Australia there are over 40 Universities or tertiary establishments offering accredited career-centred drama courses, and a host of private training schools.

An interesting sidelight to this, revealed in some recent research, is the ambivalent way professional actor training figures in the pedagogical debate. In England and Australia, many acting academies reject the notion of 'education' in favour of 'training' for stage and screen (Prior 2004: 265). Throughout the arts industry, some artists look down on arts educators, considering them second-rate or failed artists (devastatingly articulated again by Bernard Shaw: 'those who can, do; those who can't, teach'). It seems many actor trainers carry this attitude from their acting career into their teaching. They are invariably passionate about – or defensive of – their own professionalism as actors; however, their ideas about pedagogy vary from the professional and informed to the very unformed, inarticulate and amateurish, as Ross Prior has identified (2005). Throughout the twentieth century, the tertiary academies have themselves spawned an industry of private drama schools for children, and the very mixed genre of the 'elocution' or 'speech and drama' class – until the word 'elocution' became discredited in the UK and Australia too. What goes around, comes around.

The Third Pillar: Making Drama

Making Plays

Back at that 1950s' house-play festival, among the competition to our own epic, one brave house offered a 'home-made' play, devised by the group – just as in the later festival I adjudicated in the 1980s. It got even shorter shrift than R.U.R., with the adjudicator kindly but pityingly counselling the cast not to try and do what professional playwrights did so much better. And sensible advice it was, when the festival was about providing a platform primarily for demonstrating *acting* skill, and secondarily for audiences and performers to *appreciate* dramatic literature.

This is just the same, once again, as in *music*. Here too, there has been a long-established dismissiveness to child or student composition, or at least a reluctance to classify the development of their own artistry as creators of artwork, as of equal educational importance to appreciating and performing the works of others. Pleas of music educators like Keith Swanwick (1979), who have advocated the importance of composition for exactly the same pedagogical and artistic reasons as drama, have often fallen on deaf ears. Music has had a much longer establishment in the formal curriculum than drama, yet even today, in the Australian state of Victoria's Senior Music Syllabus, students do not learn composition.

Back in drama, coexisting with those performance festivals, occasionally in the same drama clubs, a quite different activity has flourished, one that we have already tracked extensively in this book, and which in effect was the casus belli for the Great War chronicled in Chapter 6, which is about to be resolved – forever, we may hope! Children no less than professional playwrights make up plays, and in other ways create their own original dramatic action; teachers help them to do it, and good teachers help them to do it well. There is a long and healthy tradition of encouraging children to engage with the art-form of theatre by making it. True, it has tended to be seen as a second-tier activity or specialised interest, an offshoot of appreciating or performing, as in those ill-fated homegrown festival offerings. In Maisie Cobby's clarion 1956 call to arms *Calling All Playmakers!* that was clearly how she saw playwrighting for secondary school students:

> You will have discovered ... [note the omission, but watch this space, however] ... from watching plays at the theatre, the cinema or on television, that drama is a subject which

covers a wide and varied range of activities. For the majority, acting a part in a play is
most popular, but on the other hand, there are some to whom other aspects of drama make a
stronger appeal. They may be interested in writing and producing their own plays, designing
the scenery or the costumes ... etc. (1956: vii.)

Though acting other people's plays has been historically the staple fare of drama
clubs, junior theatre groups and youth and student theatres, in and beyond schools,
there have been a growing number of directors of these groups who have seen the
potential of the young people working with their own material.

There is a double challenge in this, so ruthlessly exposed by those two festival
adjudicators: that any play created by the group must also be performed by the group
(i.e., usually themselves). Good scripts are a tough and appropriate task for budding
actors to wrestle with, providing both substance and support: to learn to interpret,
find the subtexts in the dialogue and action, develop the characters, explore the relationships and articulate the structure. Apprentice scripts only have these qualities in
vestigial or incomplete form. Conversely, budding *playwrights* need the same kind
of challenge and support from those acting their plays who can help them find out
what can and does work, can extend their own understanding of how to write for
performers, and can diminish or conceal some of the weaknesses. Apprentice actors
mostly can't. However, particularly in the last 30 years, the expertise has grown
immeasurably, both in understanding the kind of material and structures that young
people can create and manage, and in how to present them in ways that do show
the skills of both playwrights and actors to advantage, and allow those elements that
are beyond the capacities of either to stay insignificant, or at least unnoticed. Some
genres of drama lend themselves comfortably to this, like collage drama, popular
among community theatre too. The documented work of companies like Carole
Tarlington's *Vancouver Youth Theatre* and Errol Bray's *Shopfront* has led to a much
greater confidence in the notion of collaborative playbuilding (e.g., Tarlington &
Michaels 1995; Bray 1976, 1991; Oddey 1996).

This of course is also a challenge to the canonical wisdom of Western orthodox
drama, and a dramatic literature and traditions that have overwhelmingly been built
on the notion of the single playwright/artist who, director and actors aside, is the
'onlie begetter' of the play. Bray's name for his theatre, *Shopfront*, the titles of his
books, e.g., *Playbuilding: A Guide for Group Creation of Plays with Young People*
and his lead in establishing the ongoing *Interplay* International Young Playwrights'
Festival all proclaim his complete confidence in the ability of young people to
generate art work, and he has done a lot to encourage both solo and collaborative
playmaking. From the 1980s, there has been a generation of young people's directors outside schools, and increasingly teachers within schools, trying out various
combinations of student-devised work: individual would-be playwrights creating
material for their colleagues to perform; groups improvising or cowriting their own
material, with or without the critical assistance and red pen of the adult director;
young people writing or improvising scenes for the director/playwright to shape into
more formed theatre for them to perform; young people working with professional
playwrights and directors in partnerships and residencies. How this manifests itself

nowadays as curriculum will be looked at later in this chapter, after we have tracked another branch of the stream of playmaking back to its wellspring.

Improvised Drama

The omission in the quote above from Maisie Cobby is revealing, about what we can see in hindsight was a gap in her (and everybody's) thinking:

> You will have discovered, *both from your school dramatic work*, and from watching plays
> . . .

Now, quite a lot of that 'school dramatic work' for Cobby, by which she meant their primary school drama, was comprised of dramatic play. If we revisit what she has to say about that:

> [The child] wants to unravel situations which puzzle and interest him, to know more about the world and the people and strange places and things he sees in picture books. Above all, he needs to understand the relationship which exists between himself and these activities . . .. Always it should be remembered that dramatic play and not dramatic performance is the intention throughout (1955: 4).

we can see clearly from the final sentence that for the younger child making the play, and not playing the part, is the thing. Unlike later, performance is subordinated to an activity that is vividly described in this definition, which reads to us like a pretty good description of what a playwright (or composer, painter, poet or any primary artist) does, at least in the formative stages.

In the world of dramatic play, as Holly Giffin (1990) and Julie Dunn (2002) in particular have shown, children learn early to manage the elements of dramatic form to create original shared dramas that are enacted with gusto and sustainment, entirely self-sufficient and satisfying unto themselves, with no external audiences. Dunn has shown that 11-year-old girls can among themselves use and negotiate five different kinds of playwrighting as they *spontaneously* invent and enact dramatic narrative, often incorporating more than one genre of performance style, for periods of up to 3 hours without missing a beat or dropping the shared illusion for a second. As with adults, some children have a specially heightened talent for identifying dramatic opportunities, for enriching the drama, deepening the tension or complexifying the issues – dubbed 'master dramatists' by Barbara Creaser (1990) and 'super dramatists' by Dunn. This astonishing and humbling level of sophisticated artistic skill is usually entirely hidden from adults, though the indefatigable observers and chroniclers of children's play, Iona and Peter Opie, were on to it (1959: 1). All these writers note that the involvement or intervention of adults, or even being watched, can actively inhibit this rich and controlled inventiveness, presumably as the children automatically defer to the adult's supposed authority or become self-conscious and lose their focus and metacommunicative skills within the group. Both Peter Slade (1954) and Dunn had to use considerable patience and ingenuity in their research to counter this concealment.

And here is a dilemma for teachers. Thanks to scholars like Giffin and Dunn we can now compare the artistry of these clandestine epics with the improvised dress-up plays performed *for* adults by the really extrovert infants, or the results of the 'get-into-a-group-and-make-up-a-play-to-show-us' strategy widely used by well-meaning teachers wanting to give scope for creativity. We can see the disparity, especially in the latter category, as, without considerable trained help from the teacher, the youngsters typically parade self-consciously with simplistic characters and plots, very imperfect control of focus, narrative and tension, or management of language, movement or mood, and often an eager or anxious overuse of costume. No wonder such efforts sink without trace in drama festivals. But this negative picture actually does not at all fairly represent the effort or tell the whole story. The real problem or challenge that the activity represents often goes unidentified, the whole performance is dismissed as trivial or inartistic, and often drama with it.

Almost exactly like those youth theatre members in their playbuilding activities discussed above, the children working in school classrooms to 'make-up-a-play-to-show-us' are actually trying to do two things at once, two very different, difficult and somewhat incompatible artistic tasks, *playwrighting* and *acting* – over both of which they have at best emerging and incomplete skills. Inevitably, because 'show-us' is the driver and outcome of the activity, the performing element invariably rules … ('We'll get a laugh if we …' What will look best, cleverest, funniest, least exposing?) Moreover, children in classrooms, unlike the youth theatre playbuilders, are not always self-selected, keen volunteers. This kind of curricular activity in a public classroom contrasts with Dunn's preteenage children demonstrating such artistry in their hidden dramatic play. For them, the primary satisfaction is really in the playmaking, not the acting (though many of the children themselves would not be aware of this). They are able to concentrate entirely on the play-creation *because* their enactment is actually secondary, a moment-by-moment crystallisation of the shared creation, forgotten the moment it has happened, part of the metacommunication that makes the invention manifest. Their acting just signifies the moment and signals to each other where they are and where they are going.

In bringing an invented play to the public, three things happen to original improvised dramatic play to change the dynamic and impoverish the artistry. First, the concentration must be on the performing – especially as there are usually people in the audience whom the performers want to impress, act up to or not be embarrassed in front of. Second, these plays are usually created rather differently: with the intention of performance, or with the dual intention of performing *and* learning about some school knowledge, so they are usually planned and discussed in advance, rather than just spontaneously emerging. Third, even if in preparation they are improvised in action, the performance is invariably a conscious and self-conscious re-enactment. The teacher's help in either devising and refining the play or directing the performance sometimes merely adds another dimension of difficulty, with the young creators grappling with another generationally different vision and a new set of technical demands.

These tensions can be clearly seen in the gallant and in their own way quite rich scripts of Harriet Finlay-Johnson's children, where quite often the content weighs down the artistry:

Little boy:	Oh dad, I know something that Southey wrote. It was *The Falls of Lodore*. Do take me to see the Falls. They must be wonderful . . ..
Traveller:	Well, we will go to bed now, and tomorrow morning, first thing, we will do what Wordsworth did: we will tramp over hill and dale and see all we can.
Landlady:	Ah! That's if it doesn't rain, sir!
Traveller:	Ha ha! That's a sly hit at the climate. I know you are noted for having the rainiest climate in England. What causes it?
Landlady:	Some say it is the moist wind from the Atlantic.
Traveller:	I suppose the mountains attract the great rainfall and cause the great lakes at the same time.

(Finlay-Johnson 1907: 196).

There is much better script than this in the book, it must be said. Although it is clear through the pages that Johnson's children were highly motivated and given opportunity and encouragement to be creative and artistic, their work was firmly tied both to the learning demands of the lesson, and the structures of conventional scripted theatre.

Winifred Ward and the creative dramatics movement in their own way took the first steps towards harnessing the artistic potential of dramatic play to the educational demands of the classroom. Ward was careful to pay tribute to the theatrical traditions that represented for her the grown-up art-form of drama. Peter Slade cast caution and theatrics to the winds, and probably did more harm than good in the short term, not by his revolutionary demand that Child Drama be recognised as complete and an art-form in itself, but in his complementary dismissal of standard conventions of theatre of his time and his bellicose response to those who defended them. Brian Way's adoption of theatre exercises to manage improvised dramatic art only managed to further domesticate it rather than reassert the aesthetic, and the blood pressure of John Allen and the guardians of 'Art-form' continued to rise.

One of Dorothy Heathcote's lasting achievements, though an indirect one rarely ascribed to her, is in fact in foreshadowing how the third pillar of art can manageably take its place in the curriculum of drama in schools, right through to senior level. Back in her famous filmed manifesto, *Three Looms Waiting*, she explicitly identified the artistic demands of working in collaborative playmaking with youth theatre members. This, together with the other three excerpts of improvised drama with primary children, special needs children and young offenders, made a very strong implicit argument about the artistic potential of drama-in-education, or process drama. However, the pedagogical excitement that her techniques generated, and the fact that they were clearly allied to the improvisation/process/child drama movement, very much overshadowed this artistic statement. The teachers who followed her copied the pedagogy (or tried to), and on the whole neglected the art-form. She and her amanuensis Gavin Bolton both tried to reassert artistic credentials for her kind of drama, but they too were so focussed on the relationship with learning that their defences were overlooked by the educators and still too subtle for the theatre folk – as can be seen in that fateful 1978 Riverside Conference, where their work and their writing mystified the theatre practitioners, who couldn't see much theatre in either.

Partly in response to the growing attacks described in Chapter 6, a counter-offensive developed throughout the 1980s within the process movement. It was around this time that the term 'process drama' emerged simultaneously in several places. This was not just defensive, but at first driven mainly, especially outside the UK, by the desire to explore the artistic possibilities of process drama, and discover if in fact what we were working with was effectively a new dramatic form or genre. A number of writer/practitioners, including Bolton and David Davis in the UK decided to go back to the basic elements of dramatic art-form (as identified by Aristotle and his successors) and see if these actually fitted process drama and even children's dramatic play. In Australia, strongly influenced by Heathcote and taking up her theatre cues, Pam Gaudry and Roma Burgess were already reframing Aristotle's elements metaphorically in terms of 'the teacher as playwright' with the drama lesson (any kind of drama lesson) as 'script', categorising the basic styles as 'naturalistic', 'epic' or 'anti-theatre', and identifying such basic elements as *focus on event, focus on place, focus on time*, and *impact*, in terms of *dilemma, surprise, suspense, irony* and *symbol* (1985: 83–93). They wove these seamlessly into a secondary school drama curriculum framework that made approximately equal space for *playmaking*, with a strong emphasis on both group-devised and process work, along with *performing* and *appreciating* – a prescient move, though not explicitly signalled.

Brad Haseman and John O'Toole followed these leads in the impertinently titled *Dramawise* (1987) by updating Aristotle, constructing a model of those basic elements of dramatic form which are common to all manifestations of drama and theatre, right along the continuum, from dramatic play, through process drama and playbuilding, to classic play-text and performance. Naturally we identified largely the same elements as Bolton and Davis, and Burgess and Gaudry. These classroom textbook approaches to discovering or rediscovering the artistry of process drama were also being theorised, most celebratedly by Cecily O'Neill in her book *Dramaworlds* (1995), whose back cover blurb boldly identifies process drama as 'an essential part of today's theatre'. A little earlier, this author had followed our textbook up by using our structural model specifically to investigate the artistic dynamics and effects of processual drama forms, not their educational purposes (O'Toole 1992). Furthermore, the limitations of instructional role-play, simulation and sociodrama as either a motivating force or an effective pedagogy are a direct result of the exclusion of art-form, as we have seen. As both theory and practice were developing in understanding and sophistication, something else was dawning: that the better the grasp of the art-form, the better would be the articulation of meaning; in other words, the better the art, the better the learning.

Resolving the Conundrum: The Whole Curriculum

By the early 1990s, the conditions were ripe for a formal synthesis of *playmaking* with *performing* and *appreciating*: in the metaphor heading this chapter, standing a practical drama curriculum firmly on its three pillars. Burgess and Gaudry had shown the way. Student-devised drama, both as playbuilding and its allied forms, and as process drama, had effectively established its credentials.

Across the broader field of arts education, including music, dance and visual arts at least, the philosophers were constructing basically the same edifice, followed closely by the curriculum designers. In Australia, Warren Lett among others had already identified that when people engage with the arts, they do so effectively in one of three modes: in Lett's words as 'maker', then 'remaking or performing', then 'reception' (1982: 7) – i.e., as (a) *artist – making* art, (b) *performer – re-making, interpreting* or *communicating* art or (c) *audience – receiving, responding* to or *appreciating* art. Just at this time, the arts were forcing their way into the core curriculum as a single, more or less unified *key learning area*, and in order to be accepted needed to present a common rationale, comparable practice and equitable assessment. New South Wales and Queensland have both adopted just this paradigm and language, with the three dimensions entitled *making, performing* and *appreciating* in New South Wales, and *forming, presenting* and *responding* in Queensland, where the Senior Drama Syllabus and Years 1–10 Drama Guidelines were being written almost at the same time. These three dimensions in essence have subsequently been adopted as the organising strands right across all the art-forms in the 2002 Years 1–10 Arts Syllabus, with each art-form using its preferred terminology: dance (*choreographing, performing, appreciating*), drama (*forming, presenting, responding*), media (*constructing, producing, responding*), music (*aurally and visually identifying and responding to music, singing and playing, reading and writing . . . including arranging and composing*) and visual arts (*making images and objects, making and displaying, appraising images and objects*).

It has not quite been plain sailing. Curriculum's demand for *absolute* comparability imposes strains on the notion of the commonality of the arts and the goodwill of the art-forms towards each other. Music should actually fit very comfortably within this paradigm. However, the music educators are still fighting (and mainly in-fighting) for the full inclusion of *forming*, i.e., composing. Look at how prolix music's terminology for labelling its strands is, and also notice that unlike all the others, the *forming* dimension (composing and arranging) comes last, almost as an afterthought; this betrays the innate unease and dissension within the discipline. A genuine disparity exists between the performing and the visual and plastic arts, for which, of course, *presenting* is usually much less significant, or even vestigial. For visual arts, making and appreciating are really the only two dimensions that count. Unfortunately, school curricular and assessment structures do not permit the flexibility to recognise such natural disparities. Once more the unease is plainly visible in the language with its tortuous repetitions. This is hardly surprising, since in that curriculum, the driving force came from the performing arts, with drama's voice a dominant one, unusually. Nationally, the same uneasiness is evident. The provisional National Curriculum Framework of 1994 was effectually written by two visual artists, and so the forming and presenting dimensions have been conflated into *creating, making and presenting*; and responding divided into two distinct components: *arts criticism and aesthetics; and past and present contexts.*

In contemporary syllabuses around Australia at least, and often elsewhere, drama as art-form balances stably and comfortably on its three pillars, of roughly equal size and substance. In secondary schools, drama often gets a narrow perch on the junior timetable, where process drama turns towards playbuilding, and leads naturally to performing and responding. By senior secondary levels, all students are expected to engage with major movements of world theatre and texts as well as their own drama: in Queensland, there are three content categories of the syllabus: student-devised drama, Australian drama and world drama. For student-devised drama, they are expected to complete not only *forming* but also *presenting* and *responding* tasks, such as critical analysis of their work. *Forming* tasks in the latter two categories include pastiche scenario and scriptwriting, writing scenes beyond the texts, directing and design assignments.

In early childhood and primary education, the emphasis tends to be stronger on forming rather than performing or responding – on dramatic play and (where teachers know it and can help do it) on process drama and playmaking. Drama is rarely timetabled separately, especially in state schools, and primary drama specialists are even rarer. This means inevitably that there is a strong emphasis on drama for growth, and drama as a learning medium – where the teacher can attain the prescribed drama outcomes while actually timetabled for English, social studies or health and physical education.

In terms of performing drama, most current textbooks, exemplars and on-line resources strongly recommend playbuilding with young children and transforming process dramas in preference to the performing of scripted text written by other people. If driven by authentic emotion and understanding of situation and character, the children will find the right words for themselves, and learn and use the appropriate language registers. The 'if' is the problem, and many teachers untrained in drama feel themselves inadequate to generate authentic dramatic feeling, and besides, don't really know that drama is anything more than acting out scripts like people do in a theatre. Provision for these fearful souls has grown from the scripts for Empire Day and school assemblies put out weekly by a helpful Victorian Education Department in the 1960s. There is an enthusiastic commercial industry of scripts for children to perform, ranging from the challenging and powerful to mawkish and patronising insults to young people's intellects. As Finlay-Johnson and Cook demonstrated so long ago and so categorically, young children are quite capable of engaging with real dramatic substance, including Shakespeare and classic text. The playscript, however, grand or trivial, is not a let-off for the inexperienced teacher, but equally a minefield, as having to grapple with, learn and perform other people's text is itself a barrier to the identification and authentic understanding and emotion. The usually trenchant John Allen sums up the dilemma shrewdly and cautiously. As the most thoughtful and magnanimous defender of drama as an art-form, he should perhaps appropriately be given the last word in this chapter:

> If children can read and speak with reasonable fluency they do not find it particularly difficult to learn lines. Whether it is desirable that they should do so is another matter. Contemporary opinion seems on the whole not to favour the practice, but I think that very often contemporary opinion is being a little mealy-mouthed. To learn the lines of a play is like learning the lines of a poem or song: it is to come into sharp contact with inherited form. The extent that this is desirable is a matter of relationship with the child's own creative work. (1979: 129).

References

Allen, J. (1979). *Drama in schools: Its theory and practice*. London: Heinemann.

Atwan, R. (1999). Shakespeare: The invention of the human: Review. *The Boston Review*. Feb-March. http://bostonreview.net/BR24.1/atwan.html Retrieved 29 August 2007.

Barthes, R. (1977). *Image, music, text*. Translated Stephen Heath. London: Fontana. First published in *Aspen* (1967).

Bray, E. (1976). *Are we heroes? Experiences in educational drama*. Kensington NSW: University of New South Wales press.

Bray, E. (1991). *Playbuilding : A guide for group creation of plays with young people*. Sydney: Currency Press.

Burton, E. J. (1955). *Drama in schools – Approaches, methods and activities*. London: Herbert Jenkins.

Cook, C. (1917). *The Play Way*. London: Heinemann.

Creaser, B. (1990). *Pretend play: A natural path to learning*. Watson, ACT: Australian Early Childhood Association.

Dunn, J. (2002). *Imagined worlds in play*. Unpublished PhD thesis. Brisbane: Griffith University.

Finlay-Johnson, H. (1907). *The dramatic method of teaching*. London: Nisbet.

Gaudry, P., & Burgess, R. (1985). *Time for drama: A handbook for secondary teachers*. Melbourne: Longman Cheshire.

Giffin, H. (1990).To say and not to say: skills of dramatic play. *Youth Theatre Journal, 5*(2), 14–20.

Hornbrook, D. (1991). *Education as dramatic art*. Oxford: Blackwell.

Iser, W. (1978). *The act of reading : A theory of aesthetic response*. London: Routledge & Kegan Paul.

Kempe, A., & Nicholson, H. (2001). *Learning to teach drama 11–18*. London: Continuum.

Lett, W. (1982). The framing of realities: From actual to virtual, children's thinking and making in the arts. *NADIE Journal (now NJ), 7*(2), 6–18.

Mangeni, P. (2000). One earth one family: Drama and environmental education. In J. O'Toole & M. Lepp (Eds.), *Drama for life*. Brisbane: Playlab Press.

Oddey, A. (1996). *Devising theatre: A practical and theoretical handbook*. London: Routledge.

Opie, I., & Opie, P. (1959). *The lore and language of schoolchildren*. London: Oxford University Press.

O'Neill, C. (1995). *Drama worlds: A framework for process drama*. Portsmouth, NH: Heinemann.

O'Toole, J. (1992). *The process of drama: Negotiating art-form and meaning*. London: Routledge.

Payne, B. Iden. (1952). Theatre training in England and America. *Educational Theatre Journal*, *4*(4), 298–302, (December, 1952).

Prior, R. (2004). *Characterising actor trainers' understanding of their practice in Australian and English drama schools*. Unpublished Ph.D. Thesis. Brisbane: Griffith University.

Queensland Studies Authority. (2001). *Senior Drama Syllabus*. http://www.qsa.qld.edu.au/yrs11_12/subjects/drama/syllabus.pdf Retrieved 30 August 2007.

Royal Shakespeare Company. (2007). http://www.rsc.org.uk/learning/4487.aspx; and associated promotional materials. Retrieved 29 August 2007.

Slade, P. (1954). *Child drama*. London: Hodder and Stoughton.

Swanwick, K. (1979). *A basis for music education*. Windsor: National Foundation for Educational Research.

Tarlington, C., & Michaels, W. (1995). *Building plays : Simple playbuilding techniques at work*. Markham, ON: Pembroke.

Taylor, P. (1995). *Pre-text and story drama: The artistry of Cecily O'Neill and David Booth*. Brisbane: National Association for Drama in Education.

Willis, P. (1990). *Common culture: Symbolic work at play in the everyday cultures of the young*. Milton Keynes: Open University Press.

Part III
Drama in Action in Contemporary Curriculum

Chapter 8
Doorway Politics: Cracking an Education System

John O'Toole and Madonna Stinson

Part One: Queensland – A Case Study

It is the early 1970s. As pilots from the Southern States fly over the State border, they can rarely resist warning passengers: 'Ladies and Gentlemen, we are now entering Queensland – please put your watches back 50 years'. Sydneysiders laugh appreciatively, and Queenslanders squirm resentfully. Queensland does not have summer Daylight Saving Time. It is also known as The Deep North. It is the only State where more than half the population lives outside the environs of the capital, and the rural electorates are enormous. As a result, a gerrymandered system of government has evolved, initially to give the scattered country districts more of a voice. Started years earlier by a postwar descendant of the world's first Labour government, the gerrymander has been, for over 20 years, ruthlessly exercised and expanded by a very conservative coalition dominated by a Country Party faction that has kept Queensland culturally 'traditional' – i.e., white angloceltic. It also savagely suppresses dissent, such as anti-Vietnam and anti-apartheid protests, which are nationwide a part of the passionate debate about Australia's changing allegiances and cultural profile.

In this unlikely setting, a wonderful little irony is unfolding in the education world: a revolutionary systemic change that will make more possible the new enacted and experiential curricula described in Chapter 2, and incidentally open the door for drama to sneak into the House of Curriculum.

The old gents of the Country Party cabinet did not know what they did, which in retrospect seems to have been mainly out of anti-intellectual spite. The inner cabinet were all men, all over 50, all country-bred, and we believe that they had all left school at the end of elementary school; all except one, who had done a further education course to the ripe age of 13, so they made him Minister of Education. A few were autodidacts with a respect for culture and education. The Premier and his cronies were not. In that politically and intellectually volatile decade, the ideas that were naturally challenging traditionalism found their most energetic expression, in Queensland as elsewhere, in the University. The students and lecturers of the University of Queensland were right at the front of protest meetings and marches, some becoming popular heroes. The Premier's response was to ban the meetings

J. O'Toole et al., *Drama and Curriculum,* Landscapes: the Arts, Aesthetics, and Education 6, DOI 10.1007/978-1-4020-9370-8_9, © Springer Science+Business Media B.V. 2009

and even the right to march, which led to many ugly and violent confrontations. Those old men of the government who had always distrusted book learning and its propensity to put ideas into people's heads, how they hated the University. However, the University was federally funded, and the government could not do anything to punish it. Or could they?

The University, as was common at the time in Australia, following the British system, controlled the State school examinations. The authority of the University over the examinations was both far-reaching and educationally crippling, in terms of contemporary curricular ideas. That's the first part of the irony – the free-thinking challenge that the student and lecturer protesters represented was certainly not fostered by the University-driven school examination system. Its interest was in ensuring a continuous and well-schooled flow of compliant, literate and numerate candidates into the University, particularly to feed the increasingly ravenous faculties of Medicine, Law and Engineering. So the education systems were geared up for this task, even though only a small fraction of children would actually be able to reach the University. Objectives (for this read 'mastery of content') ruled. Tests were administered weekly. The season when the jacarandas bloomed was spoilt for generations of senior students, as this was the time of the annual public examinations. Maths and the more mechanical aspects of English and comprehension were supreme, with science next, and social studies somewhere behind, and then other humanities fitted in when and if time could be found for them.

Never mind such details. The Government had just one chance to reduce the influence of the University and they took it. They took the school examinations away from the University, and sent out their education department officers to find some other system. Preferably one that could be directly answerable and responsible to 'the people', 'the parents' – for the government was populistic – taking the power out of the hands of the intellectuals. Off went the officers, initially baffled at such a task. However, some of them did read books about curriculum, and they were hearing about experiments in School-Based Curriculum Development (SBCD), in the UK and Canada chiefly. In that system apparently schools and teachers controlled their own assessment; schools and groups of schools set their own curriculum and assessed it internally, moderating the results with other schools rather than having a single, monolithic external examination setup. In the UK, it was known as 'Mode 3' and could count for up to a set percentage (usually 40–60%) of the total assessment.

School-based assessment had other potential advantages, apart from local autonomy over the marking and results. If schools could control what they assessed, the logical corollary was that potentially they could be equally in control of what they taught, even what subjects they chose, or what branches of knowledge they chose to call subjects. More radical still, the local community and the parents might even get a say in this. Other states in Australia were toying with the idea, but no authority had gone the whole hog and completely scrapped the yardstick of an external examination that was the same for all students statewide. However, if the Queensland government wanted something entirely different, where the community and the parents were in control, this was what they could have. So, almost overnight, examinations were scrapped, along with the panoply of weekly standardised tests in maths and English, and teachers came back after the school holidays to find a new and mystifying landscape.

For a few years, it was very difficult and traumatic for many teachers, especially older ones. Nobody local had any idea how this new system would work. No teachers had been trained to think up their own long-term curriculum plans, lessons and their own assessment. Where possible, many clung to what they knew and continued to set regular tests. Others bravely ventured into the new territory. After almost a decade of flailing around and gradually settling down, a thoroughgoing review of the new system, *RoSBA* (*Review of School-Based Assessment*), was impressively executed in 1978 by the new Board of Secondary School Studies, with the assistance of the much reviled University academics, such as Royce Sadler, an expert in criterion-based assessment. The revised system was implemented from 1981 and has been in place ever since.

Since then, teachers, parents and children have flourished under school-based curriculum development and assessment. Many cannot conceive of the system operating any other way. We now have grandparents who have never known common public examinations. Like any system, the advantages are a matter of swings and roundabouts – there is still ongoing debate, for instance, about the relative amount of stress produced by facing an annual examination on which everything depends, versus the constant pressure of having all work assessed. There are few governments brave enough to follow Queensland in entirely scrapping a central examination (in Australia, only the Australian Capital Territory), but few in Queensland would want to see the assessment system changed back to common public examinations as the only measure of educational achievement. And the old men of the Country Party? Long gone, along with the gerrymander, hoist by their own petard and swept out in a scandal of corruption. Queensland is no longer the Deep North, but the Smart State.

We have described this generic educational sea-change in so much detail because it is a vivid and quite significant example of the systemic destabilisation that seems to be one of the necessary preconditions for drama to get more than a foot in the door. A similar, if not so radical, change happened elsewhere, as we will show. Other preconditions are necessary, too, one of which is a local community of drama practitioners with the readiness to take opportunities to slide in whenever or however the door or even a window opens a chink. So when drama does appear in the building, it takes shape quite diversely. We will address the synergies and disparities among the Australian states in more detail later in this chapter, as they are emblematic of the opportunities and constraints faced by drama worldwide.

Drama in the Driveway

In that significant decade when school-based assessment was replacing state examinations, the years 1–10 curriculum in Queensland public (i.e., state-run) schools, as in most states, was pretty basic, with four major areas of study: English, maths, science and social studies. Anything else was a bonus. The State education system had little money available for bonuses. Music perched just inside the door, as did physical education (with dance), and the education department managed to accredit trained primary specialist teachers in these two subjects, still the only specialist primary teachers in Queensland state schools. In one sense, this shows the respect that the arts – as much as sport – do generate in Australia: in a cash-strapped curriculum, not at the centre, maybe, but as an affectionately acknowledged add-on. It also shows that for art, music and dance, the system providers acknowledge that specially trained skills beyond the reach of garden variety primary teachers may be needed.

The merit of specialist primary arts teachers is still hotly disputed. On the one hand, they do (or should) guarantee that children will get properly skilled tuition and pedagogy in the art-form. On the other, this is usually for half an hour a week or so, in a kind of ghetto situation, which many teachers are not able to relate to the rest of their curriculum or integrate into it. Some even feel that the half-hour is enough, which absolves them from mentioning the arts, let alone teaching them.

There was virtually no mention of such a being as a drama teacher or of drama as a subject (though one survivor of that period clearly does remember being appointed as a drama teacher to a local state high school in 1976). The proposal in 1977 that there should be a curriculum for drama, presented by the recently formed Queensland Association for Drama in Education (QADIE), drew an amused laugh from the senior curriculum officer who received it. Not only there was no call for it but 'the parents would not stand for it' – they wanted their children to focus on the basics, and drama would be seen as a diversion. The proposal was neither formally acknowledged nor considered. This was understandable, since drama barely figured in Department documents or syllabuses. Three years before our smirking rebuff, there had been one quite startling near miss for drama. The Queensland government in spite of its anti-intellectualism was not altogether unsympathetic to the arts – one Education Minister was energetically supportive, and himself had (country) artistic accomplishments such as deftly playing the musical saw, as John heard with his own ears! In 1974, the Government authorised the State Department to gazette three new positions for *arts supervisors*: one for music, one for visual arts and . . . almost incredibly . . . one for drama. Only the first two were appointed; the drama position lapsed – and there was no QADIE then to fight for it.

The fledgling drama education community recognised that a different strategy was needed, a more diffuse one which took account of where drama might be received warmly within the system – if not through the front door, then through the windows; and windows of opportunity there were, in plenty, though none of them quite big enough to let in a new teaching force armed with a new subject.

There was mention of drama, certainly, within English literature syllabuses, with Shakespeare a standard component, and more nervously, contemporary Australian plays like *Summer of the Seventeenth Doll*. Not a strong argument in itself at the time for specialist teaching – would you have specialist poetry teachers? And literature was already losing ground internally in the English community to the rising tide of literacy, labelled at this time as *language arts*. For a time, the Queensland drama community looked at what they were doing in the UK and Tasmania, where drama was part of the language work.

Then there was the school play, or musical as it usually was in Queensland. In secondary schools, this was invariably extra-curricular, but quite big business sometimes, and usually with tendrils reaching into the art, music, English and even manual arts and science classrooms – somebody had to make the sets and manage the technical effects. In primary schools, good teachers and principals have always made space for children to perform to other children and to parents, in one way or another.

As ever, the Catholic and independent schools cherished arts learning, seeing it as an important part of cultural heritage. Some schools made children pay for speech and drama classes, as they had to for flute, dance or specialised sports or gymnastic coaching. *Speech and Drama* had their well-organised educational network including examinations, local (*AMEB – Australian Music Education Board*) and UK based (*Trinity College*). Some schools did incorporate them in the curriculum, and *Junior* and *Senior Speech and Drama* were the first manifestations of drama to successfully exploit the school-based curriculum and assessment system to become official 'Board'-registered subjects. Even before that, in the 1950s, *Art of Speech* – with a little drama involved – was a small elective component of the old university exam system.

The Colleges of Advanced Education (CAEs), as the teachers' colleges became known after 1973, had speech and communication departments, whose main function was to provide beginning teachers with the skills of self-presentation and managing group dynamics. These classes were invariably drama-based. Interestingly, they were usually very popular, and spawned highly popular elective studies in drama. Some of this was straight production work, often stirring, provocative and political theatre characteristic of the new and fringe theatre of the time. Productions increasingly included the more processual forms of improvisation, and community theatre, and theatre-in-education. In 1980, the first of these sets of popular electives gelled into a formal 'major study' of drama as a second teaching area for secondary schools, followed 5 years later by a 4-year specialist B.Ed with drama. By this time, it was almost too late, as drama was off and running in the secondary schools.

In 1976, QADIE was founded, in the main by lecturers from these colleges, some of whom had trained in the UK, USA and interstate, combined with passionate teachers who were advocating drama from inside their schools, and some of the more forward-looking Speech and Drama teachers. The same year the National Association (NADIE) was founded, led and dominated in the early years by the much more advanced and sophisticated state associations from Victoria and New South Wales. These states had drama advisory services and established drama courses in their schools. They were inclusive, generous and helpful, giving the stripling Queensland organisation both good advice and some bargaining power.

All the state associations were also intensely aware of their role as lobbyists and advocates for drama, and wherever possible worked opportunistically to increase drama's influence or even get a hearing. Sometimes, indeed, they worked with explicitly political nous, such as in the 'beer, beards & boots strategy' deployed by QADIE for the Queensland Education Department. At that time, all the key administrators in the department were men, and there was a very sporty, 'blokey' (male) culture. For example, one deputy director, who had been identified through QADIE personal contacts as having a potential interest in drama, was an ex-international footballer. QADIE recognised that where drama was noticed at all, it was perceived as an occupation more for girls than boys: partly because of Drama's association with *Speech and Drama* in mainly girls' private schools; probably partly due to the fact that nearly all the leading lights in theatre in Queensland and the majority of members of theatre groups were female; and partly also due to the broader social stereotypes about drama. QADIE had a number of its most high-profile members who were bearded and quite 'blokey' men. One or more of these invariably formed the spearheads of representations to the male senior administrators in the Education Department, often 'over a few beers', which proved quite a successful strategy for some years, until the culture changed enough for a less-gendered strategy, and allowed for the reassertion of women as the dominant forces in QADIE and nationally. The social forces have not changed very much, and drama is still overwhelmingly a female dominated subject in schools and universities in Australia and Queensland. At the national level, NADIE's first five presidents were male (though not all bearded!), and did most of the national lobbying. For over 30 years, both QADIE and NADIE have been a very energetic and effective network, support system and lobby group for drama in Queensland and nationally – and in the last 15 years, internationally. Jointly in 1995, both organisations hosted the second World Congress of Drama/Theatre and Education in Brisbane.

The CAEs in the 1970s were also staffed by determined and passionate drama or speech and drama professionals, who formed a large proportion of the core of these budding state and national drama education associations. Some of these CAEs had deliberately employed lecturers from what were perceived as centres of drama education and innovation, particularly the UK, and the USA. An indirect result of this (often through personal contacts of those imports) was the influential visits of a number of key overseas innovators – in Victoria, Canadian drama education scholar Richard Courtney, in New South Wales and South Australia the revered English expert Dorothy Heathcote. Queensland saw lengthy visits from other key drama and arts-in-education pioneers from the British Isles: Gavin Bolton in 1979, Robert Witkin in 1980 and Cecily O'Neill in 1987.

In Through the Porch

Coincidentally, in the Queensland Education Department 'there was movement at the station for the word had passed around', in the words of one of Australia's most famous poems. Although back at the homestead – central office – there was little but the waggish response of the curriculum officer to the thought of drama in the curriculum, out in the 'bush' a lot was happening, not least because of those calculated raids by the drama community. The Director of Pre-School Education, Gerald Ashby, whose revolutionary noncurriculum policy was noted in Chapter 1, got together in 1975 with a local theatre company and sponsored the Early Childhood Drama Project (ECDP), a theatre-in-education group for children between the ages of 3 and 8. The next year, a drama lecturer, Gail Wiltshire, returned from England where she had seen some theatre-in-education. She managed to convince the North Brisbane Director of Education of the value of locally based theatre in education, which she assured him she had invented herself (news travelled slowly in the corridors of education and he'd presumably not heard of ECDP). She launched a couple of state-funded T-i-E teams, and with them Queensland's first state school specialist drama teaching careers – including Madonna's. The following year, on the other side of the river, Brisbane South Region independently developed a drama resource project, directed by a brilliant young drama teacher, Brad Haseman. In the next few years, a similar team was started in the Special Education directorate, when Gerald Ashby moved there. Several regional drama advisors were appointed, based in sizeable districts like Rockhampton and the Gold Coast, and even the little country town of Roma. These did not usually last long, as they were lone rangers without much of a support system.

And the invitation of the School-based assessment was being fervently accepted. Teachers from four public schools who were passionate about theatre and production got together, helped by Paul Paye, a dynamic CAE lecturer with a background in American summer stock theatre, and trialled a new syllabus in *Theatre*. This was in competition with the existing *Speech and Drama* syllabuses, which were almost exclusively the province initially of the private and Catholic schools. It was a roaring success, and after a 2-year pilot it too became a 'Board' subject, so schools could choose either *Theatre* or *Speech and Drama*. Throughout the 1980s, secondary drama grew like Topsy – by far the fastest growing subject area in the state. In 1979, Years 11 and 12 (Senior syllabus) students studying drama-related subjects totalled under a thousand. In 1989, the number was over 13,000. Such growth can be attributed to student and parent choice, and a significant enticement was that study in these areas was credited toward university entrance, a circumstance that was not common to all states, e.g., Western Australia had to wait for this until 2001.

The popularity of the school syllabuses had preempted the tertiary drama training, and it was the Board of Secondary School Studies, which really helped to professionalise the drama teaching community. The Board controlled central curriculum development and school-based assessment through the 1980s and 1990s in secondary schools (and gradually accrued 'S's until it was the Board of *Senior Secondary School Studies*), with highly competent advisers[1] working for the Board and the Department of Education. They gave help, advice and stability to what was – particularly in the early days – an undertrained teaching force. These novice drama teachers had not only to teach and assess the syllabuses, but also actually conceive and structure the school programs themselves following the guidelines laid out in the syllabus documents published by the Board. Queensland was very fortunate in that these advisers worked very closely with the teacher educators and with the experienced teachers in QADIE in the ongoing establishment of drama.

---

[1] Most influentially, at the Board of Secondary School Studies: (the late) Robin Thomas, Christine Heywood; Department of Education: Sue Elmes.

In the ever-necessary positioning and lobbying, in Queensland as in other states, political opportunities presented themselves, and, about equally, political threats to be fought and averted.

By the mid 1980s too, an initiative that was already established interstate, specialist Performing Arts High Schools, had been introduced into Queensland. These offered some students an enriched program in performing arts, in 'Centres for Artistic Development' (with the rather unfortunate acronym of CADs). This was in line with current political rhetoric about 'excellence in schooling' and corresponding state moves towards the establishment of schools, which would foster selective excellence – including theatre, music, dance, science and various sports.

So much for the resistance from parents.

Drama's first real toe-hold in the Queensland primary curriculum had to wait until 1991, with the preparation and publication of a very thoughtfully conceived and consultatively written statewide *Years* 1–10 *Curriculum Guide: Drama Makes Meaning*[2] (Queensland Department of Education 1991). It was quite consonant with the current theories of curriculum as 'planned, enacted and lived' ... at least, as far as any statewide curriculum document could be, which truly was not very far. At last, an official document in primary education, and one that would at least give drama parity with visual arts and music ... well, nearly. It was originally intended that it be a 'syllabus', which would have been a momentous piece of labelling, since 'syllabus' meant that the subject was mandated – i.e., all children had to be taught according to the set curriculum. Just before its completion, the Education Department got cold feet and reduced it to a 'curriculum guide', meaning that the Department thought it would be nice if teachers would teach it. Although the document was very accessible, engagingly and clearly written and had a number of practical examples, it was not widely used. By lowering the status of the document from syllabus to curriculum guide, the Education Department was able to avoid allocating funds for implementation support – if schools *had* to teach it then teachers would need professional development, but if it was not a syllabus, then implementation support was not necessary. Mandation of drama in Queensland had to wait until 2002. And that's a whole new story, which you will find in Chapter 9.

Part Two: Widening the Case Study

This section extrapolates from the Queensland experience some of the main factors that contributed to the growth of drama across Australia, in less than 40 years, from a basically extra-curricular activity, to a subject that has at least some establishment and varying currency, throughout the years of schooling in all states. The contribution of these factors has been ambivalent or has come at a cost, and at times has provided stumbling blocks, but they are all significant. They resonate sufficiently

---

[2] Published by the Queensland Department of Education but substantively written by Debbie Wall.

with other experiences worldwide to be identified as key factors in getting the giant in through the door of the curriculum.

The snapshot of Queensland illustrates a number of important factors in the penetration of drama into the house of schooling. Like any case study, some of these key factors are common to all other cases, others only to some. Many of the same forces were working in other states, sometimes a decade or two earlier, and many of the most potent were happening during 'that halcyon period' the 1970s, so described by a survivor from the earlier days, Tasmanian Beth Parsons, herself a very influential doorway politician. The changes in go-ahead little Tasmania in the 1950s and 1960s were among drama's first real steps into the curriculum in Australia. These happened very unevenly among the states, each of which had all their schools systems (state, church and private schools) doggedly independent from any other state, as well as each other. The main winds of changes blew as usual from England. The similar changes, which had been happening in the USA throughout the century, were a less potent influence on Australia.

Consultation with numerous drama pioneers in all states of Australia has helped us to identify and corroborate a number of these key factors in operation in all or most states, though not always identically. The first four of these may be classed as 'pass key' factors, to pursue our 'house and doorway' metaphor: keys that have given drama the right to walk straight in unchallenged, and at least take up temporary residency.

The Extra-Curricular Pass-Key (in from the Garden)

In many schools in all states, drama has been very welcome in the garden, often as a source of great public pride to the householder (the principal). The more prestigious the school – especially in the private sector – the more likely it is to have a strong tradition of performance drama, as it is to have well-supported and high-profile sport. The flowers are mostly very colourful, and quite varied: school plays, school musicals, primary Nativity plays, inter-school drama festivals, junior school play competitions, speech-night dramatic presentations and extravaganzas, Rock Eisteddfods, and just plain drama clubs.

From the extra-curriculum to the cocurriculum. In many states, Wednesday afternoons is a time that is traditionally given over to sport. Drama has, in many schools, been imported in an attempt to deal with the students who resist sport or who can't make the teams. This has of course done nothing either to dismantle the polarisation between sport and the arts, which has been a feature of Australian popular cultural perception, or to promote the image of drama as a red-blooded activity for the best and bravest.

Regular assemblies, religious or secular, are part of the fabric of schooling, and primary principals especially showcase the children's accomplishments with dramatic performances. In Victoria in the 1960s, the state education department put out a regular magazine for primary schools, including a playscript, which the children could act in their classes or present for assembly: a 'play for Empire Day', or perhaps an adaptation of Enid Blyton.

Speech and Drama as a Pass-Key

In some schools, *Speech and Drama* has meant enough to the management of the schools and the parents for them to include it in their regular curriculum, rather than just as an optional extra. And that is one small step for *Speech* and *Drama*, one giant step for drama. By the 1960s, speech and drama featured quite prominently in all states at least in the cocurriculum, and we have seen how in Queensland it was in the vanguard in taking advantage of the new school-based curriculum and assessment.

Drama first used this key to get through the door in a substantive way in Tasmania, through a piece of serendipity almost as random as the Queensland revolution. Clive Sansom, a renowned British speech and drama teacher, broadcaster and writer, became ill in 1950, and came with his Tasmanian wife to convalesce there and eventually immigrate. Their poetry recitals captivated the attention of the Director-General of Education, and he promptly ordered that *Art of Speech* should be taught in all Tasmanian state schools, to University matriculation level. In 1974, new Superintendent of Speech Beth Parsons formally added the word *drama*, and in 1980 the first syllabus guidelines were for speech and drama. Oral language was still a prime focus through the next decade, with that first Australian research study of drama and language in 1984 (Schaffner, Parsons, Little, & Felton 1984 – see Chapter 3).

Sansom's influence percolated to the mainland, and combined with the private schools' Speech and Drama organisations in Victoria to form a significant part of the momentum towards drama itself. In NSW too, an Inspector of Schools with responsibility for Speech and Drama was appointed in the late 1960s. In Western Australia and Queensland at least, from the early 1970s, speech and drama was permitted as a subject component towards the University entrance examination – in WA 60%, in Queensland 100% (and that was before the shift to school-based assessment). During this period, there was a subtle but important shift in organisation and control, away from the cocurricular AMEB and Trinity College examinations, and into the state assessment systems.

The English Pass-Key

Drama's deep, parent–child relationship with English or language arts has been attended in Australia with all the struggles and negotiations for liberty of a typical adolescent. Traditionally in all states, secondary English has provided drama with its one real home in the curriculum, and (not so universally) primary English, or language arts. In Victoria, one secondary English period a week was devoted to drama, and in primary education, the UK texts on improvised drama were quite widely used by progressive-thinking teachers; for those less venturesome, those little plays printed in the Department's primary students' magazine often found their preparation and rehearsal time in language arts periods. In NSW in the same period, secondary English teachers were expected not only to study plays, but also to direct them, and towards the end of the decade, to help students develop improvised and group-written drama and theatre. In Western Australia, drama came under the direction of the English superintendent.

Chapter 7 has already explored the reasons for one major feature of Australian drama education: that Drama has left 'home' and the sheltered comforts of English and gone to make its own way in a shared house with a bunch of youngsters with similar interests and a group identity – with music, visual arts, dance and media, as the Key Learning Area of The Arts. (However, quite illogically, drama's older twin sisters 'literature' and 'creative writing' got left behind at home.) It actually means that drama can 'double dip', since drama is still included in many secondary English syllabuses. Relationships vary. There is cordial collaboration (many drama teachers also teach English, and vice versa). There is carefully demarcated territory ('we study texts, you do performance and improvisation'). Occasionally there is mutual incomprehension. A problem in several states is that English teachers 'are poorly prepared to teach drama as we know it' as one adviser tartly put it. The hegemony of English is a very powerful one, with both advantages and disadvantages. However, in Australia drama is now very much part of the arts, and perceived as such by ourselves, by all the educational systems, by most of the general public and by nearly all our other-arts colleagues.

Sharing a Pass-Key

The word 'nearly' in the last sentence is wryly used. The other arts have been a very influential factor in drama's growth, and often but not always a positive and support-ive one – sometimes they have been equivocal, occasionally hostile or obstructive. In all cases, visual arts and/or music have been the decisive forces. Drama, dance and media (and more recently multi- and hybrid arts) have in recent decades usually occupied a similar curricular position to each other, that of supplicant at the door, with – in most cases – drama making the early running and gaining the most estab-lishment. Dance usually had its perch in physical education, and media study like drama has been ambivalently growing under the hegemonic umbrella of English. New technologies and multimedia offer new horizons for convergence of science, arts and technology in multiarts and hybrid arts that are being eagerly explored by professional artists and by children in their own homes. However, these have largely been beyond the capacity of school curricula even to aspire to, let alone to implement.

Visual arts' and music's traditional curricular tenure, though often on the mar-gins, has resulted in significant and always influential liaisons and tensions with all these other arts. In some cases, art and music have taken a territorial stance, fearing that drama especially might prove a cuckoo in the nest – in one state, when a drama specialist was appointed Superintendent of the Arts, his colleagues 'thought it was the end of the world'. On the other hand, in South Australia, the late and legendary Garth Boomer, a drama and English specialist, was appointed in the 1970s as Arts Superintendent, and he is still widely remembered with admiration by curriculum theorists for his policy of 'negotiating the curriculum' (and his eponymous book from 1982). This is surely why South Australia was the first to come up with a drama syllabus for years 1–10: *Images of Life* (1981). In other states, too, very productive networking has happened, not always supported by the systems themselves. In New South Wales in the late 1990s, the old-fashioned perceptions of a meddlesome politician were enough to unravel a decade's real reform built by meticulous and supportive inter-arts networking, and drama nearly disappeared altogether. Over the Tasman Sea in New Zealand, drama's similar subordinate relationship to music and visual arts was the result of what started as a piece of opportunistic coat-tailing. This was generously permitted by visual arts, where drama sneaked in as early as the 1940s, as a Director-General besotted by the Arts-and-Crafts movement vigorously expanded the arts in schools. However, while visual arts built a comfortable establishment in schools and colleges for over half a century, drama has languished until recently.

Although the attitude to drama of other subject teachers and policy-makers has often been one of incomprehension, perhaps mixed with irritation when a noisy and flamboyant drama class distracts the quiet and decorous maths going on next door, other subjects have at times been serviceable companions, and helped to piggy-back drama in through the door. This is particularly so where drama is recognised as a pedagogy. In Victoria, back in the early 1960s two young teachers with exposure to drama were doing exciting activities in science classes, a tradition which still continues with a movement of science teachers who use drama in their classrooms, now completely independent of the drama education fraternity, each largely unaware of and unregarded by the other. (One of those science teachers became a drama lecturer, the other a celebrated action researcher.) Such unions have rarely become permanent or spread far, often owing to the inadequate grasp of drama skills and pedagogy that effective role-play and dramatic performance both demand.

Fifth Columnists and Insiders

Coming into the school under the coat-tails of other subjects is not just a matter of hitching a lift up the drive and through the door. There are a number of other gatekeepers, other key factors. First among the gatekeepers are the fifth columnists, the sympathetic and artistically inclined senior education officials, and the sympathetic principals, especially in private schools. In the Queensland Education Department, during the crucial growth period, there were about 10 senior officials, all told, seriously disposed towards drama. It is surely not a coincidence that many of these education office insiders are remembered with respect and fondness much more broadly than by the drama community. New Zealand's arts-and-crafts tragic, Clarence Beeby, is commemorated by a foundation for visual arts education that still flourishes, and has a page of his own in Wikipedia. So too does South Australia's Garth Boomer. Queensland Pre-School founding Director Gerald Ashby is remembered as 'one of the early childhood greats' (MacGowan 2007). Doug McDonell, the Principal of the Melbourne Secondary Teachers' College, who enthusiastically supported the drama training of teachers well before there were drama classes for them to take, has a building named after him at the University of Melbourne (O'Brien 1996). Perhaps more than their individual contributions, their influence emboldened other potentially sympathetic functionaries to create a network that would allow drama to develop and flourish widely enough to create a rhizomatic nourishment and support system for itself.

Overseas Influences

Inevitably in Australasia during the 1960s to the 1980s, we looked for and found inspiration from overseas, predominantly the UK, and to a lesser extent North America (Canada as much as the USA). Of course, it had already started to come of its own volition, occasionally in the flesh, such as Clive Sansom's fortuitous trip. However, in early days it came mainly in the form of textbooks and films, eagerly sought and often uncritically embraced. We have heard of the early use in Victoria of Bishop E.J. Burton's *Drama in Schools* and in Western Australia Winifred Ward's *Playmaking with Children*. Then swamping all others and by far the most influential in early times were Peter Slade's *Child Drama* (1956), Brian Way's *Development Through Drama* (1967), Dorothy Heathcote's film *Three Looms Waiting* (1971) and Gavin Bolton's *Towards a Theory of Drama in Education* (1979), especially the first two. In Queensland in 1976, there was no formal drama in state schools, but there was one book in every school – Brian Way's. In New Zealand in 2000, there were still only two drama books common to every college and university department: Peter Slade's and Brian Way's.

We didn't wait helplessly by the shore, however: in the 1970s and 1980s there were dozens of drama teachers who travelled from Australia to sit at the feet of the gurus of the time –first Slade, then Heathcote, Bolton, O'Neill and other UK centres such as Central School of Speech and Drama, Bretton Hall College and Rose Bruford College. Some went the other way, to Nellie McCaslin, David Booth and Richard Courtney in USA and Canada. These included many (around two dozen in all) who have been highly influential in the establishment of drama education in all states of Australia. Nearly all found a source of rich inspiration for their (our) own growth:

> In Britain I saw many of the leading exponents of educational drama. They are people with vision who live their subject, who are involved as imaginative and creative artists, yet who are still pragmatic educators. This combination of creative artist and committed theorist ... occurs often enough for us in this country [i.e., Australia] to be confident of the continued healthy growth of educational drama (Thorpe 1977).

Then we imported them. Literally, in the case of Tasmania, which sent over in the 1950s for a troupe of speech advisers to carry out Sansom's plans, who were all immigrated from the UK under the Ten Pound Immigrant scheme. Something very similar, but less formal, happened in South Australia, with a strong Rose Bruford College flavour. Other Britons, such as Roger Chapman and David Young, came out and founded or directed important theatre-in-education companies in South Australia, Western Australia and Tasmania. The tertiary colleges started trying to upskill their communication and drama departments by bringing in experienced teachers and lecturers from overseas. John was one of those in the mid-seventies, also brought in as a 'Ten Pound Pom' to join at least two other Britons, two Americans and two returned expatriates on the drama staffs of the Queensland teachers' colleges alone.

And we invited the stars to strut their stuff locally. It was a long way geographically and psychologically from the US and UK drama worlds to Australia, and visits were few at first. Christabel Burniston, the legendary founder of the English Speaking Board, came on a 1950s lecture tour to Australia (English Speaking Board 2007), and it is believed that Maisie Cobby also visited New Zealand and left her mark. In the 1970s, Courtney visited Victoria, Heathcote NSW and Bolton Queensland. This trickle ran much faster as soon as the NADIE had been established, with a more or less implicit policy of including at least one overseas speaker at the annual national conference, which was responsible for the important visits of experts like Ken Robinson (in 1981), David Hornbrook (who came in1983 but largely left his divisive UK influence at home), Cecily O'Neill (in 1987) and Norah Morgan and Juliana Saxton (in 1988).

The NADIE Conference of 1990, held in Sydney with a galaxy of international talent, was a watershed in terms of the relationship of Australian drama education with the rest of the world, as it more or less represented the end of the one-way traffic, and the beginning of Australia taking its place as a major exporter as well as importer of drama ideas. However, most of the story of this conference – the part over the watershed – belongs better in the next section, which explores how the local confidence grew.

State and National Associations

The first local watershed year was really 1976, when NADIE was founded, whose importance in the development of drama in Australia is incalculable. Before that, many drama teachers had found their first collegial home in the state Speech and Drama Associations from which many of the 'new' drama teachers were metamorphosing. Although parochial, drama did travel across borders, and occasionally its advocates did meet; one such significant rendezvous was New South Wales Educational Drama Association's first state drama conference at Terrigal in 1974. This was important partly because it was obviously one of those especially memorable events for those who attended – in the words of its director 30 years on: 'one of the most incredible experiences of my life – so vibrant, so exciting . . . we knew we were making history'. Just as importantly, there were a number of key pioneers from interstate, who took away not only new ideas, but a new sense of communitas that was to become embodied less than 2 years later.

In the mid-winter of 1976, in a chilly scout hut in the Adelaide Hills, South Australian Drama Adviser Gordon Foulds held a delegate meeting of members from all the (then) state educational drama associations. It was a contentious event, as such meetings are wont to be, and perhaps elegantly symbolic, in that not only was the discussion framed by plenty of active drama-sharing workshops, but the conflicts were actually played out in drama. The gentle warm-up and getting-to-know-you exercises of the conference organisers were swept away and replaced by an extended and deliberately provocative improvised drama about Middle-east terrorism – then as now a hot topic. It gingered up the debate, and robustness characterized the out-come. The new association was NADIE, a loose affiliation of the state associations, whose main purposes would be to hold an annual conference, provide regular publi-cations, and act as a cross-state lobby and advocacy group. History has proved it an ideal structure – productive, resilient and self-sustaining, able to acknowledge and utilise the diverse input of each state association.

Within 3 years, all the states and territories had affiliated with the new asso-ciation, and chipped in a proportion of their annual subscriptions to fund it. The local associations have quite distinct profiles and run their own business, their own state conferences and journals, and only appeal to the national association to help in moments of crisis, like the imminent disappearance of drama in 1989 in NSW, where the concerted lobbying from the national association and all states had some softening effect. Although all the state associations are still in existence bar the tiny, brave but underpopulated Northern Territory one, the larger ones have had the critical mass to survive and prosper best.

NADIE has flourished, too, with very few changes or breaks in the continuity. The national conference is still annual, and a very important time for teachers to get together and lose their sense of isolation as very small players of a minority game in a vast country. The *NADIE Journal* in the early 1990s reflected the growing interest in research by becoming one of the first refereed journals in the field. This caused some grumbling among the teachers who mainly scan journals for ideas for next Monday's class, and led to the publication of an annual practical magazine (ADEM – Australian Drama Education Magazine) that complements the flourishing magazines and newsletters of the state associations. There has been one solitary destabilising incident, which briefly threatened to split NADIE in 1982, a row over links with South African drama education during the period of cultural boycotts. No change more radical than consensually changing the association's name in 1998 from NADIE to Drama Australia has occurred since.

Two other events, both conferences, stand out in Drama Australia's history (and, we would maintain, drama education's history globally) as both affirmative and con-sequential in the long-term establishment of drama education. The first of these was the 1990 NADIE conference, which, as we have noted above, had a large number of overseas delegates and speakers. Rather to our surprise, some of these – notably the North Europeans – were highly respectful about the quality and sophistication of Australian drama education. We were so used to battling along with our own curricula, isolation, uninterested colleagues, etc., and clinging to each other muttering stirring words of support that we were quite taken aback by compliments. Contrastingly, we were repelled by the skirmishes these very visitors were having among themselves, as part of the Battle of the Paradigms, which was then at its height, and decided we would have none of it.

Thus emboldened, we started to reverse the trend of importing people to show us how to do it. The number of overseas experts invited to NADIE conferences took a dive. This 1990 conference also came at a time when important events were happening internationally, initiatives towards a more global presence for drama. Fifty-two Australians and several New Zealanders flooded the inaugural Congress in Porto, Portugal of what was there named IDEA (The International Drama/Theatre and Education Association). This Southern invasion of what had been intended as a restricted delegate conference was a factor in reshaping IDEA from what was intended by its founders, to what it is now. Immediately this broadened the Australian drama curriculum – for the first time we started meeting Africans, Eastern Europeans, South Americans, who were doing quite different things with drama in their schools and communities that we had not conceived of through our rather restricted pursuit of the previously dominant Western overseas models. We discovered that what we were doing was of interest to them too, and many of them, even those from the countries we had looked up to like Canada and the USA, envied us our level of curriculum establishment compared to their own (now that was a surprise). With the naive overconfidence of the toddler, we threw ourselves into the Byzantine ideological struggles over IDEA's foundation. More or less accidentally and only semiwittingly we tipped the balance of power, and found ourselves with the new global association's first Vice-President, Kate Donelan, and the next triennial Congress to host. That 2nd IDEA World Congress, held in Brisbane and incorporating the NADIE conference, was the second of the stand-out events in NADIE's history, and the more influential in terms of drama's place both in the educational establishment and in the curriculum. Its size (nearly 1200 delegates including 400 international and 500 from interstate) and its scope (13 international keynotes, 38 theatrical performances, 300 workshops and papers, a schools fieldwork program and a red-hot social club) surprised and impressed many colleagues in other disciplines until now far grander, and in education offices. In Brisbane, at this Congress, Australian drama education came of age.

Tertiary Education Influences

Drama Australia has always had a good proportion of its members in the tertiary sector, a reminder of what a potent influence the colleges and universities have been in the development of drama curriculum. Tertiary educators were often prime movers in the early days, in NSW, Tasmania and Western Australia; in Victoria, they contrived to be training drama teachers well in advance of any formal curriculum. The importance of the influence is most strikingly seen where it is absent. In the Boomer-inspired 1970s, when South Australia produced their pioneering *Images of Life* arts curriculum, there were a similar number of college drama educators to the bigger states, all of whom were influential in developing a curriculum and building a community of drama teachers. However, one might speculate that Boomer's very influence might have had a downside – since all teachers were expected to teach negotiatively and across disciplines, there was perhaps less territorialism and, therefore, less emphasis on specialist training in small subjects like drama; a perception emerged and remained that teachers did not have to be specially trained. As long as they were interested, they could teach drama – so 'people were recruited from all over the curriculum'. When one of the key early figures of tertiary education, Barbara Crompton, died in 1999, so did specialist drama teacher education; and so, to a large extent, did a thriving and dynamic drama education community. In New Zealand, the tertiary drama educators were until recently 'notable by their absence – certainly as a force for developing research or advocacy' – a definite variation from Australia, though not unheard-of in the UK.

In Australia, since 1991, all teachers' colleges and CAEs have been amalgamated into a unified University system. During all this period, drama has been fighting its own battle for recognition as a distinct discipline within the Universities, few of which, and none of the traditional ones, had established drama or theatre in the way they had mostly recognised music, literature and fine arts. As in schools, those pesky drama people were mostly under the hegemony of English, and kept bobbing up demanding self-government. That has usually eventuated in a department of Theatre or Performance Studies.

The relationship with drama education has been very ambivalent. Perhaps a dozen of these University pioneers and scholars have given real assistance to drama education, and in recent years helped to support its nervous moves into research. Sadly, there are others who have preferred to keep drama education at arms' length. It would not be going too far to suggest that some even explicitly exclude it, either just overlooking it or perhaps fearing that teachers would lower the scholarly tone. This has been much like some of the actor-training conservatories, which until recently (with a few honourable exceptions) have done little to foster the wider cause of drama in the schools and community – much less than they might have. Some of these have deliberately avoided too close contact with teachers, or corralled their actor-training off, for fear of contamination.

In fact, though, it has mostly been a two-way trade. By the time of the amalgamation, quite a number of those CAE communication and drama departments had metamorphosed into full-on drama and/or actor-training (with or without drama education), which gave the universities ready-made drama departments. Some of these have flourished and made further metamorphoses, ganging up with other forms into units with names like 'Creative Industries' and 'Drama, Media and Communication'.

Theatre's Patchy Influence

Like the Universities and actor-training conservatories, the influence of the theatre industry has been patchy and ambivalent – a matter of the best and the worst. Theatres need to put bums on seats to survive, and they know that. Many theatres actively program plays that will appeal to schools audiences, or that are prescribed examination texts, and there has been a general assumption in theatre that by encouraging school students to like theatre, their bums will return to the seats when they are grown up. This has been the main economic rationale behind the formation of theatre-in-education and theatre-in-schools companies by most major theatres. Recent evidence (Colmar Brunton 2004) suggests it may have been misplaced and the reverse may be true – that many young people come, therefore, to regard theatre as part of the schooling process and, however, much they might have enjoyed their visits, or the visits of TIE to their schools, when they leave school they put the things of schooling behind them.

Currently, most theatre companies make quite a significant and even growing commitment to schools and young people's work. There is, however, still a cultural perception, going back many years within and without the industry that theatre is basically for adults. In this conception, young people are different, and less significant as audiences – and, because they do not have the highly trained skills of professional artists, ineffectual as performers (except as dangerously charming supernumeraries: 'never work with animals or children'). Historically, in Australia as in the UK, some major companies made a token effort towards schools and education systems, but as quickly as possible turned with relief and the bulk of the dollars to the main business of catering for grown-ups. This common perception was witheringly articulated in 1988 by the late playwright Alex Buzo: 'The TIE people do a great job educating children, but it's not art, and it's not entertainment'. For the artists too, there has been a similar historical perception that theatre in schools is what you do when you're just out of acting school, or while waiting for a proper job to come along – and few actors in main house theatre can be said to look forward eagerly to the schools matinees. Fortunately, the communication between the two industries has not always been so dire, even in early days. Ashby's brilliant initiative to establish Queensland's Early Childhood Drama Project depended equally on the vision and enthusiasm of Brisbane's enterprising La Boite Theatre; the influential Magpie TIE was an initiative of the South Australian State Theatre.

Theatre does of course have the potential to inspire and irradiate education, and in the best hands, always has. A series of workshops by actor John Bell and the other founders of Sydney's Nimrod Theatre in the 1970s were crucial stimuli for the establishment of the NSW Educational Drama Association – and the Bell Shakespeare Company still provides a lavish nationwide program of workshops for both students and teachers. Melbourne's Australian Performing Group had even closer connections with drama education, with several of its foremost artists such as actor Max Gillies and playwright David Williamson lecturing on those early Victorian drama teaching courses. Illustrious actors Geoffrey Rush and Bille Brown have both worked for state theatre in education companies as artistic director and playwright, respectively. A *very* few theatre directors, like Sydney's Don Mamouney (*Sidetrack Theatre*) and Queenslander Bryan Nason (*Grin and Tonic Theatre Troupe*), have made no artistic class distinction between adult and children's work, and made it their life's work to create theatre for the communities in Australia, which do not have ready access to theatre, or the social habit of it – and that includes young people.

The growth and development of theatre-in-education in Australia has some parallels with its growth in the UK, and some differences, which are beyond the province of this book and are dealt with elsewhere (O'Toole & Bundy 1993). However, in virtually every state, there has been some theatre in schools – often one single company – that has either made a lasting impact, or been highly influential in the growth phase of drama in schools. This has taken different forms: British style participatory theatre in education; puppet theatre; early childhood theatre; hard-hitting, political performance work for older children and young adults; eclectic touring companies. Many have come and gone. It is noticeable that most of the big state theatre companies and performing arts centres are now making much more of a serious, and financial, commitment to various forms of theatre for young people and educational provision, such as seconded advisory teachers, than they would have dreamt of even a decade ago. This is presumably not unrelated to the fact that drama *is* now established nationally in the school curriculum.

Renovating the House, or Just Redecorating?

Within the house, a number of key factors also contribute to the kind of welcome drama gets when it knocks on the door. Some of these are a combined matter of luck and the mood of the times: if the educational climate is leaning towards the progressive, and there also happens to be a key influential insider or two, then there is a good chance of getting into the lobby at least. Where there is a change in the assessment or examination system, doors may creak ajar. How much money there is for development is another very crucial factor, because in the end it is money that firstly buys the amount of professional development and advisory staff, and then sustains a support system while schools, teachers and students get to grips with the unfamiliar skills of a complex art-form and aesthetic pedagogy. The money provided by states has varied wildly. It must have cost a great deal for little Tasmania to support an advisory service for nearly 30 years with up to eight full-time advisers and a superintendent in its heyday, or for Victoria's Bouverie Street Drama Centre with a Director, up to three TIE teams and a raft of advisers and resources for a decade. Some states have thoughtfully budgeted as much or more for implementation and professional development as for the drama curriculum itself, others not. What is clear is that the states that have had a tradition of effective advisory services are those that have on the whole fared best, and survived most robustly, when things have gone bad.

And that's to be remembered, and catered for. Every action has an equal and opposite reaction, as we learned in science. For every progressive Director of

Education, or accidentally benevolent government initiative, there's one of the other sort. Moreover we know how uneasy the whole relationship between drama and any official ethos or system whatever has been historically. This chapter has elicited enough stories to make us finish on a sobering note.

When John briefly worked with the New Zealand advisers implementing their new drama syllabus in 2004, there was an air of optimism and application – schools were eagerly trying out the new ideas, with the advisers backing them up; drama had achieved equal weighting in the university entrance examination; and drama was, yet again as we have seen elsewhere, the fastest growing subject in the senior secondary curriculum. However, one year earlier, Dorothy Heathcote, discussing the New Zealand curriculum with its then National Coordinator, Peter O'Connor, with her usual devastating directness 'asked me not whether young people do drama in schools in New Zealand, but "Do they do things that matter, and in doing that, do they know they matter?"'. Pondering this double-barrelled question was already causing O'Connor a deal of unease, which as he has admitted, led to him leaving this apparently promising and influential post the very next year, and even losing confidence in the whole value of drama being established in the curriculum (O'Connor 2008). Year 2007 brought three straws in the wind of a different kind. All the advisers had been retrenched as the money ran out, except the visual arts ones (old Mr Beeby's influence alive and well, evidently). A theatre-in-education company working with years 7 and 8 students in over 200 mainly disadvantaged schools reported that it had not come across even one teacher – out of 600 it had worked with – who uses drama on a regular basis as a pedagogy or a subject. Finally, there were rumours of a new educational policy change at government level (equally from the government and the opposition) that might bring in renewed emphasis on 'the basics' and make the arts optional once more.

We do not need to look far for precedents. In Victoria in the 1990s, as in the UK a decade earlier, the advent of a radical conservative government swept away all those expensive advisory services. That Victorian drama education, like the UK, has actually survived, not unscathed but tougher, is owing to many of the other factors mentioned above, such as a strong state association, a well-trained teaching force and strong links with the tertiary institutions that trained them.

Examples like this make it worth concluding with the words of the NSW EDA's founding president in his farewell speech, given in 1977: prescient words, and extraordinarily relevant to this book at the time of writing:

> A great deal will depend on membership ... and the few enthusiastic and selfless individuals without whom organisations cannot exist. But a great deal will also depend on the outcome of the present educational controversy about literacy, numeracy, back-to-basics, accountability, etc. The weather ahead does not augur well for unconsolidated areas like educational drama. It doesn't augur well because of the educational climate of crisis, with its tendency to swing the pendulum away from 'progressive' and experimental practice to a study of restricted subject areas, and the time might come when we will be looking back at the late 1960s and early 1970s as the 'Golden Age' of drama experimentation. (Fiala 1977)

Let's hope not, but now, well into the next century, it would be rash to bet against it ... and alarm bells are already ringing back in Queensland.

References

We are grateful to numerous pioneers in all states for their help in this chapter, who are named in the Acknowledgments. Although, owing to limitations on space and the capacity of an international readership to be absorbed by local history, not all have been cited or named in the text, their perspectives and memories have combined to provide what we hope is a coherent and textured overview of the very diverse and complex growth of drama in Australian education.

Boomer, G. (1982). *Negotiating the curriculum: A teacher-student partnership*. Sydney: Ashton Scholastic.

Buzo, A. (1988). *The young person's guide to the theatre and almost everything else*. Melbourne: Penguin.

Colmar Brunton. (2004). *Youth audience research: Motivations and barriers to attendance amongst 12–17 year olds*, Melbourne: Arts Victoria.

English Speaking Board. (2007). *Who's who in ESB*. http://www.esbuk.org/whoswhoinesb. htm#founder Accessed 8 April 2007.

Fiala, O. (1977). President's Report to the AGM of the NSW Educational Drama Association. *Do It*. Vol 11.

MacGowan, G. (2007). *Pre-school days – teachers remember*. Queensland Department of Education, Training and the Arts. http://education.qld.gov.au/etrf/farewell/preschool_ days.html Accessed 7 April 2007.

O'Brien, A. (1996). *The pleasure of the company*. Melbourne: The University of Melbourne.

O'Connor, P. (2008). *Silent, upon A peak in Darien: Drama education from the edge*. Keynote Address: National Drama Conference, Durham UK. April.

O'Toole, J., & Bundy, P. (1993). Kites and magpies: TIE in Australia. In Anthony Jackson (Ed.), *Learning through theatre*. London: Routledge.

Queensland Department of Education. (1991). *Drama makes meaning: Years 1 to 10 drama curriculum guide*. Brisbane: Department of Education.

Schaffner, M., Parsons, B., Little, G., & Felton, H. (1984). *Drama, language and learning: Reports of the drama and language research project*. Hobart: Speech and Drama Centre, Education Department of Tasmania.

Thorpe, J. (1977). Drama, from Terrigal to London and back. *Do It*. New South Wales EDA. Vol 10. p. 8.

Chapter 9
Drama as Macro-Curriculum: Peeking Behind the Closed Doors of Drama Syllabus Development

The Development of the Queensland Arts Curriculum (1998–2002)

Madonna Stinson

In this chapter, we continue the shift in emphasis from the global to the particular. Globalisation has impacted on education and curriculum development and recently there has been a tendency for curricula to be marketed internationally. It seems that curriculum development can be lucrative. However, the purchasing of a curriculum, which has been developed in another location, especially another country, takes little account of the context in which that curriculum will be implemented. The needs of students and their schooling vary according to distinctive social, economic and cultural contexts and any curriculum must be responsive to these needs. This chapter illustrates the particular process that one systemic curriculum authority went through to develop an arts and drama curriculum for its own specific schooling context: Queensland, Australia. At the time of going to press the curriculum document that resulted is still the mandated syllabus in Queensland schools but, as we will see later, changes are afoot.

The Queensland Context

At more than 1.72 million square kilometres in size, Queensland is Australia's second largest state with a population of nearly 4 million, most of whom are resident in the south-east corner. The compulsory school age is between 5 and 15, and all children attend primary school – Years Prep to 7; followed by secondary school – Years 8–10. More than 80% of students continue to study for the final (but noncompulsory) 2 years of secondary school, and complete their formal school education when they are about 18 years old.

Nearly 50% of Queenslanders live in rural settings and 45% of the population changed address in the 5 years between 1996 and 2001 (Australian Bureau of Statistics 2003). Most large and urban schools are in the south-east corner near the capital,

J. O'Toole et al., *Drama and Curriculum,* Landscapes: the Arts, Aesthetics, and Education 6, DOI 10.1007/978-1-4020-9370-8_10,

Brisbane, and range in size from around 300 to 2000 students. Outside the Brisbane area, while there are still some schools with several hundred students, many are very small indeed: for example, there are 133 'one-teacher' schools where the principal is the only teacher, with a class of up to 20 students. Any task of curriculum development is a complex undertaking, more so when a curriculum and materials must be found that are relevant and suitable for students who live in such diverse, and often isolated, settings and who may move locations two or three times during their schooling.

Queensland has a unique system of curriculum design, implementation and assessment within Australia, as it is the only state without common public examinations in all subject areas (as we described in Chapter 8). Until the establishment of the Queensland School Curriculum Council in 1996, curriculum development and design for the compulsory years of schooling was managed and controlled by the Department of Education (Education Queensland).

The *Years 1–10 Arts Curriculum* development project commenced in 1998 and concluded when school implementation began in July 2002. The distinctiveness of this curriculum development project centres on the degree of consultation and collaboration that characterised the decisions made at each stage of the design and development phases. That consultation was part of the government legislation at the establishment of the curriculum authority and the curriculum developers were bound by law to show that they had consulted widely and were held accountable to that consultation. The consultation process was an attempt to accommodate the needs of the two independent authorities (the Association of Independent Schools of Queensland and the Queensland Catholic Education Council) with those of the established government education department. While the Queensland School Curriculum Council reported directly to the Minister of Education, key decisions were influenced by the management structures and stakeholders within each of the three authorities.

As the 4 years of collaborative curriculum development progressed, the curriculum writers and teachers involved grappled with what Murray Print (1993: 1) calls the fundamental questions of curriculum:

- What to teach?
- How to teach?
- When to teach?
- What is the impact of teaching?

Key challenges for this curriculum development project included how to select and organise learning so that it was meaningful and pertinent to specific learning contexts.

I was a member of the team who worked on this curriculum. In 1998, I was seconded from my position as Head of Performing Arts at a large Brisbane secondary school and began working with two other colleagues to write the 'design brief' and first draft of the syllabus. At the beginning of 1999, we were joined by five other (subject expert) writers as the materials continued to be developed and refined in the trial phase, which lasted for 18 months. The final stage of the project involved the development, refinement and editing of teaching support materials.

I should point out that schooling in Queensland is not based on textbooks. Schools rarely choose to use set texts in many of the subjects, and all syllabus documents could be described as *frameworks* rather than documents that prescribe content, teaching, and assessment in substantial and sequential detail. The prevailing practice of the profession is for teachers to use the framework of the syllabus to plan units of work and prepare teaching materials according to the specific needs of the school community in which they work. at Senior level (Years 11 and 12), these become programs that are accredited by district-based panels of teachers. Teachers in Queensland value this approach because the capacity to design, implement and assess innovative teaching materials is a highly regarded professional skill.

At a systemic level of curriculum development, the organisation responsible for designing and developing the curriculum must also have the authority and power to design and implement assessment and reporting. In this project, the division of responsibilities for development (by the QSCC) and implementation, assessment and reporting (the individual systemic authorities) made the task particularly challenging. An intricate dynamic of both *influences* and *constraints*, which we had to negotiate, was created by personnel changes at senior levels, shifts in curriculum orientation at much more generic levels than *the arts*, and the unusually open process of consultation with both teachers and the community. Despite support from the Queensland Catholic Education Commission and the Association of Independent Schools at every stage of the project, the fractious and often belligerent nature of the relationship between the QSCC and Education Queensland ran contrary to the expectation of collaboration and intersystemic support. Education Queensland, the largest, best resourced, and most authoritative educational voice in the state, by insisting on the retention of control over assessment, reporting and implementation, was able to undermine the work of the QSCC.

Consultation

The consultation process was intensive and complex. The Council's aim was to involve individuals and groups at all levels in an iterative process, which allowed them direct impact on the developing curriculum. The arts team attempted to engage all stakeholders in participation in the ongoing conversation of curriculum development rather than simply providing documents, prepared by 'experts' and intended to be implemented as written.

One key reason for the legislated consultation process was to involve as many teachers as possible as co-constructors of this curriculum. Philip Taylor (1996: 5), who is critical of curriculum packages generated by 'others' for teachers to implement, asks 'Why is it that teachers do not dominate or feature widely in these documents?' In this project, teachers featured at every level and at every phase of the project contributing their lived experience, knowledge of the disciplines and particular schooling contexts.

The process of consultation was extensive and ongoing. Far more than an information sharing process, it was one that valued diversity of input, respected teachers' work, and attempted to act upon the advice from the consultative groups.

Michael Apple claims that schools act as agents of cultural and ideological hegemony, and hence curriculum developers must be conscious of the political, economic, social and cultural implications of their selections. Apple (2004:6) asks us to consider:

- Whose knowledge is it?
- Who selected it?
- Why is it organised and taught in this way?
- To this particular group?

In response to these questions, and in relation to this set of documents, the Queensland School Curriculum Council would claim that the answers are:

- ours (the teachers of Queensland);
- we did;
- each art-form will be taught differently because we collectively decided that it would be so; and
- the group depends on the context.

Or it would be arguing this, if it still existed – but as we shall see, it exists no more, swept away in the tides of political change.

Curriculum developers are 'shaped by all the experiences that have shaped them' (Ornstein 2003: 4). Because teachers as consultative partners were intrinsic to the development of this syllabus, preexisting conceptions of drama curriculum and teacher-training were significant in the shaping of the drama curriculum that emerged from the process. As one of Britain's ex-colonies, it is unsurprising that contemporary drama education in Queensland owes a great deal to its heritage of the history of drama education in the UK, particularly the work of Dorothy Heathcote and Gavin Bolton. Previous chapters have discussed this heritage and a number of drama educators trained by Heathcote and Bolton played important roles in shaping the understanding of what drama learning entails. Since many of these accomplished drama educators worked in the teacher education programs at Queensland universities, they had direct impact on the epistemology and pedagogy of teachers in schools, as well as a range of drama curriculum documents in place at the beginning of 1998.

The Curriculum Design

When the Queensland School Curriculum Council was established in 1996, most Australian states and territories were following an 'outcomes-based' model. This was based on an agreement by the (then) Ministers of Education for each state government in the early 1990s. In line with the national initiative, the Queensland

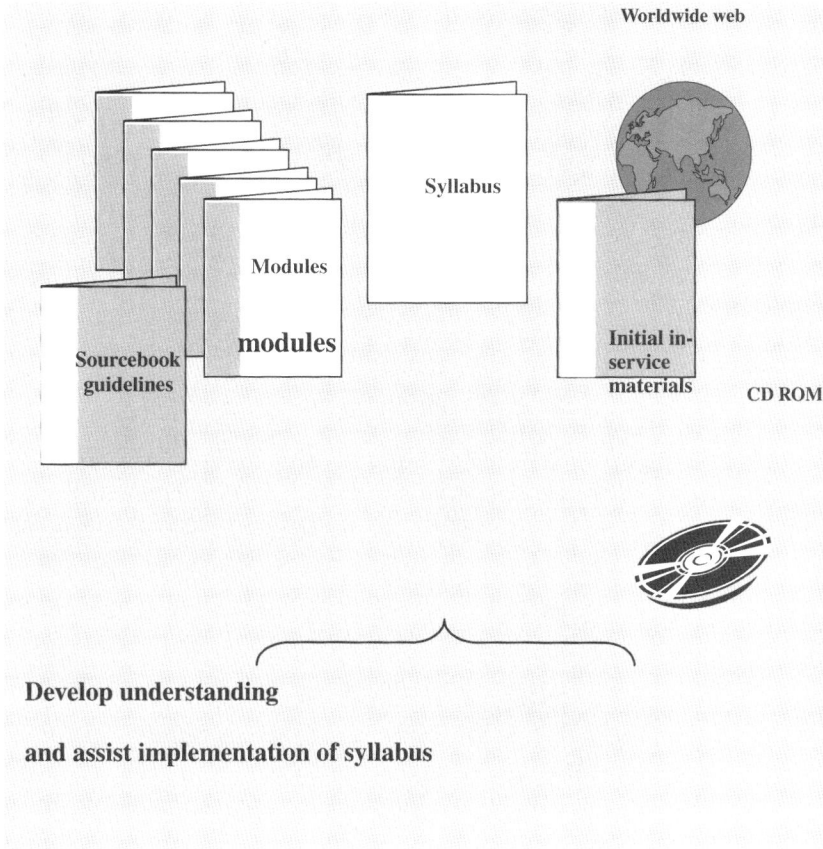

Fig. 9.1 Suite of documents

School Curriculum Council decided that all curriculum materials would be based on an 'outcomes approach to education', which was a modification of *outcomes-based education* (OBE) propounded by William Spady (1993, 1994), rather than the still-current 'objectives'-based approach derived from Ralph Tyler.

The syllabus was the *compulsory* component of a 'suite' of documents (see Fig. 9.1) and was both the focal point and the framework for the prescribed curriculum. In addition to this central document, support documents were prepared to assist teachers in understanding and implementing the syllabus. The first amongst the support documents was the *Sourcebook Guidelines*. In this book, teachers found 'elaborations' (examples and explanations of classroom practice) of the outcomes as well as detailed advice for planning and assessment.

Additional to the *sourcebook guidelines*, 60 'modules' offered examples of planned learning experiences and possibilities for integration. They contained advice on assessment, photocopiable masters and worksheets. The modules were not specific lesson plans, broken into timed sequences of activities. Instead, exemplars

provided a range of learning experiences within a provisional structure that teachers could choose from or modify to suit their schooling context. Teachers were
encouraged to plan from these for their own classes, lingering in some activities
and phases, offering others directly as planned and sequenced, or choosing to skip
or quickly move through others if they were not essential for student learning. The
modules were meant to be models of practice rather than 'teacher-proof' materials that should be implemented exactly according to plan. Giroux and McLaren
(1989) warn that the deskilling of teachers goes hand in hand with what they term
'management-type pedagogies' evident in prepackaged 'teacher-proof' curriculum
materials. These one-size-fits-all materials, so often seen nowadays, 'do not require
the use of the teacher's judgement, demean teachers and expect them to function as
automatons rather than professionals' (Eisner 2002:41).

Another printed document accompanying the *Syllabus* and *Sourcebook Guidelines* was the Initial *In-Service Materials*. This book was planned to be an independent and self-managing course of study to assist teachers to deepen their understanding of the syllabus and processes of planning and assessment. All of the documents
were reproduced on a CD Rom, which was distributed free-of-charge to all teachers
in Queensland. The CD Rom also contained video footage of students demonstrating
the outcomes, and additional materials not in print.

Phase One: The Design Brief

From January to June, 1998, the arts project team developed the 'design brief',
which provided the framework for the development of the syllabus. As part of the
preparation, the team began the process of ongoing consultation. We conducted
focus group interviews with teachers, school administrators, academics and professional associations to determine what these stakeholders wished to see in the
curriculum documents. We sent fax surveys to 100 randomly selected schools
throughout the state. An on-line consultative network of more than 200 individuals
and groups was established. Throughout the project, schools and the on-line consultative network continued to be provided with drafts of the document and were
regularly asked to provide feedback and advice.

More formal consultation was managed through the establishment of an Arts
Syllabus Advisory Committee (SAC), made up of individuals who represented each
of the schooling systems, professional associations (such as Drama Queensland –
formerly QADIE), primary, secondary and special education sectors, and the community. This committee (of about 30 people) met four times per year, for a day at a
time. Each representative drew on a substantial personal and professional network
and provided detailed feedback and input throughout the development process.

By May 1998, the draft design brief was sent to the Curriculum Council, another
representative body, this time made up of senior officers from each curriculum
authority, which met regularly to consider and approve (or provide feedback on)
the developing curriculum materials. The *arts design* brief was approved by the

Curriculum Council at the first submission, which meant that the project could proceed to the next stage: the outcomes development phase.

Phase Two: The Outcomes Development Phase

The *influences* described earlier in this chapter contributed to the decision to make this a 'role-based' curriculum. Role is considered 'that central feature of all theatre' (O'Neill 1995:69); Bolton (1982:41) claims that through harnessing what theatre and drama have in common, the teaching of dramatic form (albeit indirectly) is what occurs in role-based drama.

The syllabus we created attempts to integrate all the paradigms of purpose as described in this book, with the exception of the language focus. In the early years of schooling, the emphasis was to be on the expressive/developmental and social/pedagogical paradigms, using other subject areas to provide drama with 'serious and worthwhile content [to] . . . illuminate these areas of the curriculum' (O'Neill & Lambert 1982:16). In the secondary school years, the expressive/developmental and social/pedagogical paradigms are retained with a more explicit orientation towards the art-form as students learn more theatre conventions and forms, and work more independently as dramatic artists to form their own work and interpret the works of others.

All syllabuses developed by the QSCC were written according to the statements of *core learning outcomes* described in six developmental levels, which loosely parallel the 10 years of compulsory schooling. (These levels are akin to the four 'Key Stages' of contemporary UK schooling, but having six provides a little more fine-tuning.) In an attempt to align with a fundamental principle of outcomes-based-education (i.e., time is a constant and learning is a variable), these levels were not equivalent with years of schooling. The six levels described essential learning that need to be supported during *10 years* of planned learning experiences for all students, built in as regular 'check points', thus:

> For the purpose of planning and assessment, outcome levels typically relate to year levels as follows:
>
> - Students demonstrating Level 2 outcomes at the end of Year 3
> - Students demonstrating Level 3 outcomes at the end of Year 5
> - Students demonstrating Level 4 outcomes at the end of Year 7
> - Students demonstrating Level 6 outcomes at the end of Year 10 (QSCC 2002:18)

Writing this role-based drama curriculum, and following the particular outcomes approach developed by the Queensland School Curriculum Council, meant that it was necessary to produce a linear model of curriculum and make decisions about how learning might progress, i.e., what learning preceded important learning at higher and more complex levels, what followed on from what, and how to make the patterns and development clear for teachers so that they could use the documents effectively to plan for learning in their own schooling contexts

Table 9.1 The final set of drama outcomes

The three outcomes at a level are designed to work in a complementary and interrelated way.

Form	Present	Respond	
DR1.1 Students create and accept roles while participating in dramatic play.	DR1.2 Students share drama with others by participating, listening and watching.	DR1.3 Students describe ideas and feelings experienced during the making and shaping of their dramatic play.	**Typically by the end of Year 3**
DR2.1 Students make choices about and develop roles to build dramatic action.	DR2.2 Students share moments of dramatic action using voice and movement so that they can be seen, heard and understood.	DR2.3 Students describe drama experiences and presentations, expressing opinions and exchanging viewpoints with others.	
DR3.1 Students negotiate, in and out of role, a range of situations and narratives.	DR3.2 Students rehearse and present dramatic action for a specific purpose.	DR3.3 Students discuss and interpret the learnings and understandings developed through drama experiences.	**Typically by the end of Year 5**
DR4.1 Students select dramatic elements and conventions to collaboratively shape improvisations and role-plays.	DR4.2 Students present devised and scripted drama using performance skills appropriate for a variety of purposes and audiences.	DR4.3 Students make supported critical judgments about the application of dramatic elements, conventions in the context of their own work and that of others.	**Typically by the end of Year 7**
DR5.1 Students structure dramatic action, both individually and in groups, using elements and conventions appropriate to the selected dramatic form, style, and purpose.	DR5.2 Students present selected roles using performance skills appropriate to the selected dramatic form, style and purpose.	DR5.3 Students identify and evaluate the application of dramatic elements and conventions used in their own work and that of others, communicating an awareness of the selected form and style and purpose.	**Typically by the end of Year 10 (Levels 5 and 6 require at least 180 hours of timetabled specialist study)**
DR6.1 Students devise and refine scenarios and scripts, both individually and as part of an ensemble, using elements and conventions appropriate to selected forms, styles and purposes.	DR6.2 Students present a rehearsed, polished performance, applying performance skills appropriate to the selected form, style and performance space.	DR6.3 Students evaluate the forms, styles and processes used in dramatic action and performance, identifying the influence of purpose and context.	

Developmental learning occurs from one level to the next.

Therefore DR1.1 leads to DR2.1 and so on

The QSCC's policy was to 'outsource' the writing of outcomes to consortia with established expertise and networks, usually the relevant subject's professional association. Drama Queensland was employed to write the drama outcomes and continued the process of collaborative consultation by establishing an 'outcomes writing symposium', which was opened up to the membership. They established a committee of 21 members, representative of primary, secondary, and tertiary educators, who worked for 4 days to create the first set of drama outcomes for the syllabus and submitted this first draft document by the end of October, 1998. This level of consultation in setting policy directions is one of the more unusual features of this Syllabus development process, and an opportunity which the drama community seized much more enthusiastically than its colleagues in the other named art-forms. This disparity may be seen not only in the final syllabus documents, but also in the syllabus's much higher level of popularity and acceptance among the drama teachers.

There were 30 draft outcomes in this first set, five at each level. Because, at this stage of the project, the outcomes were intended to 'stand alone' for planning, they were detailed and quite cumbersome. For the next 2 years, they were refined during the trial process in schools and revised in light of decisions made within the Curriculum Council. The three systemic authorities were worried about the large number of outcomes and we were required to reduce the number in each of the arts strands from 30 (or more in some of the other arts) to a maximum of 3 at each level. The first draft outcomes were seen to be too 'jargony' and simplification was necessary. The (new) minister for education wanted a list of common core content, and directives from ministers had to be followed without question. Teachers in schools and members of Drama Queensland participated in the ongoing process of refinement by interpreting, planning, implementing and assessing with the outcomes and providing regular feedback to the curriculum development team.

Table 9.1 shows the final set of outcomes that emerged following the syllabus trial in schools and ongoing consultation during 1999 and 2000. The full picture is provided in the Syllabus and the Sourcebook Guidelines. You might like to download these from http://www.qsa.qld.edu.au/yrs1to10/kla/arts.

Phase Three: Trialling the Curriculum in Schools

By the end of 1998, we had written the *first* draft syllabus (there were 10 formal drafts before we were finished) and we were able to try the document out with schools to see if the materials (a) were suitable, (b) did describe the essential learning in the area, and (c) the outcomes were appropriately levelled for students. Our trialling lasted for 18 months. Schools were chosen because they were representative of diversity of location and social and cultural contexts, and came from remote Aboriginal communities in the Gulf of Carpentaria, small rural communities, and large urban communities. Thirty-six schools and more than 100 teachers were involved in the ongoing development of the syllabus and support materials.

During the trial phase, the schools had the responsibility of assessing the developing materials and suggesting modifications they felt necessary. Teachers were asked to try to plan, teach, and assess with the outcomes and provide feedback to the curriculum development team on how effective the syllabus materials were. We visited the schools regularly, helping teachers to plan, modelling teaching if necessary (or if asked), observing classes, and collecting examples of student work and teacher planning. We also continued to consult widely, beyond the school communities.

The curriculum development team continued to meet (four times per year) with our Arts Syllabus Advisory committee; we sent many drafts out to our on-line consultative network (this was open to anyone who registered with us to receive and provide feedback on the draft materials); and we consulted with Drama Queensland who continued to contribute to the modifications of the outcomes, assessment issues, and to share ideas for the sorts of support materials that teachers might find useful.

During the trial phase, we used feedback from teachers in schools and our consultative networks to inform our writing of the 'elaborations' of the outcomes that can be found in the Sourcebook Guidelines, and commenced the development of 60 modules[1] (12 for Drama) that provided models of planning and assessment.

The trial process was monitored by an independent external evaluator, EdData. This company was employed by the Curriculum Council to provide outside and unbiased advice. During the trial, EdData surveyed schools, interviewed teachers and school administrators and provided three reports, offering feedback on the developing materials. The final report concluded that:

> the draft curriculum, as defined by the draft syllabus, sample modules and draft sourcebook guidelines, is highly appropriate for a core curriculum in Years 1 to 10. It has the potential to raise the profile of the arts considerably in schools and to broaden the ambit of the arts within the curriculum, especially in the primary years. It has the potential to improve outcomes in the arts for many students. The materials are effective in defining the curriculum in terms of outcomes. The sample modules are effective in giving teachers practical ideas on how to implement the syllabus. The elaborations and typical demonstrations are highly effective in explaining the key learning area to teachers in practical terms. The curriculum is realistic in terms of resource demands and the indicative time allocation for The Arts (EdData 2000, p. 3).

The Curriculum Council approved the Arts curriculum to go ahead for editing, printing, and distribution in 2001.

Politics and the Draughts of Change

The brief description above of this lengthy process of curriculum development may give the impression that the path was smooth and uncomplicated. This is far from the truth and there is not enough space in this chapter to detail all the complications that were encountered. However, the challenges we faced due to the political influences

---

[1] See http://www.qsa.qld.edu.au/yrs1to10/kla/arts/modules.html#drama for hotlinks to the full set of drama modules.

and changes at senior levels of the department of education do warrant some discussion because of the way they inform the forces brought to bear on curriculum
development.

The change of political party following the State election in 1998 meant a new
minister for education was appointed in June, shortly followed by the appointment
of a new director-general of education in August who held the position for less than
2 years, when he was replaced in June, 2000. The new Minister issued a directive requiring the inclusion of 'Core Content' in the syllabus very soon after his
appointment and thus we began to feel the impact of political interference in curriculum documents. The new Director-General, however, had much more pervasive
influence. He indicated that new directions in curriculum were required and also
signalled a lack of support for the work of the Curriculum Council. This led to an
understandable feeling of insecurity within the schooling community.

There was a good deal of uncertainty and distrust about Education Queensland's commitment to the outcomes-based syllabuses developed at the Queensland
School Curriculum Council. This distrust was well-founded. During 1999, we
began to hear a good deal about 'New Basics' as a preferred curriculum organ-
iser (Education Queensland 2000). *New Basics* began trialling in selected Education
Queensland schools during 2000. By 2001, the architect of *New Basics*, a University of Queensland academic, had been appointed as Assistant Director-General of
Education.

In April 1999, Education Queensland published the '2010' document (Queensland Department of Education 1999), which proposed new directions for education in state schools in Queensland. Australia-wide, enrolments in government
schools had been dropping as parents, especially those who had the socioeconomic
resources, mainly middleclass, had exercised their 'right to choose', and moved
their students to catholic or independent schools, which had been strongly advan-
taged by changes in Federal Government funding under the conservative Coalition
government. The new Director-General identified this as a significant problem for
Queensland state schools:

> The drift in enrolments erodes the funding base, undermines staff morale, and leads even-
> tually to the situation in which the student population is severely skewed to the most
> disadvantaged social groups (Moran 1999: 4).

He claimed that Catholic and independent schools employed more and more
'*sophisticated marketing strategies to gain a greater share of student enrolments*',
as their education funding increased in response to Commonwealth Government
priorities. The '2010' document recognised the enrolment drift as a major problem
for government schools.

The shift in enrolments was a result of a larger and more affluent middleclass
choosing *not* to send their children to state schools because they believed that independent and catholic schools would provide their children with more opportunities
for social networking and better educational standards. The '2010' vision for education aimed to entice students back into government schools and keep them there until
they graduated. Of course, this was not entirely altruistic. The numbers of students

in schools directly impacted on the calculation of funding for education from the Commonwealth government. Therefore, the Queensland government sought a new direction, hoping to reverse the trend from state to private schools.

Constraints

From the beginning of the arts curriculum development project, Education Queensland had insisted that QSCC syllabuses be pedagogy-free and would not address assessment. Paradoxically their incoming Assistant Director-General posted the following statement on the Education Queensland website:

> [If] we want to change student outcomes, it's a key axiom in curriculum theory that ... the three message systems – curriculum, pedagogy, assessment – need to be brought into proper alignment for us to get desired education results and outcomes (Luke 1999, p. 3).

The inability to bring curriculum, pedagogy and assessment into 'proper alignment' was a specific constraint that caused us much angst, particularly during the trial process when the development team were *prohibited* from answering questions related to assessment raised by participating teachers.

Additional directives included that we were to 'adhere to the model of the State', which meant that music was taught by discipline-trained teachers, while the other arts areas were left to 'generalists'. This perpetuated a long-standing inequity for music to be, by far, the best resourced and supported of all the arts, with visual arts a close second. The 'newer' arts areas of dance, drama and media just had to make do with existing resources, human and physical.

All of these hostile pressures at the macro-level of the Department worked together to weaken the position and influence of the fledgling syllabus. This was in spite of 'our own' team of fifth columnists. The Department contained a small but energetic Visual and Performing Arts Unit – to give it advice on matters of arts curriculum, no less – and throughout the whole curriculum project they were enthusiastic and supportive, but in the end, their advice too was sidelined.

Without substantial, relevant and ongoing implementation support, new curriculum materials are doomed to sit on shelves, gathering dust. Education Queensland at first committed around $1,200,000 (including salaries) for 3 years for all five of the arts strands. This was something, though by contrast in the same year New Zealand allocated $10 million for implementing its syllabus. Even this commitment to implementation was questionable as within months, there was a threatened withdrawal of all funds, only circumvented by uproar from teachers, the tertiary arts education sector and professional associations. A reduced implementation continued (with first five, then three, then two staff) for 2 years, and $87,000 for them to make it all work.

How far drama's one-fifth of $87,000 would go can be easily calculated, in terms of 1647 schools (in 2001)[2] offering Years 1–10 across a state half the size

---

[2] 1289 state schools, 281 Catholic schools, 177 independent schools.

of Europe, and round about 15,000 teachers expected to teach the new syllabus, the great majority of whom would have had little or no prior training or practical experience. It may be true that necessity is the mother of invention, since these absurdly straitened resources did lead to some very elegant (if desperate) measures by the skeleton implementation team led (in Drama) by Julie Dunn. The team set up a statewide rhizomatic pattern of regional support networks managed by teachers. In each region, those teachers with any expertise to share in any art-form were enthusiastically winkled out, and pressed to help in the in-servicing of their colleagues on a school, cluster or district basis. While the money lasted, the team travelled exhaustively throughout the state, giving countless demonstrations and workshops, trying not just to 'show and tell' but to set up support groups simple but robust enough to sustain themselves. The team also set up many resources for teachers on the Department's on-line resource depository 'The Learning Place'[3], with a built-in discussion group. Drama Queensland enthusiastically came to the party, of course, though their strength and power base is mainly in the secondary schooling systems. To this day, the syllabus 'elaborations' and 'sourcebook modules' (or in jargon-free terms, the detailed examples and lesson plans, which we wrote to accompany the syllabus) are the most valuable and widely used aspect of the implementation. Although some teachers are reported even to find these daunting, their ongoing usefulness is not surprising: they were, after all, written consultatively, with many of Queensland's best drama teachers involved in their writing. Moreover, they have been the obvious first port of call by distressed neophytes suddenly called on to teach and report on their children's progress in a subject about which many of them knew as much as they did about nuclear physics. A few of the regional support networks managed by teachers are still functioning, even enthusiastically, with the on-line resource depository and discussion group the only sustained outcomes, but not bad for the money.

No curriculum development process can be seen to be independent of the political situation at the time. In Australia, the first decade of the twenty-first century has seen a move away from outcomes curricula developed at a state level and increased pressure for a National Curriculum Framework to emerge once more. State governments are now required to implement and report on *student performance standards* (linked to age and year level of schooling) in order to receive Commonwealth education funding. This move aligns with global trends towards the practice of ranking and comparing schools in terms of student performance. As a result, the Queensland Government has instigated the development of 'essential learning standards' common across all key learning areas, and which essentially reduce syllabuses to background documents, even while the process of embedding the pedagogy has barely started. The 'standards' become curriculum-by-assessment and reinforce control through ranking schools (and with the rankings linked to the funding). Change continues apace. On the day that I am writing this the Commonwealth government has announced a new task force, headed by an academic who has

---

[3] http://education.qld.gov.au/learningplace/

worked with the OECD and who comes from an economics background, to develop a new National Curriculum for the entire country. It will concentrate on the 'core', i.e., English, mathematics and science. So, once again, drama *will* be running hard ... to keep in the same place. We are still knocking at the door, with barely a toe on the threshold, keys in our hands.

References

Apple, M. W. (2004). *Ideology and curriculum* (3rd ed.). New York and London: Routledge Falmer.
Australian Bureau of Statistics. (2003). *Queensland in Review, 2003*. Retrieved 20 April, 2007, from http://www.abs.gov.au/Ausstats/abs@.nsf/Lookup/ CF3424B58ECB69C8CA256CC500211FCA#
Bolton, G. (1982). Philosophical perspectives on drama and the curriculum. In J. Nixon (Ed.), *Drama and the whole curriculum* (pp. 27–42). London: Hutchinson.
EdData. (2000). *Evaluation of the years 1 to 10 the arts curriculum development project: Report three*. Brisbane: Queensland School Curriculum Council.
Education Queensland. (2000). *The Queensland school reform longitudinal study*. Brisbane: Education Queensland.
Eisner, E.W. (2002). *The educational imagination: on the design and evaluation of school programs* (3rd ed.) Upper Saddle River, NJ: Merrill Prentice Hall.
Giroux, H. A., & McLaren, P. L. (1989). Teacher education and the politics of engagement: The case of democratic schooling. In H. A. Giroux & P. L. McLaren (Eds.), *Critical pedagogy, the state and cultural struggle* (pp. 301–331). New York: State University of New York Press.
Luke, A. (1999). *Education 2010 and new times: Why equity and social justice still matter, but differently*. Retrieved December 13, 1999, from http://www.qed.qld.gov.au/ news/framework/ onlineal.htm
Moran, T. (1999). Future directions for State education in Queensland: The role of research. The J. A Robinson Memorial Lecture 1999. *Queensland Journal of Educational Research, 15*.
O'Neill, C. (1995). *Dramaworlds: A framework for process drama*. Portsmouth, NH: Heinemann.
O'Neill, C., & Lambert, A. (1982). *Drama structures: A practical handbook for teachers*. Portsmouth, NH: Heinemann.
Ornstein, A. C. (2003). Philosophy as a basis for curriculum decisions. In A. C. Ornstein, L. S. Behar-Horenstein, & E. F. Pajak (Eds.), *Contemporary issues in curriculum* (pp. 3–9). Boston: Allyn & Bacon.
Print, M. (1993). *Curriculum development and design* (2nd ed.). Sydney: Allen & Unwin.
Queensland Department of Education. (1999). *2010 Queensland State Education*. Brisbane: Queensland Department of Education.
QSCC. (2002). *The arts years 1 to 10 syllabus*. Brisbane: Queensland School Curriculum Council.
Spady, W. G. (1993). *Outcome-based education: Workshop report No. 5* (No. 5). Belconnen, ACT: Australian Curriculum Studies Association.
Spady, W. G. (1994). *Outcome-based education: Critical issues and answers*. Arlington, VA: American Association of School Administrators.
Taylor, P. (1996). Doing reflective practitioner research in arts education. In P. Taylor (Ed.), *Researching drama and arts education: Paradigms and possibilities* (pp. 25–58). London: Falmer Press.

Chapter 10
The History Centre: A Micro-Curriculum

Tiina Moore

Background

In 1979 Elliot Eisner wrote:

> What I am suggesting is for curriculum designers to consider the potential of allowing students to use modes of response to historical ideas or experiences that might take shape in forms that are not indigenous to history as it is now conceived (130).

In the History Centre at ELTHAM College of Education, Melbourne, Australia, Year 3 and 4 students respond performatively to folktales, historical events and sociopolitical pressures by taking on fictional characters 'inside' a narrative curriculum framework. In the last 7 years of 'storied' interdisciplinary studies, students have been invited to:

- complete the inner chamber of an ancient Egyptian tomb;
- revitalize a ghost town on the Murray river;
- stand up to two greedy kings: one who appropriates gold; the other water;
- defend their beachside foreshore against development;
- study the transit of Venus as part of the *Endeavour* voyage and unravel cultural differences in Tahiti or the Great Southern continent;
- build the settlement of Sydney Town as convicts and free settlers;
- try their luck (and patience) on the goldfields of Ballarat; and
- reenact the walk as Chinese miners from Robe, South Australia to the Victorian goldfields.

In order to appreciate how 'it all works' in the History Centre, it is important to understand the background and culture of this relatively young, Australian independent school.

ELTHAM College of Education was founded in 1974 in what is now the urban fringe of North-East Melbourne. Its founder is a local architect who envisioned a nondenominational, coeducational school for the growing community. He foresaw an 'Australian-made' Kindergarten –Year-12 school that was not modelled on the English grammar school system. Amongst the early innovations of Eltham College were on-site day care (now off-site), recycling, and collaborations with local artists. ELTHAM now boasts its own vineyard, a permaculture course, a state-of-the-art

J. O'Toole et al., *Drama and Curriculum,* Landscapes: the Arts, Aesthetics,
and Education 6, DOI 10.1007/978-1-4020-9370-8_11,
© Springer Science+Business Media B.V. 2009

Hospitality Centre, a Year 9 City Campus, and the Year 3 and 4 History Centre. A 'knowledge era' culture now drives the school with an emphasis on skills and self-directed learning privileged over knowledge of subjects or disciplines (Warner 2006: 21).

A Timely Convergence

The seeds for the History Centre were planted in the first year of my employment as a specialist drama teacher at ELTHAM. Eisner's statement had resonances with my drama education, which had valued multimodal ways of knowing and drama as a methodology across subject areas. Significant influences on my theory and practice came from the narrative framing of David Booth's story drama (1994) and Heathcote and Bolton's use of teacher-in-role (1995) alongside the profoundly cohesive curriculum structure known as Mantle of the Expert. I will return to this structure later in this chapter.

My personal background dovetailed easily with the story form model (1988) that Kieran Egan had introduced to ELTHAM in the 1990s. Drawing on Donald Merlin's work on myth, Egan considered narrative to be *the* fundamental integrative mind tool and many primary teachers were trialling narrative curriculum frameworks in their classes. Egan foresaw units of study '. . .lasting from a month . . . to a whole term or semester'. He has recommended that several teachers cooperate in the story design such that, 'All the curriculum content will be accommodated within the overarching story structure (1997: 251). Egan's model, conjoined with the school's practice of physically building communities and settlements in the classrooms, was a dynamic welcome for a drama teacher new to the primary-aged sector. As far back as teaching staff can remember, the first 'built environments' at Eltham were devised for the *Australian Pioneers* unit. Students would secure upright timber poles to the four corners of a large rectangular work-table, thereby creating a structure for a shopfront. The overhead signs created from butcher's paper or plasticised paper would signal a bakery, dairy, or ironmonger's shop. The following year, they might be recycled into the thatched huts of South Pacific islanders.

I marvelled at the way that students learned mathematics, language, the arts, and social sciences while enthusiastically investing in what I came to regard as symbolic theatre sets. None of the teachers were themselves drama trained nor had they ever come across the strategy of teacher in role. Clearly this was a timely convergence of a personal history with the evolution of a progressive school.

The principles of narrative framing and integrated curriculum, which were firmly established in Years 4–6, encouraged collaborations with specialists. My collaboration with Geraldine, the Year 5 teacher, was particularly important to the development of the History Centre. We established a partnership whereby her class lesson, for example, based on the nature of crime in nineteenth-century London would develop in drama into flashbacks of personal stories of transported convicts. Not only did class knowledge directly impact on drama tasks, but Geraldine, who attended most drama lessons with her year level, carried over drama content for further reflection in class. The reflections might take the form of discussions, journal writing or displays. The cycle of knowledge, embodied practices and reflections formed the foundations for our teaching and learning relationship. There is no doubt that this somewhat spontaneous way of working owed some of its success to experience and to an available process drama repertoire. Despite the limitations of working across two settings with one timetabled drama lesson each week, the engagement of students and the meaning making were satisfying for all concerned and so we continued for many years.

With a simultaneous change of millennium, principal, and strategic plan, we were ready to extend the principles of the collaboration to the next stage. Our submission to set up large group 'living through' experiences in a teaching and learning context using the foundations of Mantle of the Expert, was approved.

An Interdisciplinary Curriculum

The Victorian Essential Learning Standards (VELS 2005) supports teaching and learning behaviours, which cross discipline boundaries and engage students in real-world issues and problems. Interdisciplinary studies are an integral part of assessment. Included in this strand of learning are communication, design, creativity and technology, ICT and thinking processes. Heathcote's Mantle of the Expert, introduced in Chapter 5, provided a model of how these goals may be achieved. The Mantle of the Expert strategy models ways whereby self-direction is preserved in mastering skills not as students, but in role as members of a community in which dedication and pride are brought to the enterprises of being, for example, villagers of a quiet Victorian coastal community. 'Everyone is grown up . . .' states Heathcote, '. . . carrying the responsibilities of adults and facing up to the results of their decisions' (2000: 35). As a result, curriculum work is purposeful and important and 'students not only do what is necessary but they examine the nature of the doing' (p. 34). In this model, the pressure of completed tasks comes from an external pressure (the deadline for the opening of the summer season), and the teacher–student relationship resembles that of a master and apprentice with common community interests.

Gavin Bolton's biography of Dorothy Heathcote was published in 2003. In it, he has written, 'We do not know of any regular teacher who has managed to conduct a full scale M of E (Mantle of the Expert) in her own school' (128). Since Bolton made that statement, Mantle of the Expert has been 'discovered' by the broader educational community and over 100,000 Internet sites can be accessed. Heathcote's teaching and learning paradigm added method and substance to the calls for inquiry, differentiation, shared power and authentic student research that have prevailed in writings on designing curriculum (Aoki in Pinar & Irwin 2005; Doll 1993). To my mind, the community context and the use of Mantle of the Expert structure for a minimum of a school term sets the History Centre apart.

The History Centre

At the time of Bolton's observation, the History Centre was in its second year of operation and four classes of Year 3 and 4 students were time travelling to ancient Egypt to complete an unfinished tomb as builders, artisans, scribes and priests. The unit of work was planned as a term's enterprise (10 weeks) and the final burial of the sarcophagus would involve a procession, formal readings and the creation of hieroglyphic panels, canopic jars and offerings for safe travel to the afterlife. Having said that our planned units rarely fit neatly into the Australian terms and we have learned over time to plan for three loosely connected units in a year, with some room to manoeuvre.

A number of features make the History Centre different from a weekly specialist drama class. The geographical design is most important, comprising four separate classrooms each of which has access to a central, carpeted gathering space – the History Centre itself. This is inhabited by four classes, with the class teachers (two Year 3, two Year 4–8–10 year olds) and a drama specialist (myself) forming a close team. The collaborative planning includes week-by-week renegotiation. The five teachers work together in and out of role. The whole curriculum is narratively framed, with the holistic pedagogical design allowing a great deal of 'flow', and opportunities for cross-age task groups. There is one full day of uninterrupted time each week for drama workshops and a full group 'living as if in role' session. A key part of this is the built environment, which is an integral part of each unit – effectively the theatrical set and much more. Two additional whole-group 'in role' sessions are run by the class teachers for their own classes.

Because the Year 3s and Year 4s work together within this narrative curriculum design, the History Centre operates on a two-year curriculum cycle. Each year begins with a folktale that sets up the concerns and the metaphors for the year's work. The year that focuses on convict history, for example, uses *The Sea People*, a tale of colonisation (Muller & Steiner 1982), to set the scene for Captain Cook's *Endeavour* voyage, the First Fleet of Australian convicts, then the European settlement and the stories of the goldfields of Victoria. In alternate years, *The King's Fountain*, a picture storybook by Lloyd Alexander (1971), illustrates the preciousness of water, which is then followed up with an investigation of our Australian coastal community and the entombing of the pharaoh along the Nile River. The messages of the story pretexts are reviewed again at the end of the year with all the experiential layers of learning folded into their embodied and reflective understandings.

St. Rhyio by the Sea

Note the anagram.

It was the last Thursday before the Easter break and I remember looking around the centre area with pride and amazement. The term had been a bit rushed because Easter fell early. As a team, we knew that the unit of work would extend into second term. Behind me was a large fishing net interlaced with sea creatures of all sizes and materials. On the display board to my left was the view facing inland from our fictional community. It was decked out in hessian and natural materials to symbolize the fragile coastal scrub and wildlife habitat. In front of the computer pods were murals and 'beach boxes' two metres tall cut from fibreboard and painted brightly with individual features. Taking 'centre stage' was a seaside jetty assembled from donated wooden pallets, which stood about half a metre high. It extended from a seaside backdrop for about 7 metres down the middle of the centre area. It had been the gathering place for our village, our 'story stage' and a symbol of weeks of hard work of physical and emotional investment.

The visual imagery for our quiet fishing village had come from the coastal town of San Remo, the gateway to Phillip Island near Melbourne where we had enjoyed our Outdoor Education camping experience. The stories that we shared in drama workshops layered our fictional 'sea change' stories with the spooky tales that we inherited from St. Rhyio old-timers. The three sessions of 'in role' (our scheduled interdisciplinary blocks) folded descriptive writing from camp recollections with the physical labour of sprucing up the town for the summer season. Once the students had fully invested in the town as villagers, we teachers decided to threaten its peace. We were a little too effective.

On the penultimate day of term, the four classes of students were gathered in the centre area sharing the progress of their groups. Tyres had been roped alongside the jetty (for the boats) and the last of the beach boxes was positioned on the sidewall. These 'work crew' reports were an important feature of bringing students (real) and townsfolk (role) together at the end of the day. Students and adults shared information, processes, hardships and humour. Then, the external door opened, Gordon, the new maintenance man came in and without a word, cordoned off the jetty with orange builders' bunting and answered student questions monosyllabically. His final words were, 'I've just been told it's unsafe!'

Students looked to the teachers for reassurance. We feigned confusion. Their connection and ownership of the space was in no doubt. Unfortunately they were ready to riot. Fearful of sending four classes of young people on holiday in a fury, the teachers diffused the situation by redirecting students to 'get the facts' before storming the principal's office. In any event, the students hopped on to computers and recorded their feelings.

> Upset, distressed, pressured, annoyed. What is going on? We took ages lifting, tying and cleaning? Who organized this? It was our environment. They have no right to stop us from using it.
>
> We built this pier all by ourselves and it took ages and lots of effort. I feel really annoyed and angry. What is the point of this?
>
> We built the pier so we should get to use it. SAVE THE PIER!!!!!!

The teachers of the History Centre had spent several weeks creating the personal connections and the physical environment of St. Rhyio (building belief). We knew that for dramatic tensions to occur that would provide positive learning outcomes, the students would need to invest in the community. In other words, the jetty and the peaceful nature of the coastal town would have to matter to them before we could introduce a threat. This stage took longer than we expected, but the physical environment looked terrific.

When we came back from the Easter break, the St. Rhyio pier was still cordoned off. Students were confronted with the blueprints for the development of the foreshore. It was with this new pretext that the integrated curriculum swung into action. Students were split into four large groups to choose firstly whether they would:

1. defend the development; or
2. argue against the development on the basis of impact on
   a. infrastructure – roads, traffic, the nature of the community;
   b. sea life – permanent and migratory species;
   c. bush animals – variety of species and threatened habitats.

The four large groups further split into smaller groups depending on the topic and the style of 'presentation to Council' that they preferred. All students combined research with their chosen medium of communication (poster, written text, Power-Point, model, performance, display book, etc.), which they presented 'in role' to the St. Rhyio council and a representative from the developers. They were hot-seated further about details that arose from their presentations.

Individual or pair 'Council submissions' leaned towards poster or PowerPoint presentations designed to advocate for the preservation of habitats of pygmy possums, shearwaters, and fur seals. One large group of about a dozen students used elastic to show the webbed connections between animals and their environment. They prepared a script, which combined the physical representation of life cycles and food chains with the knowledge they had accumulated from library and Internet sources. They included the threats to permanent wildlife, migratory species, bushland habitats and livelihoods such as marine tourism, fishing charters, surfing competitions and the dairy industry. Other presentations included models and dioramas of increased congestion and rubbish and designed community action T-shirt messages and billboards.

There is no doubt that the group who defended the proposed seaside development had a difficult task. Nonetheless, their arguments for employment, for sympathetic architecture, for minimal environmental impact, were treated seriously and gave everyone additional food for thought. In the end, the town councillors elected to delay further development 'at this time'.

A year-3 student reflected on the work defending St. Rhyio:

> St Rhyio was fun. I loved making all those things and I could feel the teamwork. I also loved making my poster with my friends. We made fish, landscapes, trees and lots more. I loved taking care of the environment and making things to save the Earth.
>
> At the start of the year we) created St. Rhyio when some people wanted to build a city instead of a beach with a nice view. But we got our way, luckily they didn't.

The story of St Rhyio is the most recent of the story frames that have been developed in the History Centre. The stages of story building included:

- sharing the visual imagery of a quiet coastal town;
- physical investment in creating our own seaside village;

- multimodal exploration of personal and communal history;
- dealing with the dramatic tension caused by the threat to lifestyle while students were engaged in sharing 'working bee' reports (this with a shared memo among all the teachers to make it less real next time!);
- symbolic representation to the village by the community members, of the proposed development;
- town meeting to share 'environmental impact' responsibilities for the council presentations;
- accumulation of data and work tasks in varied sizes of groups;
- presentations to council (electronic, print and performance modes);
- pool party and fish and chips to celebrate the success of our efforts.

Reflective Practice

As it happened, the restructuring of the Year 3 and 4 program into the design of the History Centre coincided with some reflective practitioner research of my own. This had started by investigating the Centre's precursor, known as the Playhouse, which had operated for several years, and where the seeds of the cross-curricular collaborations had been sown with Geraldine. However, drama was still structured temporally and physically into single weekly classes, one class at a time, in a nominated drama space. That provided a very valuable yardstick by which to evaluate the Centre. The second year of data collection then coincided with the inaugural year of the History Centre, thus affording me an opportunity to compare my processes and practices as a drama teacher in a traditional specialist structure with that in a narratively framed, interdisciplinary learning community.

My research questions focused on the nature of my teaching interventions and the way that they impacted on student autonomy (known as self-directed learning at ELTHAM). While it is not my intention to outline the details of my case studies, my findings have implications for process drama, integrated approaches and curriculum design. In comparing my drama practices and interventions in weekly, drama specialist classes with those that emerged in role experiences and workshops conducted over a full day, I discovered that in the History Centre:

- power relationships are more likely to be shared or overturned;
- student authorship over content and form becomes more evident; and
- teachers make greater use of liminal or 'twilight roles'.

The findings will not be particularly surprising to those teachers who are familiar with the ways that Mantle of the Expert assumes shared knowledge and contextualised authority of young people when they are positioned to solve adult challenges. To that end, the students make decisions, find the information and share the expertise that they need to build a case for (let's say) St. Rhyio. When that expertise is performative, publicly voiced and witnessed, they take authorship over the content and the form of the stories. I can think of instances where story 'seeds', which were planted by teachers, were conveniently ignored and even overturned for those that students have preferred to pursue. Author and ELTHAM principal Dr. David Warner holds the view that for students to be able to lead change in the twenty-first century, schools must be prepared to share knowledge and authority; have time space and freedom to explore; model the world and enable students not only to cope with change, but be agents of change (2006: 45).

Interestingly, the third key finding of my research, which concerns the fanciful notion of 'twilight' role, is compatible with these knowledge era goals.

Twilight Role

I have resurrected Heathcote's notion of *twilight role*, which I first encountered while studying in Durham, England, in the early eighties. It has not been evident in drama publications although the term is recognised by former students of Heathcote. Twilight role is perhaps incorporated implicitly in the notion of *shadow* or *shadowy role*, which is explained by Bowell and Heap, who claim:

> This serves largely as a device which injects information into the drama so that it can develop further without needing to interrupt the action. It also provides the teacher with a means of activating the frame tension of the drama and the opportunity to model language and emotional engagement for the pupils (2001: 98).

More recently Heathcote, in conversation with the author (2008), has confided that she did not ever consciously reject 'twilight role' but that other passions would have taken over as priorities at the time. The significant gap in time notwithstanding, Heathcote proceeded to clearly differentiate between five different stages of twilight role as she imagined the ways that a teacher might sidestep into full role.

The images of twilight and shadows are appropriate for the 'potential space' (Winnicott 1980) that exists between the explicit teacher/instructor and the teacher in role. Carroll has described it as a shift in vocal register without making any particular role explicit (2007).

Twilight role as an image, a label and a strategy has been largely overlooked. In a narratively framed curriculum structure, there are times for straightforward teacher instruction and times for full role. What has been surprising is the frequency whereby all teachers occupy the liminal space, which forewarns with a shift of position, demeanour, or questioning style that 'we' are sliding into a fictional realm. When Gordon put the barrier around the St. Rhyio pier, there was no registration of fiction, only 'real'. Students were outraged. Perhaps a simple 'twilight' statement such as, 'I'll just go check and see if he's mending the boardwalk for the summer season, shall I?' might have tempered the outrage. Students used to my 'narrational' voice would have recognised the shift if I had stated, 'And so it was, that many citizens happened to witness the stranger who came to examine the lie of the land around the foreshore.' The oversight aside, it became evident that twilight role comes into play more frequently when time is on one's side. The pressure of 'getting something done' in a single weekly specialist lesson overtakes the more gentle exploratory stage of discovery. The teacher is more likely to instruct, list, and shortcut learning processes in the name of efficiency.

The time, the shared space, the collegiality and the school culture with its emphasis on self-directed learning were administrative factors, which certainly enabled the teacher's stepping back 'into twilight' thereby allowing the advancement of student authority and expertise to come to the fore. As teachers retreat from natural authority, students have opportunities to take greater responsibility for their knowledge. Teacher judgment comes in the form of knowing how and when to scaffold learning without creating frustration.

The Physical Environment

Perhaps the least familiar but surprisingly significant addition to my ongoing repertoire of 'building belief' is the importance of the physical environment. For ancient Egypt, we have painted a backdrop, built a sarcophagus and printed hieroglyphic panels to line the tomb. The Endeavour was built from tyvek sails, ropes and bamboo. The King's fountain had a foam well as a village gathering place. The Goldfields encompass large sand trays where symbolic mining (in miniature) takes on all the excitement of the real thing. I have mentioned how important the evocation of the physical environment was to making the Sydney Town and St Rhyio dramatic learning units effective. As a drama teacher trained for secondary education, the only set building that I had previously experienced came by way of extracurricular productions and varying sizes of rostra. I can't help but feel angry about the dungeons and leftover classrooms that I have inhabited. The 'empty space' may be appropriate for adults, professionals and Peter Brook (1972), but it limits opportunities in an educational context.

The environments that we build in the History Centre offer investment, a sense of community, visible 'distance travelled' and achievement in the public arena. Students can informally mentor each other in a way that would occur naturally in any communal project. I have come to learn that a sense of place is not incidental but central to the engagement and commitment to our work.

I started this chapter with a quote from Eisner written in 1979. More recently, Kath Murdoch has reinforced Eisner's and Egan's counsel for a coherent, engaging curriculum. She has stated:

> . . . at its heart, integrating curriculum is about designing curriculum, teaching and learning in such a way as to minimise unnecessary fragmentation and maximise authentic connectedness across the learning experience for students in relation to both 'content' (what is being learned about and for) and 'process' (how and with whom this learning is taking place). (2007: 67)

At the time of writing, History Centre staff are preparing for the fourth round of the 2-year curriculum cycle. The incoming Year 3s had an orientation and an introduction to the lifestyles of the islanders in *The Sea People*. After the summer break, they will become those islanders. The island experiences should serve as an interesting contrast with the new outdoor education program, which will focus on the cultural traditions, values and experiences of an aboriginal community. Next year, Dreamtime stories will live alongside those of Pacific Islanders, explorers and astronomers. In the History Centre, we will continue to unravel the mysteries of history by 'living through' the challenges of the past in the present.

References

Alexander, L. (1971). *The king's fountain*. New York: E.P. Dutton & Co. Inc.
Bolton, G. (2003). *Dorothy heathcote's story*. Stoke on Trent, UK: Trentham Books.
Booth, D. (1994). *Story drama*. Markham, Ontario: Pembroke Publishers.
Bowell, P., & Heap, B. (2001). *Planning process drama*. London: David Fulton Publishers.
Brook, P. (1972). *The empty space*. Harmondsworth: Penguin.
Doll, W. E. Jr. (1993). *A post-modern perspective on curriculum*. New York: Teachers College Press.
Egan, K. (1997). *The educated mind*. Chicago: The University of Chicago Press.
Egan, K. (1988). *Teaching as storytelling: An alternative approach to teaching the curriculum in the elementary school*. NY: Routledge.
Eisner, E. (1979). *The educational imagination*. New York: Macmillan Publishing Co. Inc.
Heathcote, D. (2000). Contexts for Active Learning: four models to forge links between schooling and society. In Chris Lawrence (Ed.), *Drama research number 1* (pp. 31–45). London: National Drama Publications.
Heathcote, D. (2008). Private conversation April 8, 2008, National Drama conference, *Body, Mind, Soul*. Durham, England.
Heathcote, D., & Bolton, G. (1995). *Drama for learning: Dorothy heathcote's mantle of the expert approach to education*. Portsmouth, NH: Heinemann.
Muller, J., & Steiner, J. (1982). *The sea people*. New York: Schocken Books.
Murdoch, K. (2007). Journeying towards integrative curriculum. In *Curriculum Perspectives* (Vol. 27, No. 1, pp. 67–70). Canberra: Australian Curriculum Studies Association (ACSA).
Pinar, W. F., & Irwin, R. L. (Eds.). (2005). *Curriculum in a new key: The collected works of Ted T. Aoki*. Mahwah, New Jersey: Lawrence Erlbaum Associates, Publishers.
Victorian Curriculum and Assessment Authority. (2005). *Victorian essential learning standards*. Melbourne: VCAA
Warner, D. (2006). *Schooling for the Knowledge Era*. Camberwell, Victoria: Acer Press.
Winnicott, D. (1980). *Playing and reality*. New York: Penguin Books.

Chapter 11
Pasts, Present and Futures: Which Door Next?

John O'Toole and Madonna Stinson

The reader will have noticed that we have deliberately avoided the battle-worn territorial cartography of trying to define the boundaries of both/either drama and/or theatre, in favour of what we believe are much more usefully blurred edges, and ambiguous, even paradoxical perimeters. However, so that we've got something to talk about, our map does have some common features. Words like acting, performing and role-play come to mind, and have been often used. It's something to do with presenting human images in public, something to do with exploring relationships and feelings, but it's also something to do with cognitive models and fictional situations, it's something to do with the body and sensory and kinaesthetic activities, something to do with aesthetics and something to do with play and playfulness. Well, mostly ... sort-of. Oh yes, and people do it by forming, presenting and responding and sometimes all three simultaneously. No wonder it shape-shifts. Does it have a basic, proper shape at all? And what shapes might it assume in the future, and why? Time to call on Proteus's other magic capacity, twist his tail a bit and see if he'll foretell something of where we might be heading.

Applied Theatre

We might start with a scrutiny of particular contemporary drama and theatre practice, and that should probably begin with what at the time of writing is a very fashionable redefinition of the territory, known as 'applied theatre' (though a couple of British scholars in the field prefer 'applied drama' for the same phenomenon). Starting more or less simultaneously in many places, the applied theatre movement was formalised – also simultaneously – in the UK and Australia, in university 'Centres for Applied Theatre Research'. This movement is an attempt to find and acknowledge the commonality in the myriad current manifestations of live theatre and dramatic events, which occur outside traditional theatre venues. That, of course, includes the work of educators such as Augusto Boal, Theatre for Development, the theatre-in-education movement ... and should or can also include all the applications of theatre manifested in educational contexts such as schools – in other words, everything that this book is about. A quite neutral definition of applied

J. O'Toole et al., *Drama and Curriculum,* Landscapes: the Arts, Aesthetics, and Education 6, DOI 10.1007/978-1-4020-9370-8_12,

theatre would be: *Dramatic and theatrical performance for specific context, purpose and audience, usually taking place beyond conventional theatres, usually involving interactivity*. This definition – quite deliberately – does not in itself acknowledge any educational component and, therefore, includes forms such as street theatre, busking, sporting openings, and interval entertainments, the increasingly popular manifestations of both theatre and dramatic role-play in conferences and corporate presentations, and perhaps even the highly theatrical processions and military parades orchestrated and produced by governments to encourage patriotism or loyalty to the status quo – what the late Kuo Pao Kun (the 'father of Singapore theatre') called 'theatre that governs' (1996: 169). However, virtually all the other current definitions in the burgeoning literature perceive a very strong essential educational component, sometimes didactic, together with an agenda for social change and betterment, such as the Griffith University, Brisbane, Applied Theatre Research Program:

> Applied Theatre is the use of theatre in a non-traditional way to bring about changes in human behaviour, usually in some direct participant manner. (Griffith 2007).

Even more so, the Manchester University UK definition:

> 'Applied Theatre' refers to the practice of theatre and drama in non-traditional settings. It refers to theatre practice that engages with areas of social and cultural policy such as public health, education, criminal justice, heritage site interpretation and development. Applied Theatre at Manchester has included theatre in education, prison theatre, theatre in places of conflict, theatre in museums and heritage sites, theatre for development and theatre with refugee communities and artists. This diverse range of practice exists at the intersection of performance studies and community, participatory, educational and political theatre practice (Manchester 2007).

Why are we connecting applied theatre and curriculum? Most key writers in the field so far also acknowledge or privilege purposes of broad education and/or social change. Philip Taylor's *Applied Theatre* (2003) is actually subtitled *Creating Transformative Encounters in the Community*, and Helen Nicholson's *Applied Drama: the Gift of Theatre* has as its third chapter 'Pedagogies, praxis and performance' and a strong social transformation message throughout. The forthcoming *Applied Theatre Reader* (Prentki & Preston 2008) may be expected to have a similar broadly educational focus, as Tim Prentki is a long-time key scholar, teacher and practitioner of Theatre for Development and Sheila Preston an experienced colleague who defines as a major research interest 'critical pedagogies for global citizenship'.

Indeed, some members of the Theatre for Development crowd, especially those in Africa, feel that a new term, particularly *applied* theatre, is quite unnecessary (and certainly any notion of a 'new' movement). In discussions with the authors, Ugandan drama educator Mangeni Patrick pointed out that African traditional theatre has always had specific social and in the broadest sense educational purposes, rather than 'just' entertainment, and that is why from the start of TfD, government agencies and NGOs, as well as social reformers and liberators, have *applied* theatre as a natural medium for specific educational purposes. Victor Ukaegbu puts it pithily:

Traditional African performances straddle sacred-secular boundaries but by commanding some form of investment in efficacious outcomes, most performances can serve ritual and aesthetic functions. What is needed is not a new concept or definition but the re-introduction of production strategies and collective concerns that created the traditional performances that audiences attended as participants instead of as detached spectators (2007: 53).

This reevaluation also reminds us that audience participation was not invented by contemporary drama and theatre practitioners.

The first volume of the *Applied Theatre Researcher* (2000) contains two interesting early attempts to pin the beast down that on the surface at least presuppose a natural educational purpose. Bjørn Rasmussen notes that

the wish to facilitate drama and theater as a powerful medium, affecting changes for the attendants, is a family resemblance found by those exercising the practice of applied theater. Moreover, a typical wish for positive changes recalls a vital, still modern and educational project.

More eclectically, Judith Ackroyd provides a deliberately broad-based definition, one which strongly yet not exclusively emphasises educational and social change purposes:

I suggest that it is an intentionality which all the various groups have in common. They share a belief in the power of the theatre form to address something beyond the form itself. So one group use theatre in order to promote positive social processes within a particular community, whilst others employ it in order to promote an understanding of human resource issues among corporate employees. The range is huge, including such as theatre for education, for community development, and for health promotion, and dramatherapy and psychodrama.

Is the future of drama education to be found in applied theatre, then? Certainly the emphasis placed by the welter of convergent sentiments above would seem to suggest that our earlier definition is much too neutral and that education is indeed integral to applied theatre. The 2007 *International Symposium on Applied Theatre: Engagement and Transformation* (note the pedagogically grounded subtitle) held in Sydney had lively discussions about whether drama education formed a subset of applied theatre, or vice-versa. However, this marriage of true minds perspective is not only optimistic but ill-founded, and the relationship between drama education and applied theatre is nothing if not problematical, and growing more so – something that Ackroyd has herself put her finger on, in a recent trenchant reevaluation of her own 2000 article.

I guess I feel a bit cheated to have embraced the term because I saw it bringing a range of practices together with drama education and then find it has eased my dramatic preference out (2007).

Perhaps applied theatre has become a cuckoo in the nest, or is in danger of becoming so. Ackroyd makes a pertinent observation: 'Drama in education doesn't seem to get a significant stake. Nothing in the classroom.' Certainly there has been a quite remarkable and wilful shift in scholarly interest and academic literature away from the school and towards adult and community – nonformal educational – contexts, especially in the UK (a little less so in North America and Australasia, though the trend is noticeable there too). The shift is so pronounced that the journal

Research in Drama Education is rebranding itself with the subtitle *The Journal of Applied Theatre and Performance* and is even having to devote a 'special edition' in 2008 to drama education; so pronounced has the emphasis in its pages on applied theatre become. The triennial international *Researching Drama and Theatre in Education* conference has been completely rebadged for 2008 as *Researching Applied Drama, Theatre and Performance*: *Performance, Cross-cultural dialogue and Co-existence*. Although that title certainly invokes some of the grander themes of education, the word itself has been conspicuously dropped, together with any reference whatever to schools, teachers or even young people in the Conference Focus statement (Exeter 2007). This bears out vividly Ackroyd's accusation that:

> The [applied theatre] discourse now delineates a restricted and exclusive type of radical practice, enshrined in an evangelical frame. ... There's no mention of gospel street theatre nor work with the police, nor drama for business ... because these would mitigate against the politics of the discourse being constructed. These are not ideologically suitable (2007).

There may be in all this nothing much more than the old territorial status game, familiar to Western drama educators and referred to often in earlier pages. On the one hand, the educators among us are trying to gain status in the world of arts policy and strategy, where schools and children rank low in the pecking order; and conversely, the artists among us are trying to retain our status as adult professionals while proving that our artwork has 'efficacious outcomes', in Ukaegbu's useful phrase. Certainly many leading applied theatre practitioners do still proudly refer to themselves as drama educators, such as New Zealander Peter O'Connor, whose company's name is 'Applied Theatre Consultants' and its primary business is working in schools with children (O'Connor, Holland, & O'Connor 2007). All the authors of this book line up alongside O'Connor, working in and teaching both drama education and applied theatre, and ourselves very unsure of where one ends and the other begins – or even if there is a boundary at all. However, 'line up' suggests battle, and this would be a very unnecessary one, and like other phantom dichotomies encountered in these pages can be quickly resolved with the 'application' of intelligent and magnanimous analysis, as Penny Bundy shows in a cogent editorial for the *IDEA Journal/Applied Theatre Researcher* – evoking strong echoes as she does so of Dorothy Heathcote's '5 Ws':

> If one sees the rhetoric of applied theatre as a story – a created thing – then ... one of the five terms ... the *who, what, where, why* and *how* of a story can often be identified as the organising element by which the others are given meaning (2007).

She illustrates this with an elegant set of questions, which could well be used as a template for constructing any theatre or drama work driven by Ackroyd's 'intentionality' and focuses on its participants rather than its artists – as all that we are talking about in this book does, or should. She sums up:

> Like Ackroyd, we are not seeing Applied Theatre as a specific and bounded form or practice. Rather, the articles represent a range of ideas and practices in a number of different contexts. Interestingly, the authors do place different emphasis on the who, what, where, why and how of the work they discuss.

Culture, Politics and Technology

That excursion into another language, though not really another landscape, may not seem to get us far in spotting futures, but it does point to some important future indicators, and highlight another one of those characteristics that go towards defining 'drama'. Applied theatre is very self-consciously aware of its social responsibilities, and its role as a cultural barometer.

All drama is protean and shape-shifting, yes, but not randomly. It is always intricately (if not always popularly) tuned into the cultural and social mores of its times and contexts. It also reflects and refracts the political paradigms dominant and current. One may assume that the medieval monks who generated the miracle cycles, and particularly their successors who wrote the morality plays, were strongly supportive of (their version of) a stable society and the social and intellectual status quo in which they had their own comfortable place. Harriet Finlay Johnson and Winifred Ward did not carry any explicit messages of social change – on the contrary, Johnson in particular wanted the best for her working class children *within* their social milieus and likely futures. On the other hand, in the 1970s and 1980s in Britain, heavily influenced by post World War II theatre and by Bertolt Brecht, many drama education and especially theatre-in-education practitioners used explicitly Marxist arguments in promoting an agenda of radical social change through drama – and strongly influenced many others who were not Marxists. This contributed in no small measure to the heat of the 'British debate', though not to the light. In several memorable conferences, John observed that members on both sides passionately used Marxist ideology to support their high-ground, diametrically opposite stand in the phantom dichotomy. Some, particularly T-i-E companies, went further, and no small number of these were closed by their sponsoring education authorities or theatres, after too aggressively and relentlessly biting the hands that fed them.

That left-wing political impetus, of course, had its effect on what happened to drama in the schools in the UK – where drama perished as a separate subject under the wheels of the Black Paper juggernaut. No less than the late Professor Richard Courtney, effectively drama education's first philosopher, claimed – in conversation with John, 1998 – to have evidence that right-wing Prime Minister Margaret Thatcher herself gave orders for drama to be dropped from the New National Curriculum. Somebody did, anyway. The energetic rebuilding of drama in that country has seen it positively thriving under the wing of English. So, back to the future by going back to Chapter 3, perhaps? Certainly one at least of the leading contemporary UK drama educators, Professor Jonothan Neelands – also in conversation with the authors – thinks that so far this has been a highly positive move, and quite possibly English is the place where drama should find (or re-find) its curricular home. That undoubtedly gives us pause in Australia, having cast ourselves adrift from English and made our bed in the arts. On the other hand, not just politics, but history and culture also play a major role in where drama does or does not fit, and perhaps the UK is a special case. After all, England does possess the world's most valuable tourist commodity, in the person of its most famous playwright; according to a recent media poll, Shakespeare is still the second-most popular English man or woman (after Winston Churchill) and even though few adult Britons go to see his plays live, still less study them, many children have to, as Shakespeare is a compulsory part of English Literature curricula throughout the world.

The last three decades have seen the rise of poststructuralism and of critical theory in the academies, and the adoption of a dominant social constructivist agenda in schools, and even in curriculum design. The result in the world of drama and theatre, including drama education, has been a growing critical eclecticism, a blurring of definitions and a slipperiness of genre, including much more openness of form, collaborative generation of artwork and a readiness for cultural border crossing. As Brad Haseman puts it, the whole landscape of drama and theatre is being changed by at least five contemporary factors:

1. ... by hybridity – the impulse to collaborate and produce hybrid works ... 'slash arts' – music/theatre, dance/theatre and so on,
2. ... by interactivity – the creation and integration of content into engaging, immersive environments,
3. ... as it becomes an input into other industries ... the latest in a range of drama-facilitated interventions in education, health and business known as applied theatre,
4. by new forms of cultural production ... the traditional form of drama production is being unsettled as the technical dimensions of production embrace projections of text, still images, animations and moving images (More on this below),
5. by multiplatform, cross-promotional means of producing and distributing cultural products .... Increasingly innovative artists and producers are creating opportunities for multiplatform delivery and cross-promotion of their work ... dramatic action created for one context can be reversioned for another ... it can use the enabling technologies of a digital environment to connect with larger and technically savvy audiences everywhere (2004: 19–21).

It cannot be stressed too strongly that *all* these are already long-time characteristics of drama pedagogy, as Haseman himself emphasises. Largely unnoticed by the mainstream worlds either of art or curriculum, we have been playing in the margins, experimenting and formulating 'new' forms with all of these characteristics. Moreover, like the educational and cultural scholars most frequently quoted (such as bell hooks, Patti Lather, Michel Foucault, Henry Giroux), drama educators still maintain a central interest in the nature of power and the possibilities of change, partly inherited from the Marxists. This does not necessarily change much of what goes on in schools, but it has certainly added to the diversity and depth of analysis.

Any peek into the future obviously has to take into account the new communication technologies. Drama educators have been quite swift to embrace the opportunities that have been offered for a long time by video and audio systems, and more recently by the Internet, blogs, interactive and multiplayer game platforms, online simulated environments, and even mobile phones and digital assistants, which are so often the bane of classroom teachers. (Examples of all of these may be found in Carroll, Anderson, and Cameron (2006); and even more imaginative variants in Anderson, Carroll, and Cameron (2008).) This is not as surprising as it might seem;

on the contrary. Live theatre has for many decades now regularly used new media as part of its standard design and even playwrighting equipment: slides, video, film and computer projection. New technologies continue to offer new vistas for visual and aural effects, and even integral dramatic content. There is another natural attraction: technology offers virtual reality – of which, as we are realising more and more, drama is the first form. Brenda Laurel pointed this out years ago with her seminal book *Computers as Theatre* (1993), with the earnest plea that people like us take the technology out of the hands of the young-male-dominated commercial interests, which were ensuring that violent and fantastical combat were its staple fare. Interactive multiplayer role games like *Everquest* and *World of Warcraft* are just role-drama really, with great opportunities for simplified action and strong linear narratives, and rather more limited opportunities to explore character, motives and deep human relationships – but they do allow interesting changes of point-of-view. James Gee (2003, 2005) and other technologically minded educators have taken the message and endorsed the forms for educational purposes without really recognising that at least part of the driving force is drama. Virtual environments like *Second Life* offer the opportunities not only for the collaborative creation of effectively complete dramatic contexts, but for the 'avatars' which inhabit them to converse and interact in real time.

A few process drama teachers sniffed the breeze long ago. As far back as 1986, Julie Dunn discovered the dramatic potential of some early interactive computer learning packages like *Where in the World is Carmen Sandiego?* and she was not content to leave them behind the screen for students to engage with in solitary and virtual mode. Using *Carmen Sandiego* along with some similarly stimulating maths packages, she set about inventing a new form of process drama, where the students took roles and took on something of the 'mantle of the expert'. Together they made the dramatic context of a crime and Carmen's mysterious disappearance come to life in the classroom, with the computer providing prompts and clues for the sleuths in the real-time group-based teaching context, and the dramatic tension shared by the characters in their very visceral tasks (Wood & Dunn 1986). Since then, there has been a growing number of progressively more sophisticated explorations of the multidimensional interactivity between live classrooms and computers, well summed up in the title of Sue Davis's article: *Cyberdrama: Exploring Possibilities* and led by some of the most distinguished drama pedagogues such as John Carroll, student of Dorothy Heathcote (e.g., Carroll 2004; Davis 2006; Raphael 2008). The doyenne herself, still ahead of the game in her eighties, provides a visionary foreword to Carroll's and his colleagues' book *Real Players? Drama, Technology and Education* (2006).

Drama Research and Drama as Research

The last two decades have also seen another very significant change in drama and theatre education. Prior to the 1990s, most drama educators saw ourselves primarily and often exclusively as practitioners, who, if we had a theory at all, derived it a posteriori, from our practice. Apart from Richard Courtney (1968), that is. Otherwise, if you don't count Peter Slade's vivid on-the-run documentation, the first research text was Gavin Bolton's ground-breaking attempt to theorise how drama works and how children learn through it, very tentatively titled: *Towards a Theory of Drama in Education* (1979). Journals, such as there were, were mostly practice oriented, such as *Young Drama*, *2D* (UK) and *NADIE Journal* (Australia) – though the slightly later *Youth Theatre Journal* (USA) was the first to recognise the need for a refereed publication.

For various reasons, mostly as usual quite unrelated to drama, research has become a major factor worldwide. In a number of countries, including Australia, the UK and Scandinavia, professional training, such as teaching, nursing and business, has been brought under the wing of Universities, with an immediate demand to develop a culture of research and publication. The newer generation of drama teacher educators have had to get busy along with their colleagues and learn to be researchers. *Young Drama* and *2D* disappeared, to be replaced by *Research in Drama Education*, *Drama Research*, and *The Applied Theatre Researcher. NADIE Journal* morphed into the refereed *NJ*. Ironically, all the professional associations sponsoring these journals have had to respond to the plaintive appeals of their membership for the continuation of a practical journal that would provide teachers with ideas for planning classes or schemes of work (*Stage of the Art* by the American Alliance for Theater and Education, *ADEM* by Drama Australia, and *Drama – one forum, many voices* by the UK's National Drama). Eventually, schoolteachers too have started to move towards research, some driven by the ambition to join the now research-credentialled world of teacher-educators; some because their employers have started taking account of higher credentials in their payment and promotion scales.

This process has been perhaps more organic and less pronounced in the USA, where as we have noted, there has been a longer tradition of research into practice in drama education, and which has exerted its own influence on the world scene. Two key figures in this have been Betty-Jane Wagner and Cecily O'Neill. While the rest of us (apart from Bolton) were bedazzled by Dorothy Heathcote's breath-taking practice and knock-em-down charisma, Wagner started shaping Heathcote's wise but often whirling words firstly into a consistent description of her practice (1974), and then into Wagner's own scholarly practice, particularly in the teaching through drama of language (1998) and ethics (1999). Originally based in London, local Drama Adviser Cecily O'Neill had been taking a lead in making Heathcote's and Bolton's radical praxis into a user-friendly and manageable pedagogy for teachers (1977, 1982). For a decade, she was lured to Ohio State University, and turned her own natural scholarship into much more formal research, elegantly articulated in her 1996 chapter *Into the Labyrinth* and her seminal book *Drama Worlds* (1995). In the process, her research supervision skills mentored a startling number of today's leading American scholars in the field, such as Cris Warner, Chris Anderson, and Pam Scheurer, and coauthoring important research texts with Anita Manley (Manley & O'Neill 1997) and Taiwan's Kao Shin Mei (Kao & O'Neill 1998). The links between her research and practice have been recently recognised in the elegantly and appropriately titled *Structure and Spontaneity – The Process Drama of Cecily O'Neill*. (Taylor & Warner 2006).

The dominant drama research methodologies have changed markedly too, all over the world, as they have in humanities and arts education generally. The quantitative and quasi-quantitative studies driven by positivistic paradigms and goals that were once staple diet in the USA, and in every educational research methods class anywhere, have been supplanted by forms of qualitative case study and action research and reflective practitioner research. These methods are much more responsive to and mirror much better the ways of drama itself, being grounded in practice rather than hypothesis, processual rather than goal-oriented, seeking conditional insights rather than positivistic conclusions or absolute truths. They welcome contradictions and paradoxes, rather than seeking to exclude them as uncontrollable variables, and strive to provide 'rich description' and 'thick data' rather than paring the data and conclusions to unarguable essentials with Occam's razor. There is a lively debate in the academies about what extent art-making itself can be regarded as research, research-rich or research-equivalent, which has led to new and fashionable forms of arts-based and arts-informed inquiry. This enthusiastic embrace by drama educators of research as a congenial and compatible bedfellow is sometimes as much driven by fear of statistics as by the recognition of the social agency of dramatic enquiry (drama people tend to do better with words and social interactions, and not so well with numerical equations). Quite a few advocates of drama, and arts generally, who are aware of the policy games necessary to get the arts in through the curriculum doors and keep them there, are beginning to feel that the research pendulum has perhaps swung a bit too far, and that a few crisp and well-defended metrics and statistics tend to pack more punch with those who make policy decisions than any amount of anecdotal evidence of life change or elaborate insights into complexities of learning habits and social behaviour change (e.g., Deasy 2002; Robinson 2006). Bureaucrats and politicians don't have time to read those, even if they are sympathetic to them.

Drama scholars are making some interesting new connections within the tertiary academies, which might in time enrich the work in schools and colleges. Perhaps the most significant, and certainly the most fashionable, of these contemporary hook-ups is between drama and theatre scholars on the one hand, and anthropologists and sociologists on the other. We have found some common territory that both are embracing perhaps with more zeal than critical caution. The manifestations of this liaison are variously called 'ethnographic performance', 'performed ethnography' and even 'ethnodrama' (differences in title which as usual embody definitional and territorial claims). Anthropologists were on to this first, some while ago. They wanted some means to encompass and convey to their audience something of the complexity and life of their research subjects. Ethnographers in particular became aware that the rich life of a community, and the dynamic immediacy of people relating to each other and communicating, which gives it that life, cannot be properly or effectively contained within the impoverished confines of a retrospective and static written research report. Perhaps, they thought, something of this life could be 'recreated', three-dimensionally and in real time, through drama?

There was a synchronous convergence at the time with another anthropological preoccupation of the late twentieth century, which is not unrelated to drama: performativity – the recognition that people's actions do not just 'happen', but almost invariably have some kind of public dimension, as a form of signalling that is both individual and as part of the ongoing rites of any society. There's nothing really new in this, of course, the notion that we perform much or all of what we do with audience in mind, and thus perform ourselves publicly with varying degrees of self-consciousness. The idea of the 'teatro mundi' or 'theatre of the world' was very popular in the middle ages – just a little googling produced a tantalising reference to a Latin grammar book of 1246, which referred in the same verse both to this phrase and a 'scripta theatro' concerning Faustus (Born 1939: 315). Shakespeare gave the idea a couple of outings, with 'All the world's a stage' and Prospero's set piece in Act V of The Tempest. From the 1960s, it gained currency in another scholarship too: that of role-theory, particularly Erving Goffman's *The Presentation of Self in Everyday Life* (1959). This has already proved valuable to the process drama movement, helping to establish and map the relationship and differences between *role* as a function of real-life self-presentation, and *role* as a fictional character, function, or point-of-view within drama.

The key anthropologists of the performativity studies movement have also been acutely aware of their dramatic connection: e.g., Victor Turner (*Dramas, Fields, and Metaphors: Symbolic Action in Human Society* 1974); Dwight Conquergood (*Performance Studies: Interventions and Radical Research* 2002); and Don Handelman (*From Models to Mirrors: Towards an Anthropology of Public Events* 1990). As a research opening, the drama opportunists were on to it like a flash. Richard Schechner, of course, was first out of the blocks (*Between Theater & Anthropology* 1985), but his interest has always been primarily researching theatre, rather than theatricalising research. By the 1990s, several of the new research-savvy drama educators, such as Jim Mienczakowski (e.g. 1995) and Johnny Saldaña (e.g. 1998), sniffed the opening, and introduced it to the top-line ethnographers such as Norman Denzin, who have seized on it with wild enthusiasm (e.g. 1997). Since then, it has become intensely and increasingly fashionable as a way of researching human behaviour, especially the researcher's own ('auto-ethnography').

Initially researchers took timid steps into forms like reader's theatre, with actors vocalising and cautiously enacting the transcribed data provided by the 'witnesses' of the community being studied. This was usually for closed audiences of researchers, such as Cozart, Gordon, Gunzenhauser, McKinney, and Patterson's presentation of a school evaluation program to the 1998 American Educational Research Association. Before long, researchers were recreating whole cultural environments into theatrical and quasi-theatrical happenings (Madison 2005, Haseman 2000), and even Broadway was getting into the act with the smash-hit *The Laramie Project* (Kaufman 2001), which was in essence a very publicly performed ethnodrama. Schools have been enthusiastically targeted as recipients of performed ethnography with educational or therapeutic purposes (e.g., Mienczakowski 1993; Goldstein 2002). Rather belatedly, a critical edge to the enthusiasm is appearing. Sheryl Cozart and her colleagues reviewed their 1998 AERA performance with some disquiet in the light of audience comments like: 'I'm concerned about what I saw. I'm not happy, not thrilled. It's not what you did but what you said.' As they shrewdly noted, there were ongoing tensions between their roles as evaluators and researchers (Cozart, Gordon, Gunzenhauser, McKinney, and Patterson 2003). There are in fact more tensions than that, very few of which have yet been properly acknowledged by the advocates of ethnographic performance. By definition, there is bound to be tension between a form of research (ethnography), which seeks to provide scrupulously authentic data on the life of a community using the words and actions of its members and a form of art (theatre) which transforms any data it receives into something that will engage and hold an audience. The audience member's response to Cozart was in fact expressing the resentment of a research witness who saw her own contribution being, as she perceived it, demeaned on stage in public. Add to that tension those engendered by the other potentially conflicting purposes, which the researchers and the researched carry into the activity, such as education, therapy or evaluation, and you have a thoroughly problematic hybrid.

And that's not all. The distinguished American educational sociologist Patti Lather (2000) questioned the propriety of ethnographic performance for presuming to know and show how the original community or individual felt, for colonising and appropriating that 'other'.

What Is 'Appropriate'?

Perhaps recognising this problematic is just recognising the problematic in all drama, which is that drama is both rude and improper. Drama, whether in performance or in dramatic role-play, does colonise and appropriate 'the other'. That's the whole point of it. Drama's double face allows *both* empathy and distance – so that we not only identify with the written 'other' but also deconstruct and interrogate the 'other's' otherness – revealing and reengaging with it, and making it negotiable (the danger of stamping one's 'own' on it is there, yes, but that too becomes negotiable). The very word 'appropriate' has acquired a derogatory ring of moral disapproval in contemporary cultural scholarship . . . to improperly make one's own, to steal. But of course it also means to make proper and appropriate – to give new life in a new age. To go back to before Plato, Homer's texts – originally performed live by one of those 'pantomimic gentleman' (Homer himself, presumably in the first place) – have been appropriated and made modern from the word go. A couple of hundred years after Homer was finally written down, Sophocles was living and writing in the new, contested, and not entirely stable democracy of Athens. So he borrowed the obscure story of *Philoctetes* from Homer's Iliad, and turned it from a story of a victim of the Gods into a debate on personal feelings, interpersonal loyalty, and political necessity that was entirely appropriate to his time and the political context of his audience. Shakespeare took Homer's love tragedy of *Troilus and Cressida* and appropriated it into an entirely Jacobean exposé of disease and corruption and political chicanery.

And yes, drama is a politically incorrect and corrupting medium – it corrupts the certainties of received truths and identities ... with both dangers and possibilities. It pokes into hidden business, plunders cultures, strips icons, and drags out secrets for ironic examination. It even-handedly shows the commonalities as well as the differences – our common humanness within the very otherness. More than that, it can give us new stories, stories that we do not yet know are our own, and then provide us with the shock of recognition that we are involved in the stories, and complicit in their manufacture as much as their performance. While that unconscious human performativity, which Conquergood and company have identified, has us acting out those stories willy-nilly, and largely unconsciously, throughout our real social lives, at least drama provides a relatively safe virtual space, mostly free from consequences in the 'real world', to freeze for examination, reconstruct and rearrange and analyse and evaluate some of the happenings in that real world.

By now, you might be asking – what happened to the book about drama and curriculum? What we have been trying to explore, as we wrote this book, is the complexity and diversity of this art-form that we love so much and has been our obsession for many, many years. What connections can we make from there to curriculum in schools? To those of you who were hoping to find a book that described content, processes and skills – all delineated neatly in assessable standards – we apologise. Or rather, we don't! Our sense of drama aligns with our sense of curriculum: both allow for multiple interpretations; both are experienced as lived and not absorbed from the pages of a book (or a PowerPoint presentation or computer screen); both are or can be responsive to diversity of time and location, contexts and participants' needs, desires and purposes. Like Courtney and Pinar and a host of others, we recognise and celebrate the 'lived' and 'living' curriculum. After all, that is one of the fundamental purposes of drama. It is a 'divergent' curriculum, encouraging translation and transformation of content, forms and processes. It acknowledges local constraints and contexts (Stinson 2008).

One of the dominant insights to emerge from our investigation in this book is that the shape-shifting quality of drama, perhaps endemic to its marginalisation in systemic curricula traditional and contemporary, also keeps our current circumstances and the future filled equally with challenges and opportunities. We're still there on the edge – whoever we are .... There is no simple, common agreement or shared understanding of what drama is, what it does and why it is important. But that does not mean that we don't know.

This makes it hard to explain, justify and advocate for. The 'hybridity' we are so proud of also diffuses our capacity for cohesiveness. Other 'discipline areas' within school curricula can claim a body of knowledge: concepts, content. We are particularly challenged by our reliance on processes, habits of mind, and – dare we say – skills, but without a coherent and easily stated conceptual framework. This is equally a strength, allowing for the diversity so evident within the field, but as it contributes to the 'slipperiness', it also compounds our problems with advocacy. We acknowledge that it may be important to know how to annotate a script – but not for every student and not for every context. We acknowledge the importance of sustaining a role – but not for every student and not for every context. The list goes on. And maybe the slipperiness is a positive. It allows us to do what we say we want to do: focus on the students and assist them to work with and learn within the art form – living the curriculum.

Drama's opponents like Plato fear it as a Pandora's box. Open it and the ills of the world will spill out. We think not. If it is such a box, it is one in reverse, into which we make a conscious decision to step. What we find inside are the social, cultural and political values and mores of our society, and our own desires and fears and dreams, which are all potentially available for us to rearrange into those new stories. Pandora's drama box is morally neutral – so we have to be careful how we put the bits together. But perhaps we can step back out a little wiser, more knowing and better recognising our complicity in the values, culture, and politics of our real society. Our dramatic experience may have affirmed and reinforced them (the smiling mask of Aristotelian drama); or it may have confronted and subverted them (the scowling mask of Plato's fears and Boal's intentions). It is a truism – probably still worth stating – that which of these masks is being worn, and exactly how it manifests itself in performance, depends not only on those cultural mores, but also on the political context. That is particularly true of contexts of systemic education, which is always setup to reflect and perpetuate … and very, very occasionally to develop … the dominant ethos and power structures.

Whatever the local cultural and political mores and conditions, a significant challenge for the international drama education community is to engage in this conversation about exactly what drama *is* and why we think it is so important for students to have access to this way of knowing the world *within* the curriculum. That argument must still be made afresh in each educational context – as it has down through time.

We'll finish this book, therefore, by briefly engaging in the conversation with two distinguished contemporary drama educators, both from states where drama has made it right into the house as part of the standard curriculum, about the nature of our challenge once we do get in through the door. In most societies we know, the dominant pattern of school curriculum is still technicist and positivistic, and in spite of all the new theory and all the efforts of some education systems themselves, there has been little change from the curriculum-as-planned towards the curriculum-as-lived, as we hinted at the end of Chapter 2. In this continuing context, one of the biggest challenges that drama faces is that once it does get through the door, it must avoid being domesticated. Peter O'Connor, after watching a drama lesson on death in war, which was full of inauthentic emotion, exaggerated acting, and tasks that had no relevance to the students' lives or the world and the wars just beyond the classroom, wrote despairingly:

> As each child died we demonstrated our acting deaths to each other in heights of melodramatic activity. (Many were done at level two, 'great consistency and flair demonstrated'). As I watched the young people leave with their tidy, written hand-out sheets of melodrama techniques taught (although doubtfully learnt) I wondered what we had achieved by moving drama into the middle. What had we sacrificed when drama becomes a subject just like every other subject? And as we work through the curriculum with our measured outcomes the opportunity for empathy is lost as we measure other things. Michael Fleming's warning

of what is the point of learning King Lear, if we at the end of it don't understand what it is to be an old man going mad, rings true in drama classrooms where such questions get lost in the functionality of learning about a discipline in the arts. Because technique is what is so easily measured, the spirit of drama evaporates (2008).

Part of the answer to O'Connor's challenge is that to some extent, this is a problem of pedagogy rather than curriculum – it is very unlikely that this travesty had either been prescribed by the syllabus designers or negotiated with the students, and any good working drama teachers would shudder at the lesson's excesses, which he describes in graphic detail. To discredit a whole system by a worst-case example is a kind of sophistry, which we hoped to leave behind after Chapter 6. However, his challenge cannot be shrugged off as easily as that.

> For although drama needs to sit at the centre of what we do in education it would appear to me that this does not equate to simply making it a subject in the curriculum. Despite the rhetoric, schooling . . . has become places where the monologue of the teacher's voice has all but totally silenced kids who sit waiting for the next learning intention to be realised. Where the freedom to do [drama] work has been co-opted into safe and predictable accountable outcomes (ibid).

As we see it, the problem isn't that drama is *necessarily* constrained by becoming a subject in a curriculum. Rather, it is that the curriculum, which we are often forced into creating with our systems' and governments' current modernist/technicist approach to schooling, is just not drama. We *are* too often forced to comply with the language and layout and assessment requirements that are the boundary objects, which demarcate the 'essential' content and learnings, and whatever the essence of drama is, it is certainly not to be found in those.

Often forced perhaps we may be, but not always, and there are less bleak prospects to be found inside the House of Curriculum as our final conversation demonstrates, with Jo Wise, Drama Queensland's ex-President, a sage and experienced player in the game, responsible herself for organising many of drama's successful excursions into the house in recent years. Her heartfelt plea to the members of that association serves us up with yet another challenge from inside the house . . . how to stay there!

> Many of you have been very lucky to live in a state where drama stands equally with four other arts subjects from P-12. You have enjoyed the status that comes with being valued and regarded as equal members of whole school curriculum communities. You have been able to create assessment that makes sense to you, your kids and values the capacity of young people and teachers to work as artists.
>
> We all acknowledge that in schools we are continually faced with the core/other curriculum debates, the space issues, the struggles for timetabling and on-going explanations that we have to give regarding the cognitive, social and emotional impact of drama practice for all young people. . .etc . . .. Regardless of all this (or perhaps because of it) many of us stand strong and successfully in schools with great spaces, large numbers, parents and other teachers supporting us.
>
> The reasons why we can design good curriculum and assessment, work collaboratively with whole school communities and relate our classroom work with the real world is because people before us wrote good quality, evidence based, relevant curriculum and we have had quality specialised drama teachers train us. There are no guarantees, no policy or future plans that enshrine this good luck.

University places that specialise in Arts education, particularly drama are being actively cut [in other states, not yet Queensland]. Drama education/Arts education generally is not on the agenda of the National Curriculum Board yet. It is you as Drama educators who have benefited from good curriculum and well trained specialised teachers at schools and universities who need to put it there (Wise 2008).

We believe that we drama educators can and *will* continue to put drama and much more into the curriculum conversation about children's entitlements to those multimodal ways of knowing and understanding the world which are called learning. When the world of academia 'discovered' multiliteracies, we were the ones saying 'yes of course'. Our belief remains strong despite the (re)current back-to-basics pushes, which always threaten to reduce drama once again to a helpless watcher at the door of Wonderland, or rather that strange Looking Glass land called schools, where:

> . . . it takes all the running you can do, to keep in the same place. If you want to get some-where else, you must run twice as fast as that . . . and . . . the rule is, jam tomorrow and jam yesterday, but never jam today;
> (Through the Looking Glass, and what Alice found there).

The co-history of drama and curriculum has lasted for centuries, shifting and modifying according to the dominant society of the time, going underground when it had to, but always surviving. And so we believe it will continue. We drama educators are now able more than ever before to draw on our international community of prac-tice, our growing body of research and literature, and our well-developed capacities as expressive and communicative teaching artists, as we continue to fashion that key to the curriculum door. To what extent, we wonder, can we choose through which door we will enter, and what we can do once inside the house?

References

Ackroyd, J. (2000). Applied theatre: Problems and possibilities. *The Applied Theatre Researcher* Vol 1. http://www.griffith.edu.au/centre/cpci/atr/journal/article1_number1.htm

Ackroyd, J. (2007). Applied theatre: An exclusionary discourse? *The IDEA Journal/Applied The-atre Researcher*, 8. http://www.griffith.edu.au/_data/assets/pdf_file/0005/52889/07-ackroyd-final.pdf

Anderson, M., Carroll, J., & Cameron, D. (Eds.). (2008 in preparation). *Drama education with digital technology: Applying theatre, drama and technology to learning*. London: Contin-uum Books.

Bolton, G. (1979). *Towards a theory of drama in education*. London: Longmans.

Born, L. K. (1939). Quotations and citations in the accentarium of John of Garland. *Transactions and Proceedings of the American Philological Association* (303–317).

Carroll, J. (2004). Digital pre-text: process drama and everyday technology. In C. Hatton & M. Anderson (Eds.), *The state of our art: NSW perspectives in educational drama*. Sydney: Currency Press.

Carroll, J., Anderson, M., & Cameron, D. (Eds.). (2006). *Real players? Drama, technology and education*. Stoke on Trent: Trentham.

Conquergood, D. (2002). Performance studies: Interventions and radical research. *The Drama Review*, *46*(2), 145–156.

Cozart, S. C., Gordon, J., Gunzenhauser, M., McKinney, M. B., & Patterson, J. A. (1998). *Performing reform: Presenting the polyphony*. San Diego, CA: Performance presented at the annual meeting of the American Educational Research Association.

Cozart, S. C., Gordon, J., Gunzenhauser, M., McKinney, M. B., & Patterson, J. A. (2003). Disrupting dialogue: Envisioning performance ethnography for research and evaluation. *Educational Foundations, 17*(2), 53–69.

Davis, S. (2006). Cyberdrama: Exploring possibilities. *NJ (Drama Australia), 30*(1), 91–103.

Deasy, R. (2002). *Critical links. Learning in the arts and student academic and social development*. Washington DC: Arts Education Partnership.

Denzin, N. (1997). *Interpretive ethnography: Ethnographic practices for the 21st century. Chapter 4: Performance Texts*. Thousand Oaks, Cal: Sage.

Exeter (The University of) (2007). Focus of the conference. *Researching Applied Drama, Theatre and Performance*: *Performance, Cross-cultural dialogue and Co-existence*. Conference website: http://www.spa.ex.ac.uk/drama/appliedconf/focus.html Retrieved 6 January 2008.

Gee, J. (2003). *What video games have to teach us about learning and literacy*. New York: Palgrave Macmillan.

Gee, J. (2005). *Why video games are good for your soul: Pleasure and learning*. Altona, Vic.: Common Ground.

Goffman, E. (1959). *The presentation of self in everyday life*. New York: Doubleday.

Goldstein, T. (2002). Performed ethnography for representing other people's children in critical educational research. *Applied Theatre Researcher* Vol 3. http://www.griffith.edu.au/centre/cpci/atr/

Griffith University (2007). *Applied Theatre Research*: *About us*. http://www.griffith.edu.au/centre/cpci/atr/ Retrieved 6 January 2008.

Handelman, D. (1990). *Models and mirrors : Towards an anthropology of public events*. Cambridge: Cambridge University Press.

Haseman, B. (2000). Uncertain truths: Facing palliative care through drama. In J. O'Toole & M. Lepp (Eds.), *Drama for life: stories of adult learning and empowermment*. Brisbane: Playlab Press.

Haseman, B. (2004). Cooking drama and drama education in the global kitchen. *NJ (Journal of Drama Australia),28*(2), 15–24.

Kao, S. -M. & O'Neill, C. (1998). *Words into worlds: Learning a second language through process drama*. Westport, CT: Ablex.

Kaufman, M., & members of Tectonic Theatre Project. (2001). *The Laramie Project*. New York: Vintage.

Kuo, P. -K. (1996). Uprooted and searching. In J. O'Toole & K. Donelan (Eds.), *Drama, culture and empowerment: The IDEA dialogues*. Brisbane: IDEA Publications.

Lather, P. (2000). *Reflective Keynote*. International Drama in Education Research Institute, Ohio, July. Unpublished.

Laurel, B. (1993). *Computers as theatre*. Reading, Mass.: Addison-Wesley.

Madison, D. (2005). *Critical ethnography: Method, ethics, and performance. Chapter 7 – Performance ethnography*. Thousand Oaks, Cal: Sage.

Manchester (The University of) (2007). *Centre for Applied Theatre Research. About us*. http://www.arts.manchester.ac.uk/catr/about/index.htm Retrieved 6 January 2008.

Manley, A., & O'Neill, C. (Eds.). (1997). *Dreamseekers : Creative approaches to the African American heritage*. Portsmouth, NH: Heinemann.

Mienczakowski, J. (1993). Ethnography or drama: An account of a research performance project into schizophrenia. *NADIE Journal, 17*(3), 14–18.

Mienczakowski, J. (1995). The theatre of ethnography: The reconstruction of ethnography into theatre with emancipatory potential. *Qualitative Inquiry, 7*(3), 360–375.

Nicholson, H. (2005). *Applied drama: The gift of theatre*. Basingstoke: Palgrave Macmillan.

O'Connor, P. Holland, C., & O'Connor, B. (2007). The everyday becomes extraordinary: Conversations about family violence, through applied theatre. *The IDEA Journal/Applied Theatre Researcher, 8*. http://www.griffith.edu.au/centre/cpci/atr/journal.htm

O'Neill, C. (1977). *Drama guidelines*. London: Heinemann.

O'Neill, C. (1982). *Drama structures*. London: Hutchinson.

O'Neill, C. (1995). *Drama worlds*. Portsmouth, NH: Heinemann.

O'Neill, C. (1996). Into the labyrinth. In Philip Taylor (Ed.), *Researching drama and arts education: New paradigms and possibilities*. London: Falmer.

Prentki, T., & Preston, S. (2008). *The applied theatre reader*. London: Routledge.

Raphael, J. (2008). Case study 2: How to change the world. In Chapter 10. N. Jeanneret, J. O'Toole & C. Sinclair (Eds.), *Education in the Arts: Principles and practices for teaching children*. Melbourne: Oxford University Press.

Rasmussen, B. (2000). Applied theatre and the power play. *The Applied Theatre Researcher* Vol 1. http://www.griffith.edu.au/centre/cpci/atr/journal/article2_number1.htm

Robinson, K. (2006). *Back to Basics: Arts Education in the 21st Century*. Keynote address: UNESCO 1st World Conference on Arts Education, Lisbon, March.

Saldaña, J. (1998). Ethical issues in an ethnographic performance text: The dramatic impact of 'juicy stuff'. *Research in Drama Education, 3*(2), 181–196.

Schechner, R. (1985). *Between theater & anthropology*. Philadelphia: University of Pennsylvania Press.

Stinson, M. (2008). *The shifting sands of curriculum development: A case study of the development of the Years 1 to 10 The Arts curriculum for Queensland Schools*. Unpublished PhD Dissertation: Griffith University.

Taylor, P. (2003). *Applied theatre: Creating transformative encounters in the community*. Portsmouth NH: Heinemann.

Taylor, P., & Warner, C. (2006). *From structure to spontaneity: The process drama of Cecily O'Neill*. London: Trentham Books.

Turner, V. (1982). *From ritual to theatre: The human seriousness of play*. New York: Performing Arts Publications.

Ukaegbu, V. (2004). The Problem with Definitions. *Drama Research*, National Drama UK. Vol. 3. Cited in Ackroyd, J. (2007). Applied theatre: An exclusionary discourse? *The IDEA Journal/Applied Theatre Researcher, 8*.

Wagner, B. -J. (1998). *Educational drama and language arts: What research shows*. Portsmouth, NH: Heinemann.

Wagner, B. -J. (Ed.). (1999). *Building moral communities through drama*. Westport, CT: Ablex.

Wise, J. (2008). Extract from email posted on Drama Queensland internal e-group. Accessed 7 July.

Wood, G., & Dunn, J. (1986). Where in the world is Carmen Sandiego? In P. Stevenson & J. O'Toole (Eds.), *Pretending to learn: A resources pack for teachers beginning drama*. Brisbane: Brisbane CAE. [*Where in the world is Carmen Sandiego*? Broderbund Software Inc. http://www.broderbund.com]

Author Index

A

Aaltonen, Heli, 84
Ackroyd, Judith, 36, 59, 195, 196
Adams, Antony, 39, 55
Aeschylus, 23
Allen, John, 76, 100, 117, 118, 122, 138, 142
Anderson, Chris, 200
Anderson, Michael, 59, 111, 198
Aoki, Ted, 29, 43, 185
Apple, Michael, 41, 172
Aristotle, 14, 15, 17, 18–19, 21, 97, 139
Ashby, Gerald, 12, 152–153, 159

B

Balfour, Michael, 92
Bamford, Anne, 67
Barcan, Alan, 31, 32, 33
Barnes, Douglas, 55, 56, 59, 60
Barta-Martinez, Federico, 80
Barthes, Roland, 131
Beeby, Clarence, 159
Beerbohm Tree, Henry, 60
Bell, John, 164
Benjamin, Harold, 37
Benjamin, Walter, 102
Berne, Eric, 91
Bernstein, Basil, 38
Bishop of Chester, the, 21
Blatner, Adam, 90, 92
Bloom, Harold, 130
Blyton, Enid, 156
Boal, Augusto, 17, 80, 109, 112, 113, 124, 193, 205
Bolton, Gavin, 22, 52, 60, 72, 74, 81, 82, 92, 101, 102, 103, 105, 106, 109, 117, 118, 119, 120, 121, 122, 139, 152, 159, 160, 172, 175, 184, 185, 186, 200
Bond, Edward, 109, 121
Boomer, Garth, 59, 107, 158, 159, 163

Booth, David, 58, 74, 78, 104, 124, 159, 184
Bowell, Pam, 104, 190
Bray, Errol, 135
Brecht, Bertolt, 39, 102, 109, 110, 120, 121, 197
Brice Heath, Shirley, 51, 87
Brown, Bille, 164–165
Bruner, Jerome, 11, 40, 50
Bundy, Penny, 92, 93, 165, 196
Burgess, Roma, 104, 123, 124, 139, 140
Burniston, Christabel, 160
Burton, Bishop E.J., 77, 78, 86, 88, 100, 102, 129, 159
Burton, Bruce, 86, 104
Buzo, Alex, 164
Byron, Ken, 59

C

Caldwell Cook, Henry, 52, 55, 60, 100, 118, 129, 132
Carroll, John, 26, 51, 111, 190, 198, 199
Chalmers, Frank, 110
Chapman, Gerald, 121
Chapman, Roger, 160
Chekhov, Michael, 81
Chinyowa, Kennedy, 14, 112
Chomsky, Noam, 58, 65
Church, Esme, 100
Churchill, Winston, 198
Cobby, Maisie, 71, 88, 100, 134, 136, 160
Coleridge, Samuel Taylor, 72
Comenius, Jan, 11, 12, 22–23, 97
Conquergood, Dwight, 202, 204
Cook, Henry Caldwell, 52, 53, 55, 60, 100, 118, 129, 132, 142, 186
Corneille, Pierre, 23
Courtney, Richard, 29, 107, 152, 159, 160, 197, 200, 204
Cox, C.B., 84

Cox, Tim, 52
Cozart, Sheryl, 202, 203
Creaser, Barbara, 136
Crompton, Barbara, 163

D
Dalrymple, Lynn, 14, 112
Damasio, Antonio, 82
Davis, David, 102, 109, 139
Davis, Sue, 111, 199
Deasy, Richard, 201
de Mott, Benjamin, 55
Denzin, Norman, 202
Deverall, John, 123
Dewey, John, 33, 84
Dickens, Charles, 23
Disraeli, Benjamin, 129
Dobson, Warwick, 92
Dodgson, Elyse, 83
Doll, William, 41, 185
Donelan, Kate, 111, 162
Doughty, Peter, 57
Dumas, Alexandre, 90
Dunnington, Hazel Brain, 73
Dunn, Julie, 13, 71, 72, 102, 136, 137, 181, 199

E
Eastman, Arthur, 55
Eisner, Elliott, 2, 36, 40, 41, 174, 183, 184, 191
Euripides, 17, 21
Evernden, Stanley, 88

F
Fiala, Oliver, 166
Finlay Johnson, Harriet, 52, 53, 82, 87, 97, 98,
    99, 100, 103, 104–105, 138, 142, 197
Fleming, Michael, 50, 205
Florida, Richard, 85
Flory Kelly, Mary, 74
Fogerty, Elsie, 133
Foucault, Michel, 41, 198
Foulds, Gordon, 161
Freire, Paolo, 38, 39, 109
Froebel, Friedrich, 12, 22, 23

G
Gallagher, Kathleen, 86
Galván, Liliana, 80
Garrard, Allen, 76, 77, 81, 88, 108
Gaskill, Bill, 121
Gatto, John Taylor, 37, 42
Gaudry, Pam, 104, 123, 124, 139, 140
Gee, James, 111, 199
Geertz, Clifford, 13

Giffin, Holly, 71, 72, 136, 137
Gillham, Geoff, 105
Gillies, Max, 164
Giroux, Henry, 42, 174, 198
Goethe, Johann von, 90
Goffman, Erving, 202
Goode, Tony, 92, 93, 124
Grady, Sharon, 86, 109
Greene, Maxine, 2
Grimmelshausen, Hans, 90
Grindal, Archbishop, 20, 21
Groos, Karl, 12
Grumet, Madeleine, 24, 42, 43
Grundy, Denis, 32

H
Halliday, Michael, 50
Handelman, Don, 202
Harwood, Ronald, 14
Haseman, Brad, 59, 87, 104, 124, 139, 153,
    198, 202
Heap, Brian, 104, 190
Heathcote, Dorothy, 51, 52, 72, 74, 92, 101,
    102, 103, 104, 105, 106, 109, 119, 120,
    121, 122, 123, 138, 139, 152, 159, 166,
    172, 184, 185, 190, 196, 199, 200
Herrad of Landsberg, 20, 21
Hodgson, John, 74, 102
Holt, John, 38
Homer, 203
Hooks, bell, 198
Hornbrook, David, 122, 123, 124, 129, 160
Hughes Mearns, William, 73
Huizinga, Johan, 71
Hunt, Albert, 39, 109, 110

I
Iljine, Vladimir, 90, 92
Illich, Ivan, 38, 39

J
Jackson, P., 35
Jackson, Tony, 103
Jennings, Sue, 91
Johnstone, Keith, 78
Jonson, Ben, 129
Jordan, Robert, 32
Jung, Carl, 74

K
Kao, Shin-Mei, 66, 200
Kapek, Karel, 132
Kase-Polisini, Judith, 74
Kempe, Andy, 129

Kenneally, Thomas, 32
Krashen, Stephen, 64, 65
Kuo, Pao Kun, 194

L
Laban, Rudolf, 88
Landy, Robert, 92
Lather, Patti, 198, 203
Laurel, Brenda, 111, 199
Lester, John, 53
Lett, Warren, 140
Liu, J., 66

M
McCaslin, Nellie, 73, 74, 78, 79, 159
MacConnell, James, 31
McDonell, Doug, 159
McGowan, G., 12
McGregor, Lynn, 101
McIntyre, Barbara, 73
McLaren, Peter, 174
Mamouney, Don, 165
Mangeni, Patrick, 112, 133, 194
Manley, Anita, 104, 200
Marlowe, Christopher, 23
Marshall, Anne, 31
Marzano, R., 66
Mencken, H.L., 37, 42
Merlin, Donald, 184
Mienczakowski, Jim, 202
Mitchell, John, 31
Moffett, James, 55
Montessori, Maria, 23
Moreno, Jacob, 85, 90, 91, 92, 102, 110
Morgan, Norah, 58, 89, 103, 104, 160
Murdoch, Kath, 191

N
Nason, Bryan, 165
Neelands, Jonothan, 59, 104, 124, 197
Neill, A.S., 37
Nelson, Murry, 34
Nicholson, Helen, 129
Noddings, Nel, 41
Nolte, Nick, 91, 92

O
O'Connor, Peter, 92, 93, 101, 111, 166, 196, 205, 206
Odhiambo, Chris, 13, 111
O'Mara, Joanne, 5, 107
O'Neill, Cecily, 66, 74, 89, 102, 103, 104, 124, 139, 152, 159, 160, 175, 200
Opie, Iona, 136

Opie, Peter, 136
Østern, Anna-Lena, 12, 22

P
Parry, Christopher, 53
Parsons, Beth, 50, 72, 155, 156
Paye, Paul, 153
Perls, Fritz, 91
Piaget, Jean, 11, 12, 50, 71
Pick, John, 119, 122
Pinar, William, 29, 41, 42, 185, 204
Plato, 4, 15, 16, 17, 18, 20, 21, 30, 108, 127, 203, 205
Plautus, 21, 23
Postman, Neil, 38, 39
Prentki, Tim, 112, 194
Preston, Sheila, 194
Print, Murray, 170
Prior, Ross, 133, 134

Q
Qoopane, Francis, 13

R
Racine, Jean, 23
Rasmussen, Bjørn, 195
Read, Herbert, 33
Reid, Louis Arnaud, 33
Reimer, Everett, 39
Reith, Lord, 62
Rembrandt, 122
Richards, Ernest, 102
Robinson, Ken, 101, 121, 160, 201
Rugg, Harold, 34, 35
Rumbley, R., 60
Rush, Geoffrey, 164

S
Sadler, Royce, 149
Saldaña, Johnny, 202
Sansom, Clive, 156, 159, 160
Saxton, Juliana, 29, 58, 89, 104, 160
Schaffner, Megan, 50, 156
Schechner, Richard, 13, 202
Scheurer, Pam, 107, 200
Schwab, J.J., 40
Scofield, Paul, 132, 133
Shakespeare, William, 23, 42, 43, 53, 62, 90, 98, 118, 129, 130, 131, 132, 142, 150, 164, 197, 198, 202, 203
Shaw, George Bernard, 130, 133
Siks, Geraldine Brain, 73, 74, 88
Sills, Paul, 102

Slade, Peter, 60, 73, 74, 75, 76, 77, 78, 81, 85,
    88, 89, 90, 91, 92, 99, 102, 105, 118, 119,
    136, 138, 159, 200
Smigiel, Heather, 111
Smilansky, Sara, 11
Snyder, Benson, 39
Sophocles, 17, 23, 132, 203
Southey, Robert, 138
Spady, William, 173
Spolin, Viola, 78, 102
Stanislavski, Konstantin, 81, 102
Stevenson, Paul, 29, 111
Summerfield, Geoffrey, 55
Sutton-Smith, Brian, 71
Swanwick, Keith, 134
Swortzell, Nancy & Lowell, 78

T
Taba, Hilda, 35, 40
Tarlington, Carole, 135
Taylor, Evelyn, 111
Taylor, K., 111
Taylor, Philip, 104, 107, 124, 171, 194, 201
Terence, 21, 23
Thatcher, Margaret, 58, 197
Thompson, James, 92
Turner, Victor, 202
Tyler, Ralph, 35, 36, 38, 39, 40, 41, 173

U
Ukaegbu, Victor, 194, 196

V
Voss Price, Lucy, 72
Vygotsky, Lev, 12, 50, 65, 72

W
Wagner, Betty-Jane, 11, 51, 57, 101, 103,
    105, 200
Walker, Decker F., 40
Ward, Winifred, 58, 73, 74, 75, 77, 78, 80, 81,
    84, 85, 100, 102, 105, 138, 159, 197
Warner, Cris, 107, 200, 201
Warner, David, 184, 190
Way, Brian, 76, 77, 78, 81, 82, 83, 85, 88, 102,
    104, 119, 138, 159
Weingartner, Charles, 38
Wertembaker, Timberlake, 32
Whitehead, Frank, 55, 56, 57
Wiles, John, 77, 81, 87, 108
Williamson, David, 164
Williams, Raymond, 130
Willis, Paul, 130
Wiltshire, Gail, 153
Wise, Jo, 206, 207
Witkin, Robert, 152
Wittgenstein, Ludwig, 50
Wordsworth, William, 138
Wright, Nicholas, 121

Y
Young, David, 160

Subject Index

A

Aboriginal Australians, 62
Academy, academies, 15, 36, 60, 85, 127, 133
Activity Rhymes, 55
Actor training, 85, 133, 163, 164
Aesthetics, 2, 4, 33, 54, 97, 99, 124, 127, 130, 138, 141, 165, 193, 195
Affective filter hypothesis, 64
Africa, 6, 13, 14, 62, 72, 93, 161, 162, 194, 195
Alice in Wonderland, 1
Alliteration, 99
AMEB, *see* Australian Music Education Board (AMEB)
American Alliance for Theater and Education (AATE), 200
American Educational Research Association (AERA), 202–203
Ancient Egypt, 183, 186, 191
Angels in America, 130
Animation, 198
Annie's Coming Out, 109
Anthropology, 51, 201, 202
Apartheid, 147
Apology, The, 109
Applied drama, 193
Applied theatre, 92, 93, 101, 193–196, 197, 198
Applied Theatre Researcher, The, 195, 196, 200
Arithmetic, 31–32, 33, 98, 99, 100
Artistic curriculum, 2
Arts-and-Crafts movement, 158
Art of Speech, 151, 156
Arts Syllabus Advisory Committee, 174, 178
Assessment, 13, 30, 36, 43, 57, 58, 63, 117, 140, 141, 148, 149, 151, 153, 156, 165, 170, 171, 173, 174, 175, 178, 180, 181, 185, 206
Australia, 2, 6, 24, 30, 31–33, 34, 35, 37, 42, 54, 55, 58, 59, 62, 63, 75, 76, 78, 79, 84, 85, 91, 100, 101, 104, 108, 109, 123, 130, 131, 132, 133, 134, 139, 140, 141, 148, 149, 150, 152, 153, 154, 155, 156, 157, 158, 159, 160, 161, 162, 163, 164, 165, 169, 170, 179, 181, 183, 193, 197, 200
Australian Association of Teachers of English, 59
Australian Capital Territory (ACT), 149
Australian Commonwealth Government, 179–180, 181–182
Australian Drama Education Magazine (ADEM), 161, 200
Australian Music Education Board (AMEB), 63, 87, 151, 156
Australian Performing Group, 164
Auto-ethnography, 202

B

Ballarat, 183
Basics, the, 33, 58, 166
BBC English, 62
Behaviourism, 65, 110, 112
Bell Shakespeare Company, 164
Benedictines, 19
Big Ben, 62
Big Sur, 91
Birmingham, UK, 60
Black Papers, 84–85
Blogs, 198
Board of Secondary School Studies, 149, 153
Board of Senior Secondary School Studies, 153
Bonnington Hotel, 118, 120–121
Book-keeping, 31
Botany Bay, 31
Bouverie Street Drama Centre, 165
Brazil, 80, 112
Bretton Hall College, 159
Brisbane, 37, 152, 153, 162, 164, 170, 194

Brisbane, 2nd IDEA World Congress, 162
Brisbane Independent School, 37
Britain, 22, 23, 25, 30, 31, 34, 57, 58, 61, 62, 91, 101, 104, 123, 172, 197
British Association of Dramatherapists (BADTH), 89, 91
British Medical Association, 89
Bullock Report, The, 57

C
Calvinism, 22
Canada, 6, 25, 51, 55, 58, 76, 78, 85, 148, 159, 162
Carmen Sandiego, 199
Carnivals, 18
Catharsis, 17, 89
Catholic schools, 153, 179, 180
Central School of Speech and Drama, 60, 117, 133, 159
Centre for Applied Theatre Research, 193
Centre for Artistic Development (CAD), 154
Centre for Intercultural Documentation, 39
Chaos theory, 79
Chicago, 102
Child-centred curriculum, 73
Child Drama, 74, 75, 85, 89, 138
Children's theatre, 74, 117, 118
China, 79
Christianity, 19
Citizenship education, 108
Civics, 108
Classics, 32, 130
Clergy, 32
CLTAs, 65
Co-curriculum, co-curricular, 2, 13, 54, 62, 63
College of Advanced Education (CAE), 151
Commedia dell' Arte, 22, 102
Communication, 2, 49, 61, 63, 65, 66, 67, 72, 86, 87, 92, 107, 137, 151, 160, 163, 164, 185, 188, 198
Community schools, 37
Complicity, 205
Comprehensible input hypothesis, 65
Comprehension (exercises), 55, 148, 157, 158
Computers as Theatre, 111, 199
Concert party, 33
Confucius, 24, 79
Conservation of the illusion, 72, 107
Constructivism, constructivist, 40, 106, 198
Conventions, 75, 89, 99, 105, 106, 107, 138, 175, 176
Convicts, 31, 32, 183, 184, 186
Cookery, 98

Cooling Conflict, 92
Cop-in-the-head, 112
Corporate theatre, 194
Corpus Christi Day, 20
Coventry Belgrade Theatre, 103, 109
Craftwork, 54
Creation, Play of the, 20
Creative dramatics, 72–78, 79, 80, 85, 88, 138
Creative Industries, 163
Creative Power, 73
Creative writing, 100, 157
Creativity, 35, 56, 58, 73, 78–80, 84, 85, 137, 185
Critical literacy, 49, 59
Critical theory, 41, 198
Cromwell, Oliver, 21–22, 87
Crucifixion, Play of the, 19
Cultural boycotts, 161
Currambena School, 37
Currere, 29
Currick(-ing), 29

D
Dance, 2, 13, 21, 23, 24, 31, 41, 59, 75, 76, 80, 88, 89, 129, 140, 150, 151, 154, 157, 180, 198
Death of the author, 131
Debating, 61
Democratic curriculum, 58
De-schooling society, 109
Dialogue, 3, 5, 19, 20, 49, 55, 56, 59, 63, 64, 135
Didactic, 17, 20, 108, 194
Digital environment, 198
Digital narrative, 111
Dionysus, 14, 18
Dithyramb, 14
Drama Australia, 161, 162, 200
Dramaide, 93
Drama – one forum, many voices, 200
Drama and Oral Language (DOL), 66
Drama Queensland, 174, 177, 178, 181, 206
Drama Research (Journal), 200
Drama therapy, 89, 91, 92, 93
Dramatherapy, dramatherapist, 80, 89, 91, 92, 195
Dramatic episodes, 34, 35
Dramatic play, 11, 12, 13, 21, 50, 56, 71, 72, 73, 74, 75, 76, 100, 102, 103, 105, 120, 124, 136, 137, 138, 139, 141, 176
Dramatis personae, 106
Dramawise, 139
Drawing, 33, 42, 54, 104, 119, 133, 184

Dreaming, Dreamtime, 31, 192
Drill, 33, 83
Dual affect, 72, 107
Durham, UK, 101, 190

E

Early childhood, 2, 13, 25, 71, 72, 88, 103, 131, 141, 159, 165
Early Childhood Drama Project (ECDP), 12, 13, 152, 153, 164
EdData, 178
EDERED (European Children's Theatre Encounter), 84
Educational Drama Association (NSW EDA), 160, 164, 166
Eisteddfod, 132, 155
Elaborated codes, 38
Elijah and Ahab, 51–52
Elizabethan drama, 21
Elocution, 32, 57, 60, 133, 134
Eltham College, 183
Emotion, authentic, 65, 82, 89, 141, 205
Empathy, 90, 105, 109, 119, 203, 205
Encuentro Primero, Lima, 80
Engagement, 35, 55, 82, 113, 131, 185, 190, 191
Engineering, 108, 148
England, 22, 25, 30, 31, 37, 52, 55, 60, 61, 62, 78, 80, 101, 129, 130, 133, 138, 153, 155, 190, 197
English (language), 2, 21, 22, 25, 38, 39, 49–53, 55, 56, 57, 58, 59, 60, 61, 62, 64, 66, 67, 107, 128, 129, 130, 131, 132, 141, 148, 149, 150, 151, 152, 156–157, 158, 182, 198
Epic of Gilgamesh, The, 130
Esalen Institute, 91
Ethics, 3, 97, 110, 200
Ethnodrama, 201, 202
Ethnographic performance, 201, 203
Ethnography, 201, 202, 203
Evanston, Illinois, 73, 74
Everquest, 26, 199
Everyman, 20
Experiential curriculum, 58, 147
Expression scenique, 91
Extra-curriculum, -curricular, 2, 25, 33, 151, 154, 155–156

F

Falls of Lodore, The, 138
Faustus, Doctor, 202
Film & TV Studies, 131
First Fleet, the, 31, 32, 186

Folk-rites, 18
Forum theatre, 112, 113
Forwards, The, 109
French, 19, 22, 31
Fuzzy logic, 79

G

Game, games, 14, 26, 65, 71, 88, 89, 91, 99, 100, 101, 104, 111, 112, 119, 161, 196, 198, 199, 201, 206
Gardening, 32, 98
Geese Theatre, 92
Genre theory, 59
Geography, 33, 98, 100, 101
Gestalt theatre, 91
Gods, 15, 18, 203
Gold Coast, The, 153
Goldfields, the, 183, 186, 191
Gradgrind, Thomas, 131
Grammar, 29, 32, 33, 53, 61, 64, 65, 183, 202
Grammar schools, 32, 183
Griffith University, 194
Grin and Tonic Theatre Troupe, 165
Group-devised theatre, 76
Group dynamics, 3, 151
Guardian, The, 11, 16, 85, 89, 138
Gulf of Carpentaria, 177
Gymnastics, 33, 57

H

Hadow Report, The, 54, 60, 88
Hamlet, 52, 63
Handicraft, 54
Hard Times, 23
Health promotion, 195
Heartbreak High, 109
Heartbreak Kid, The, 109
Heroes, 15, 46, 147
Hidden curriculum, the, 39, 42
History, 2, 3, 4, 17, 22, 23, 29, 30, 36, 37, 41, 54, 61, 87, 98, 100, 107, 108, 117, 128, 161, 162, 172, 183–192, 197, 207
History Centre, the, 183–192
HIV-AIDS, 14, 111
HMS *Endeavour*, 186, 191, 199
Holbrook, David, 55, 56, 57, 60
Hollywood, 133
Homo Ludens, 71
Hong Kong, 79, 80, 108
Hopes for Great Happenings, 39
Humanities, 148, 201
Hungary, 11, 84
Hybrid arts, hybridity, 157, 198, 204

I

IDEA, 79, 80, 162, 196
Iliad, The, 203
Images of Life, 158, 163
Immersive environments, 198
Inclusive education, 3
Independent Schools of Queensland, 170
India, 62
Indigenous drama, 13, 31
Instructional design, 110, 111
Instructional role-play, 140
Intentionality, 195, 196
Internet, 111, 185, 188, 198
Interplay, 135
Issues-based education, 34

J

Jacobean drama, 21
Japan, 79
Jesuits, 22
Jesus, 19
Joseph (Biblical), 81

K

KACES, Korea, 79
Key Learning Area (KLA), 2, 59, 79, 89, 131,
      140, 157, 177, 178, 181
Key stages (UK), 6, 33, 53, 54, 56, 57, 58,
      62, 63, 73, 74, 76, 77, 79, 84, 85, 88,
      92, 101, 109, 117–120, 123, 132–134,
      139, 148, 150, 151, 152, 156, 159,
      160, 163–166, 172, 175, 193, 194, 195,
      197, 200
Kinaesthetic, 11, 49, 193
King Charles II, 22, 23
King James VI, 21
King Lear, 206
King's English, 62
King's Fountain, The, 186, 191
KITE, 13

L

La Boîte Theatre, 164
Labour Party (Australia), 147
Language, 1, 4, 11, 12, 18, 24, 32, 36, 38, 43,
      49–67, 72, 74, 85, 88, 98, 100, 104, 124,
      132, 137, 140, 141, 150, 156, 157, 175,
      184, 190, 197, 200, 206
Language arts, 51, 150, 156, 157
Language immersion, 65
Language interactionism, 65, 67, 102, 201
Laramie Project, The, 202

Latin, 19, 21, 22, 23, 29, 30, 38, 42, 53, 80,
      198, 199, 201, 202
Law, 16, 32, 35, 36, 37, 148, 170
Learning to learn, 79
Learning Place, The, 181
Legislative Theatre, 112
Liberal studies, 2, 108, 128
Library, 32, 98, 110, 188
Linguistic competencies, 51
Linguistics, 50, 51, 57, 59
Linguistics, anthropological, 51
Linguistics, applied, 59
Linguistics, systemic, 50
Listen to your Mothers, 112
Literacy, 1, 38, 49, 58, 59, 111, 112, 128, 131,
      150, 166
Literature, 2, 6, 38, 52–54, 57–60, 85, 88, 98,
      100, 110, 128–131, 134, 135, 150, 157,
      163, 194, 195, 198, 207
'Living-through' role-play, 105
London, 21, 58, 61, 62, 83, 118, 122, 132,
      184, 200
Long-form improvisation, 102
Looking Glass Land, 207
Lyndhurst, St Mary's College, 32

M

Magpie TIE, 164
Makhampom Theatre, 25
Manchester University, 194
Mantle of the expert, 51, 103, 106, 184, 185,
      189, 199
Manual arts, manual work, 98, 100, 151
Marbles, 71
Marking lessons, 148–149
Marxism, Marxist, 109, 117, 197, 198
Master dramatists, 136
Master of Wakefield, 20
Mathematics, maths, 31, 34, 35, 103, 128, 148,
      149, 158, 182, 184, 199
Maturation, 50
Maya Centre, 25
Medea, 17
Media, 2, 22, 24, 59, 79, 131, 140, 157, 163,
      180, 197, 199
Media studies, 131
Medicine, 90, 148
Medieval, middle ages, 18, 30, 72, 97, 102,
      106, 131, 197
Medieval re-enactment, 72
Melbourne Secondary Teachers College, 159
Mental health, 92, 93
Meritocracy, 62

Metacommunication, 72, 107, 137
Microsoft, 79
Midsummer Night's Dream, A, 99
Mimesis, 15, 18
Ministry of Education, England, 58, 66, 117
Miracle plays, 19, 21
Mode 3, 148
Modernism, modernist, 41, 206
Monologues, 62
Morality of Wisdom, The, 20
Morals, mores, 13, 15, 91, 112, 197, 205
Motor development, 88
Muggletonians, New, 122
Multi-literacies, 131, 207
Multimedia, 157
Murray river, 183
Museum, 32, 90, 194
Music, 2, 24, 31, 33, 41, 54, 59, 63, 79, 85, 88,
    127, 128, 131, 132, 134, 140, 149, 150,
    151, 154, 157, 158, 180, 198
Mystery plays, 19

N

NADIE Journal (NJ), 161, 200
Narrative, 3, 5, 11, 14, 15, 16, 20
National Association for Drama in Education
    (NADIE), 151, 152, 160, 162
National Curriculum (Australia), 30, 181
National Curriculum (UK), 197
National Drama (UK), 152, 200
National Institute of Dramatic Art (NIDA), 133
Nativity, 33, 155
Natural science, 98, 100
Nature study, 97, 98, 100
Needlecraft, needlework, 31, 32, 33, 98
Negotiated curriculum, 58
Neurology, 82
New Basics, 107, 179
Newcastle upon Tyne, 101
New English Movement, 55
New Media Studies, 131
New South Wales, 37, 140, 151, 152, 158, 160
New York University, 92
New Zealand, 6, 24, 101, 158, 159, 160, 162,
    163, 166, 180, 196
Nile River, 186
Nimrod Theatre, 164
Noah's Flood, 19
Nordic sagas, 18
Norfolk Island, 31, 32
Northern Territory (NT), 161
Null curriculum, 41
Numeracy, 58, 166

O

Objectives, 34, 35, 36, 40, 73, 74, 103, 106,
    148, 173
Occam's razor, 201
OECD, 182
Office, The, 111
Ohio State University, 200
Oracy, 50, 52, 58, 60, 61
Our Country's Good, 32
Outcomes-based education (OBE), 173

P

Pacific Islanders, 184, 192
Pandora's box, 205
Pantomime, 20
Paralanguage, 59, 64
Parramatta, 31
Pedagogy of the Oppressed, 38, 112
Peddiwell, J. Abner, 37
Peekaboo, 11
Performance Studies, 163, 194, 202
Performativity, 202, 204
Performed ethnography, 201, 202
Perse School, Cambridge, 52
Personal play, 89, 91
Peru, 80
Phaedra, 17
Phillip Island, 187
Philoctetes, 17, 203
Physical Education (PE), 24, 89, 100, 141,
    150, 157
Physics, 13, 181
Pickpockets, 32
Pinners' guild, 19
Playful, playfulness, 21, 110, 193
Playhouse, Eltham, 189
Playmaker, The, 32, 134
Playmaking, 73, 99, 120, 135, 136, 137, 139,
    140, 141, 159
Playscript, 99, 142, 155
Play Way, The, 53
Playwright, playwrighting, 72, 80, 106, 120,
    121, 129, 133, 134, 135, 136, 137, 139,
    164, 197, 199
Plowden Report, The, 56, 84, 88
Poetics, The, 14, 17
Poetry, 13, 14, 16, 17, 18, 33, 41, 54, 150, 156
Polished improvisation, 75
Popular Theatre Troupe, 110
Portia, 132
Porto, 1st IDEA Congress, 80, 162
Portugal, 80, 162
Post-modernism, post-modernists, 130

Post-structuralism, post-structuralists, 41, 117, 130
Potential space, 190
Powerpoint, 188, 204
Pre-school, 11, 12, 13, 23, 24, 152, 159
Presentation of Self in Everyday Life, The, 202
Preshil school, 37
Private schools, 23, 61, 62, 63, 79, 152, 155, 156, 158, 180
Process drama, 65, 66, 67, 76, 89, 99, 101, 104–107, 110, 111, 113, 122, 124, 139, 140, 141, 185, 189, 199, 201, 202
Productive Pedagogies, 107
Professional practice, 3
Progressive education, 33, 34, 54, 56, 73, 74, 84, 85, 123
Projected play, 99
Prospero, 202
Prostitutes, 32, 90
Protagonist, 17, 112, 118
Proteus, protean, 3, 6, 18, 21, 23, 193
Proto-drama, 11, 13, 64
Psychodrama, 25, 80, 85, 89, 90, 91, 92, 110, 195
Puppet theatre, 165
Puritanism, 21
Pyschology, 91

Q

Queen Elizabeth I, 21
Queen's English, 61
Queensland, 5, 12, 13, 36, 50, 63, 76, 87, 108, 120, 127, 128, 140, 141, 147–166, 169–171, 172, 174–181, 206, 207
Queensland Arts Syllabus, 140
Queensland Association for Drama in Education (QADIE), 150, 151, 152, 153, 174
Queensland Catholic Education Commission, 171
Queensland Department of Education (Education Queensland), 12, 13, 120, 154, 170, 171, 179, 180
Queensland Early Childhood Branch, 13, 164
Queensland School Curriculum Council (QSCC), 170, 171, 172, 175, 177, 179
Quem quaeritis, 19

R

Racism, 86
Reading, 7, 21, 31, 33, 53, 54, 57, 63, 65, 76, 77, 81, 82, 83, 98, 127, 129, 132, 140, 186
Reading lessons, 65, 76, 77

Rea Street Drama Centre, 60, 75
Received pronunciation (RP), 62
Reconceptualism, 41
Re-enactment, 72, 137
Reflective practice, 3, 189
Reflective practitioner research, 189, 201
Religious studies, instruction, 24, 25, 32, 35, 43, 55, 65, 66, 106, 110, 111, 140, 190
Remedial Drama, 90
Republic, The, 15, 17
Research in Drama Education (RIDE), 196, 200
Restricted codes, 38
Resurrection, 20
Review of School-Based Assessment (RoSBA), 149
Rhetoric, 36, 42, 61, 84, 85, 154, 196, 206
Rhyme, 33, 55
Richard II, 98
Rio de Janeiro, 112
Riverside Conference, 120, 122, 139
Robe, 183
Rock Eisteddfod, 155
Rockhampton, 153
Role-training, 25
Roma, 104, 123, 139, 153
Romans, Roman Empire, 18
Rosalind, 132
Rose Bruford College, 159, 160
Royal Academy of Dramatic Art (RADA), 60, 85, 133
Royal Court Theatre, 121
Royal Shakespeare Company, 129, 131
R.U.R., 132, 134

S

Saber-tooth Curriculum, The, 37
St. Rhyio by the Sea, 186–189
San Francisco Mime Troupe, 102
San Remo, 187
Scaffolding, 75
Scholae Pansophicae, 22
School-Based Curriculum (SBCD), 148, 149, 151, 156
School is Dead, 39
School musical, 25, 132, 155
School play, 13, 23, 33, 54, 118, 119, 151, 155
Schools Council (UK), 6, 33, 53, 54, 56, 57, 58, 62, 63, 73, 74, 76, 77, 79, 84, 85, 88, 92, 101, 103, 109, 119, 120, 121, 123, 132, 133, 134, 139, 148, 150, 151, 152, 156, 159, 160, 163, 164, 165, 166, 172, 193, 194, 195, 197, 200

Science, 33, 81, 100, 107, 108, 128, 148, 151, 154, 157, 158, 165
Scola Ludus, 22
Scotland, 62
Scripture, 19, 20, 100
Sea People, the, 186, 191
Second City Company, 102
Second Life, 26, 199
Second Shepherd's Play, 19
Self-expression, 23, 25, 73, 82, 83, 121
Sensory, 11, 49, 193
Sewing, 33
Shadowy role, 190
Shipwrights' guild, 19
Shopfront Theatre, 135
Side Effects, 109
Sidetrack Theatre, 165
Simplicissimus, 90
Simulation, 25, 110, 111, 140
Singapore, 66, 79, 80, 133, 194
Slash arts, 198
Social studies, 34, 141, 148, 149
Sociodrama, 85, 140
Sociology, 201, 203
Sociometry, 85
Sourcebook Guidelines, 173, 174, 177, 178
Sourcebook modules, 181
South Africa, 14, 62, 72, 93, 161
South Australia, 59, 152, 158, 159, 160, 161, 163
South Australia, 59, 152, 158, 159, 160, 161, 163, 164, 183
South Australian State Theatre, 164
South-East Asia, 24
South East England, 61
Spain, 80
Special needs, 3, 90, 91, 139
Spect-actors, 112, 113
Speech and Drama, 2, 33, 54, 60, 61, 63, 87, 117, 133, 134, 151, 152, 153, 156, 159, 160
Speech and Drama Centre, 60
Speech therapy, 61
Spiderweb curriculum, 41
Spiral curriculum, 40
Stage of the Art, 200
Standard Attainment Tests, 130
Standard English, 61, 62
Stegreiftheater, 90, 91
Still images, 198
Stones, The, 109
Stratford on Avon, 132
Strelly Aboriginal Community School, 37
Student-devised drama, 140, 141

Student performance standards, 181
Suicide, 93
Summerhill school, 37
Summer of the Seventeenth Doll, 150
Super dramatists, 136
Sydney (Australia), 160
Syllabus elaborations, 173, 181

T
Tahiti, 183
Taiwan, 6, 18, 24, 64, 66, 79, 108, 200
TALK Project, 58
Tambour work, 31
Tasmania, 33, 50, 51, 63, 72, 104, 150, 155, 156, 160, 163, 165
Teacher education, 1, 2, 50, 163, 172
Teacher-in-role (TIR), 51, 66, 103, 106, 184
Teachers' colleges, 151, 159, 160, 163
Teacher talk, 51
Teamwork, 188
Teatro mundi, 22, 202
Technicism, 205, 206
Tempest, The, 42, 202
Tension, dramatic, 49, 65, 99, 105, 187, 189, 199
Terrigal NSW, 160
Testing, 58, 79, 108
Texas, 60
Theatre Centre, 78, 102
Theatre for Development, 14, 25, 97, 111–113, 133, 193, 194
Theatre for liberation, 111–113
Theatre of the Oppressed, 97, 112, 124
Theatre of oppression, 17
Theatre science, 128
Theatresports, 78
Therapeutic theatre, 90
Thespis, 14, 18
This Rare Earth, 109
Three Looms Waiting, 52, 138, 159
Tiger economies, 78–79
Toastmasters, 61
Transactional analysis, 91
Transit of Venus, 183
Travelling players, 19
Treatment of Dr Lister, The, 51
Trinity College, 151, 156
Trinity Guildhall, 63
Troilus and Cressida, 203
Trudgill, Peter, 62
Twilight role, 189, 190–191
Two Noble Kinsmen, The, 90
Tyneside, 62

U

Uganda, 133, 194
UNESCO, 67
UNICEF, 111
United Kingdom (UK), 6, 24, 33, 53, 54, 56,
   57, 58, 62, 63, 73, 74, 76, 77, 79, 84, 85,
   88, 92, 101, 109, 117, 119, 120, 123, 132,
   133, 134, 139, 148, 150, 151, 152, 156,
   159, 160, 163, 164, 165, 166, 172, 175,
   193, 194, 195, 197, 200
United States (USA), 6, 25, 30, 37, 38, 51, 55,
   73, 79, 85, 91, 133, 151, 152, 155, 159,
   162, 200, 201
University of Melbourne, 159
University of Paris, 20
University of Queensland, 147, 179

V

Vancouver Youth Theatre, 135
Vanity Fair, 102
Victoria (Australia), 32, 33, 134, 151, 152,
   156, 158, 160, 163, 166, 186
Victorian College of the Arts (VCA), 85
Victorian Education Act, 1872, 33
Victorian Education Department, 141
Victorian Essential Learning Standards
   (VELS), 185
Vietnam War, 147

Visual arts, 2, 20, 24, 33, 36, 59, 76, 79, 85,
   100, 122, 128, 140, 141, 150, 154, 157,
   158, 159, 166, 180
Voluntary suspension of disbelief, 72

W

Wakefield Cycle, 19, 20
Wales, 37, 140, 151, 152, 158, 160
Wat Tyler, 98
Western Australia, 37, 153, 156, 157, 159,
   160, 163
Western Canon, The, 130
Who's handicapped?, 92
Wikipedia, 159
Wonderland, 1, 207
World of Warcraft, 26, 199
Writing lessons, 98
Writing-in-role, 36

Y

Years 1–10 Drama Guidelines (Queensland),
   120, 140
York Cycle, 19, 21
Young Drama, 153, 200

Z

Zeal Theatre, 109
Zone of proximal development (ZPD), 50,
   65, 72